The Translator's Handbook

The Translator's Handbook

Third edition

Edited by Rachel Owens

 THE ASSOCIATION FOR INFORMATION MANAGEMENT

Published in 1996 by
Aslib, The Association for Information Management
Information House
20-24 Old Street
London
EC1V 9AP

***

A CIP Catalogue record for this book is available from the British Library
Hardback ISBN 0 85142 352 3, Paperback ISBN 0 85142 363 9

Aslib, The Association for Information Management, has some two
thousand corporate members worldwide. It actively promotes better
management of information resources.

Aslib lobbies on all aspects of the management of and legislation
concerning information. It provides consultancy and information
services, professional development training, conferences, specialist
recruitment, and the Aslib Internet Programme, and publishes primary
and secondary journals, conference proceedings, directories and
monographs.

Further information about Aslib can be obtained from :
Aslib, The Association for Information Management
Information House, 20-24 Old Street, London, EC1V 9AP
Tel: +44 (0) 171 253 4488, Fax: +44 (0) 171 430 0514
Email *aslib@aslib.co.uk*, WWW *http://www.aslib.co.uk/aslib*

Printed by Bell and Bain Ltd, Glasgow

Contents

THE TRANSLATOR'S HANDBOOK
(THIRD EDITION)

Erratum Slip

We regret to inform you that a number of errors have appeared in the latest edition of Aslib's *The Translator's Handbook*. The correct text appears below, and we apologise for the inconvenience caused.

pp vi and 199

'Sián Marlow' should read 'Siân Marlow'. We apologise to the author for the incorrect spelling of her name.

p 10

2. Information texts
(b) should read
(b) '... ordered but <u>unstandardised</u> (as discussed later)...'

p 14

Quote from Baudelaire should read
'He was not bent, but broken, with the <u>spine'</u>

p 205

'Current high-speed ... more pleasant to use those ...'
should read 'Current high-speed ... more pleasant to use <u>than</u> those ...'

p 261

5 lines from the end of the page
'... evaluations of (Systran van Slype...)...1986...'
should read '...evaluations of Systran (van Slype...1986)...'

p 271

Mid page
'...grammatical in a, nor even,...'
should read '...grammatical, nor even,...'

p 315

'Institute of Linguistics' should read 'Institute of Linguists'

Editor's Introduction

RACHEL OWENS

Seven years since the publication of the second edition of *The Translator's Handbook*, Aslib has brought out what is hoped will be both a reflection on the state of the profession and a useful tool to translators and aspiring translators alike.

In the space of seven short years the profession has evolved quite dramatically with modems becoming all but mandatory, quality becoming something of a buzzword, and the Internet giving us access to seemingly unlimited information. The approach adopted in the third edition is similar to that of the first in that the contents have been divided into five parts, each with a specific theme. Each part was subsequently subdivided into up to four chapters covering various aspects of the subject in question.

In time-honoured tradition Professor Peter Newmark opens with his Introductory Survey in which he guides us through the nature of translation, approaching different types of text, the literature about translation, and translation in education.

Part II on training and development kicks off with my discussion of what makes a good translator, and the type and level of training required at all levels. This is followed by Catriona Picken's chapter in which she looks into the various career options open to translators, investigating what is currently required in the translation market and reporting on the opportunities on offer to full-time, part-time and other members of staff. Chris Schröder wraps up Part II with his discussion of the role and importance of professional organisations worldwide as seen by translators and the organisations themselves. Both Chris and Catriona undertook surveys to support their chapters and threw up some surprising and interesting results.

Moving on to the burning issue of quality in translation, Geoff Samuelsson-Brown writes for us on working procedures, quality and quality assurance. Here, he takes the opportunity to analyse the translation process (and what can go wrong at each stage), offers guidance on how to go about checking work and discusses quality control and ISO 9000 in depth. Geoffrey Kingscott continues on the issue of quality in translation by, somewhat controversially, calling into question the way in which the industry operates, examining the question of added value, and ultimately asking whether the client is actually getting what the client wants.

Part IV, The Personal Touch, raises the thorny issues of educating the client, and raising the profile of translation and translators. Lucas Weschke offers plenty of tips and advice in his chapter on how you and your clients can work together to ensure that you are both in the "translator wins/client wins" box. In doing so he offers four very practical action plans to help optimise working relationships with clients. The two following chapters are dedicated to the much-discussed issue of raising the profile of translation and translators. Eyvor Fogarty and Tristam Carrington-Windo have tackled the same issue from different perspectives, with Eyvor describing the situation in Britain where the profession is still very much in a state of evolution, and Tristam discussing working in a mature market, in this case Germany. Eyvor writes from the perspective of the translator, while Tristam has the client very much in mind.

The final part takes a closer look at the day-to-day work of the translator, terminology management, machine translation and computer aided translation. Siân and Sean Marlow provide us with an overview of the basic tools of the trade in which they discuss software, hardware, office ergonomics and reference material. Professor Klaus-Dirk Schmitz takes us through the background to terminology management systems, their concepts, types and features, and points to consider when buying them. Machine translation and machine assisted translation follow with Dr. Harold Somers and Clare Rutzler providing us with an insight into the history of MT, the limitations (past and present) of MT and the latest research directions. Geoff Samuelsson-Brown rounds off the book with a look at voice-activated software and computer-aided translation in his chapter on new technology for translators.

I would like to take this opportunity to thank Aslib and all the contributors to this, the third edition of *The Translator's Handbook*, particularly Chris Schröder and Geoff Samuelsson-Brown who stepped in at the last minute to save the day.

Part I – Introductory Survey

1. Introductory Survey

PETER NEWMARK

Background

Six years since Catriona Picken brought out the second edition of the *Translator's Handbook*, 12 years since the first edition and 24 years since John Sykes published the original *Technical Translator's Manual*, Rachel Owens was commissioned to produce a complete revision of the *Handbook*. It is to some extent a reflection of the exponential growth of the occupation. As UN membership of nation-states increases from 51 in 1945 to 185 in 1996, with further additions impending, more countries 'devolve', federalise or split up (Germany is a significant exception), more languages become national (11 succeeding two in South Africa), assert their identities and require translation. Multi-nationals; world charities; international organisations; the technological turn to the written word (faxes, telexes, electronic mail, the Internet, the Information Super Highway); the rise in literacy; the spread and improvement of transport and communication; the grants, prizes, bursaries, funds... all contribute to the increased world demand for translation.

It is difficult to produce significant statistics about the development of translation. Unesco has abandoned its intermittently published *Index Translationum*. The difficulties of the European Union's translation and interpreting budget have become legendary, and will become unmanageable unless Member States agree to limiting the provision at conferences to three or four vehicular or working languages, when every delegate or member has a right to read or listen to translated texts in German, French or English, but not in any other languages. Every day more than 400 regular staff and approximately 300 freelances work in the 40-50 meetings which take place in Brussels, in the Member States or elsewhere. In 1994 they supplied about 120,000 interpreter-days, a figure which increases from year to year. (See Noel Muylle's

3

Multilingualism – an advantage for Europe? *The Linguist*, 34/3 1995). Lawrence Venuti (*The Translator's Invisibility*, Routledge, 1995) has stated that a recent estimate values the US corporate and government translation industry at $10 billion, far exceeding the translation of literary texts in volume and in financial value. He has noted that while British and American book production increased fourfold between 1950 and 1990, the number of translations remained approximately between 2 per cent and 4 per cent of the total, although in the early 1960s there was a marked increase to between 4 per cent and 7 per cent. In 1990 British publishers brought out some 64,000 books, of which 1,600 were translations (2.4%), while American publishers brought out 46,750 books, including 1,400 translations (3%). On the other hand, the translation rate in France has varied between 8 per cent and 12 per cent, two thirds of which was from English. In Italy the translation rate was 25 per cent, more than half from English. In Germany the rate was 14 per cent, and again, well over half from English. Such a comfortable position for American and British English is illusory when one considers it in relation to the British economy. 'We are to languages as *East Enders* is to elocution', Geoffrey Kingscott has warned in *The Guardian* (7/6/95). 'The British people always assume that English is acceptable.' Admittedly the Department of Trade and Industry with its National Languages for Export Awards has made great efforts...since 1994! The Trade Minister, Richard Needham, has pointed out that a recent survey found that 74 per cent of the foreign language calls received by UK companies were abandoned at the switchboard. The DTI has also produced the delightful headline: 'Vicar of the Nation (Minister of State) sorts out watery sheep (hydraulic rams) from emergency snakes (coils)', showing that translators have to be experts in clarifying misprints as well as puns, but may be rewarded by a good laugh. Further, through the initiative of Language Line, a telephone based interpreting service which provides instant telephone interpretations in more than 140 languages, customers of Anglian Water can ring the head office on a freephone number in their own language, whether Polish or Punjabi, and proceed instantly with a three way conversation. In the last two or three years, *The Guardian* has been regularly publishing translations of articles in the leading European newspapers, but its literary editor is indifferent to the quality and authorship of translated fiction.

Nevertheless, many business people still cannot distinguish the separate requirements of oral language fluency and the cultural and linguistic skills required by professional interpreters and translators.

This new edition of the Handbook is more compact than its predecessors. It focuses on the translator's concerns: training and career, methodology, technological tools and reference works, terminology, collaboration with terminologists, the uses of MT, post-translation procedures, and relations with clients and third parties. This is a contrast to the last edition which ranged discursively from the translation 'scene' in various parts of the world to the affinities between cognate languages.

What is translation?

Translation is the transfer of the meaning of a text (which may be a word or a book) from one language to another for a new readership. No definition would appear to be more obvious or straightforward than that one, yet to my knowledge it does not occur in any dictionary, which is regrettable but understandable for several reasons. Firstly, meaning can be synonymised only by 'sense' or 'significance' or 'purport'. As soon as it is defined ('the purpose intended by a written or spoken statement'), it splits up into qualifications and reservations: whose purpose? Is the meaning the full content or the (illocutionary) message to the reader? Are we talking about denotative meaning ('He found his way'...to the bathroom) or connotative meaning ('He grasped the nettle'...he tackled the difficulty courageously), or both ('He was in a mess'). Or illocutionary or pragmatic meaning? ('Game and match')? Or sound as meaning ('the murmuring of innumerable bees')? Or is the meaning nonsense ('Miles of pram in the wind and Pam in the gorse track' – Betjeman)? Secondly (start yawning), nothing can take place in a social vacuum: what is the 'context of situation', when is the text being translated, and for whom? Thirdly, as Goethe was the first to point out, this process or act of translation is strictly (completely, precisely, perfectly, correctly) not possible, however necessary it may be. So perhaps 'as accurately as possible' should be added to my dictionary definition, along with 'keeping approximately the same length, to reproduce the impact'. Fourthly, the definition of translation, including the sense of the term 'meaning', is merely academic if the text is defective, untrue, illogical, badly written, harmful, factually or linguistically inadequate – in which case the translation may or may not become a correction of the original. But, if the translator were working in isolation, one could claim that the minimum meaning is the denotation of the text, whilst if this does not make sense, the meaning is the connotation, as in Chomsky's emblematic sentence:

"Colourless green ideas sleep furiously",

and the weirder and more apparently contextless the sentence, the more literally it has to be translated. Therefore:

"Farblose grüne Ideen schlafen wütend" and;

"Les idées vertes sans couleur dorment furieusement".

In fact, literal translation is the closest possible interpretation of any obscure proposition, or at least the closest approach to the comprehension of its meaning, which in the above case may well be: Unformed and immature ideas may be dormant until they work their way quickly to violent realisation. And so, by now, my reader may have dismissed my definition altogether.

Furthermore, my brief definition takes no account of the two types of translation and the two types of translator – one concerned with reality, the other with fiction; one with facts, the other with fantasy; one with singular denotative, the other with multiple recursive and connotative meaning; one with objects, the other with society and individuals; one in silence, the other in significant sound. Historically, translation was first concerned mainly with the second, now it is, at any rate quantitatively, mainly concerned with the first, and this change has caused some confusion, made more confounded by the fact that so many people and books on translation have ignored the difference.

Here I must point out that the translation of poetry is a third type, since poetry uniquely makes use of all the formal resources of language (metaphor, denotation and connotation; metre or rhythm, rhyme, repetition, alliteration, assonance, onomatopoeia, where the tone of the human voice is the essence of the meaning). Thus the translator of poetry has an embarrassment of factors to take into account, and is usually not able to get as close to the denotative original as in the other genres. Nevertheless, poetry and translation have always been and will always be 'close'; an unusually high proportion of poets have been and are translators, particularly those, beginning with Shelley, who have said the translation of poetry is not possible. In fact Shelley famously wrote:

> 'Hence the vanity of translation: it were as wise to cast a violet into a crucible that you might discover the formal principle of its colour and odour, as seek to transfuse from one language to another the creations of a poet. The plant must spring again from its seed, or it will bear no flower – and this is the burden of the curse of Babel.'
>
> (A Defence of Poetry, 1821).

Ironically, the above contains a recipe for poetry translation – and Shelley himself translated Homer, Euripides, Plato, Virgil, Dante, Cavalcanti, Calderon, as well as two scenes from Goethe's Faust.

Translationally considered, there are three types of language or text: non-literary, literary, and poetic. Ideally, all should be closely translated, but in fact, my categorisation represents an order or degree of closeness of translation, since in principle, non-literary translation can grasp more of the meaning of the original than literary translation, and literary certainly more than poetic translation.

Thus far I have been defining full translation. There are also many types of partial translation or summary now increasingly required: globally in many cases people are not interested in the word – they want only the facts or the message. Many academic and scientific journals include abstracts in English and other languages: others, printed in English but published abroad, include abstracts including in the language of origin. Newspaper and general periodicals contain translated summaries or quotations from articles. Comedies and farces are often adapted, since their humour may have an intractable cultural element (banana skins) which are not funny when translated: sometimes (*The Misanthrope, The Importance of being Earnest*) they should be translated straight. Translators are employed in press agencies, ministries and embassies to produce summaries of the leading articles in foreign opinion-makers. Surtitles of operas and subtitles of TV and cinema films almost always abbreviate their originals.

Translating Text Types

Before dividing translation topics into six broad categories and giving some general principles for translating them, I first propose a theory and methodology, related both to the process of translating and the product – the completed translation. My theory will cover any text in broad terms, and has the characteristic of being neither dualistic nor rigid, but it requires some qualifications and explanations: the more important the language of the text, the more closely it has to be translated.

Firstly, I assure myself that the text is 'solid'/trustworthy in its factual or imaginative base.

Secondly, I gloss the term 'language' as the linguistic substance, the words and their order, as opposed to their thought-content: the lexical words ('full' nouns, verbs, adjectives, adverbs, single or compounded) as opposed to the function words (determiners, modals, pronouns, connectives, prepositions, equational verbs). I bear in mind that language has denotative and/or connotative and/or sonic and rhythmic meaning, – I use the term 'sonic' in its recent sense of 'related to sound' – which the translator has to assess. I also consider that for the translator there are two kinds of language, non-literary, which is concerned with reality and facts and largely denotative, and literary (1. prose, 2. poetry), which is concerned with human beings and the imagination, is connotative and is an indirect criticism of human behaviour.

Thirdly, I relate 'important' to the situation, the context and sometimes the extra-textual authority of the author. Language is important in authoritative and well known, often quoted, texts, in illocutions (check!), although the standardised formula may be different in translation (*échec au roi!*), in all serious poetry, in literature and good writing, and when the customer or the employer decides it is. The translator will recognise that language in legal texts and in serious poetry is more important than it is in informational texts, whilst the language of the translation is always important.

Lastly, there are degrees of close translation (but no exact translation). The closest is a word transferred from the source language which still retains the same meaning in the target language; after that, there is literal translation at any rank (from the morpheme 'post'- to the sentence 'there is a bull in my garden'), again provided the same denotative and pragmatic meaning is retained; then transpositions of structures ('after his departure', après son départ, après être parti), then often a series of synonyms from the closest to the farthest, and a number of other translation procedures until we reach paraphrase and adaptation, always with the assumption that the degree of naturalness and seriousness is retained.

Translation topics can be divided into six broad categories: cultural texts; information texts; social texts; legal and official texts; literary texts; and poetry. In respect of translation method – as I shall attempt to show – one category begins with some overlapping, where the previous one finishes. Furthermore there is a gradation from 'detached' to 'proximate', from a narrow source text semantic range in cultural texts (where the translation need only capture a summary of the meaning) to a dense semantic range in poetry (where the poem is absorbed in the translation, but can take in only a multi-layered but small part of the original meaning).

1. Cultural texts

Cultural texts include adaptations of comedies and farces, many advertisements, propaganda and public notices. In principle, since a particular language group is being targeted, source language cultural expressions and styles (now discourses) are replaced by equivalent receptor language expressions and styles. Traditionally, the equivalent of cricket was baseball or *Boules*; of English beer was French wine; of bacon was ham. But any equivalent effect could be obtained only at the expense of accuracy. Now the force of the socio-economic-cultural factor is being gradually eroded by the global village, the 30 channel TV, the Internet, the multiplication of transport and communications, international organisations, multi-nationals, non-governmental organisations, language with its interlanguage, translation with its translationese, so that ... A diamond is for ever ... Un diamante es para siempre ... Un diamante è per sempre ... *Un diamant est pour toujours ... Ein Diamant ist für immer ...* and cultural texts, like minority languages (carefully, not by artificial nationalism) have to be cherished.

2. Information texts

In information texts – which may be (a)standardised, or (b)ordered but (as discussed later) – the facts are all-important, and the purpose of the language is to clarify them and make them agreeable to the readership. If the text is well written, i.e. concise and plain, the descriptive and qualitative words that define the facts, and the syntactical structures and word and clause order that indicate time sequence and emphasis, have to be respected. A sentence such as:

> *"Grâce à cet ordinateur et son logiciel personnalisé, les médecins disposent désormais du premier fichier médical confidentiel"*

could be translated as:

> "Doctors now have their first confidential medical files, due to computers and personalised software", or as:

> "The first confidential medical files are now at every doctor's disposal, thanks to computers and personal software", but it would be better left alone as:

> "Thanks (due, owing) to the computer and personalised software, doctors now have their first confidential medical files",

where all the emphases and connections with the context are left intact.

If, on the other hand, an information text is poorly written, the translator has to rewrite and restructure it:

> *"Mon propos ici vise a récuperer la parole qu'ils on perdue"*

> "I intend here to redress their inability to express their views".

(Illustrations adapted from Beverly Adab's *Annotated Texts for Translation, French-English,* Multi-Lingual Matters, 1993)

Information texts can have a standardised, or ordered but unstandardised form. Standardised texts include medical reports, technical reports, the agendas and minutes of meetings, recipes, directions for use, instruction manuals, higher degree theses/dissertations, menus, algorithms, rites and ceremonies, patents, treaties, laws, specifications, valuations, expert evidence, and judicial sentences.

Such texts are normally dominated by nouns and noun compounds, and have little affective vocabulary. An example, for medical reports, is: Papers and Originals/Medical Practice, Title, Authors, Source, Summary, Introduction, Present Study, (Patients and) Methods, Results, Discussion, References. The style is formal (no phrasal verbs, many passives) but the 'we' form is used in the Discussion; the past tense is used for narrative, the present for generalisation.

Ordered but unstandardised texts should have a clear time or priority sequence, whatever their degree of formality. The translation's putative readership should be assessed, and the appropriate additional explanations should be given intratextually, since the language of the original is not sacrosanct.

3. Social texts

Here I include texts ranging from psychology and sociology to texts about the arts and the humanities. In these texts psychological and cultural nuances cannot be regarded as less important than the bare facts, whether their language is descriptive or critical. These are the texts which require, as their aim, a full denotative translation, where all elements of meaning in the original are captured, but the connotative, polysemous factor is avoided, unless the text is designed to be suggestive and creative rather than straightforward and critical. A scrap example would be:

"L'apparence physique joue un rôle essentiel pour guider l'opinion que nous avons des individus que nous ne connaissons pas. Tous les racismes se nourrissent d'ailleurs de ces formes primaires d'identification".

"Physical appearance has an essential role in guiding the opinions we have of individuals we don't know. Besides, all kinds of racism feed on these simplistic forms of identification".

Note that in texts of literary criticism, the full metalinguistic literary vocabulary (e.g. register, genre, form, comedy) may be denotatively translated, but the 'new' terms from post-modernism (e.g. deconstruct, discourse, negotiate, space, the other) have to be preserved in spite of their polysemy.

4. Legal and official texts

Legal texts are the tightest univocal and monosemous denotative texts, to such an extent, that the sense of their terms frequently has to be defined therein.

Broadly, there are two kinds of legal text; those deriving from international authorities such as the EU, which have the force of law in all Member States; and those of national states, which may conform with Islamic, civil, case or other legal systems, where the translation may be descriptive and explanatory, unless it is certificated by a competent authority and may also be valid in the target language country.

The EU has its own international institutions, which are kept free of the peculiar institutional terms of their Member States. More often than not they are made up of transparent greco-latinisms which are barely modified in the languages of the Member States.

Legal language is turned towards verb-nouns, classifying adjectives and copulative verbs; qualitative adjectives and adverbs are not drawn on. There is a heavy focus on verbs such as 'determine', 'propose', 'advise', 'recommend', 'give a ruling', 'dispose', 'provide for', 'define', 'limit', 'restrict', 'distinguish' plus their nouns, so that legal language and defining language often appear to overlap. The niceties of distinction have to be rendered in translation.

Where one country's laws have to be described for information purposes in another language and the translation has no legal status, the translator can transfer peculiar source language terms, often against a background of law; thus, as Martin Weston has shown, whether 'juge d'instruction' is translated, as it usually is, as 'examining magistrate' or 'investigating judge', neither of them are standard British legal terms, and therefore some gloss on the term is appropriate.

The translator has to bear in mind that English laws are still formulated in the 'absolute shall' future tense.

Essentially, English law is impersonal (passives) and dignified, eschewing the personal language of literature ('strive to') and the superlatives of colloquialism.

5. Literary texts

Since literary texts are concerned with the world of the imagination and are centred in human beings, sometimes reflected in their physical characteristics and their natural and climatic backgrounds, whilst non-literary texts describe the facts of reality, modified by human intelligence, the translator cannot take literary language at its 'face' singular denotative value, and has to bear second often multiple connotative meaning in mind. Other particularly important elements are: the allegorical and symbolical nature of the language, often regarded as typical, or a moral comment on human behaviour; sound, in general terms; personal and emotional language; closeness to speech rhythms and spoken language (particularly phrasal verbs/nouns/adjectives); the balance of sentences and paragraphs; retention of the functional sentence perspective, i.e. the theme/rheme sequence and the emphases; concision. Scrap example:

> *"J'étais dans des dispositions étranges et tristes. La vie m'apparaissait du haut d'une sorte de piédestal qui me maintenait dans les nuages."*

'I was in a strange and sad frame of mind. Life appeared to me from the top of a sort of pedestal that kept me up in the clouds'

(P. Sollers, *Le Défi..* Adapted translation by Jean Stewart. *Penguin Short Stories,* 1966, pp. 216-7).

6. Poetry texts

Poetry calls on all the resources of language, and, in parallel, these become the factors that the translator has to weigh up and prioritise differently for each poem, depending on its nature and function. Thus metre, rhyme, rhythm, assonance, alliteration, onomatopoeia all relate to form and sound, and these, together with the denotations and connotations of the language joined in a continuous metaphor, make up the total, the meaning. All the factors of literary text mentioned in the previous section are included, so that normally each word of the original is irreplaceable and unmoveable. Most translators first retain the metre or a similar metre, attempt to keep the rhyming scheme, and compromise or sacrifice alliteration, assonance and onomatopoeia. The struggle to reconcile the semantic and the aesthetic persuasively, if not naturally, in sound and form, is at its most intense, and can sometimes be maintained only for single lines:

> "Il n'était pas voûté, mais cassé, son échine
>
> Faisant avec sa jambe un parfait angle droit,
>
> Si bien que son bâton, parachevant sa mine,
>
> Lui donnait la tournure et le pas maladroit...'

> 'He was not bent, but broken, with the spire
>
> Forming a sharp right angle to the straight,
>
> So that his stick, to finish the design,
>
> Gave him the stature and the crazy gait..."

(*Les sept vieillards* by Charles Baudelaire. Translated by Roy Campbell)

The literature about translation

The literature about translation grew slowly, apparently beginning with a few remarks (Cicero, Horace), then turning to letters (St Jerome, Luther) and to essays or introductions to translation. These remained the main literary forms until the early 20th Century, absurd genres for such a complex subject (art, craft, science, matter of taste). Gradually, starting with Dolet (1540) and Tytler (1790), books on translation appeared, but the first solid study after Tytler, *Towards a Science of Translating* was that of a linguist, Eugene Nida, not a man of letters. From the beginning, the main subject of controversy, admirably summarised in T. H. Savory's *Art of Translation* (1957), was whether translation should be free or literal, creative or servile, domesticating or foreignising, as though it were purely a dualistic process. It seems obvious that any theory of translation has to take a stand on this question, and therefore some theory of translation is as necessary as a theory of grammar is to language. From the beginning, and often now, the question of whether the text was intended to describe an aspect of the real or of an imagined world was ignored. And again from the beginning, translators tended to identify their readers with themselves (i.e. educated and intelligent), and since the earliest translated texts were authoritative or religious (the voice of God), the earliest translation tended to be literal whilst the earliest writers on translation (broadly from Roman times until the beginning of the 19th Century) tended to react against literal translation. To my knowledge, the importance of assessing the intelligence and the requirements of this readership was not seriously discussed until Eugene Nida wrote his book in 1964.

In view of the evidently increasing political and social importance and the expansion of translation, it is not surprising that the literature has grown exponentially (see the chronological bibliography to George Steiner's *After Babel*, 1975). It is a dynamic and controversial topic and takes many forms, ranging from theoretical and philosophical works to textbooks and translation criticism, and traditionally, annotation and glossing of classical works. Since linguistics took over from philology in the 1960s, and started concerning itself with synchronic language and generating various kinds of applied linguistics, the linguistic study of translations became useful. Linguistics began to have a powerful influence on the writing about translation theory and methodology, though it was initially viewed with suspicion by translators and translation teachers. Since international organisations and serious other employers now look for diplomas in translation as necessary qualifications, the discipline or interdiscipline is to some extent habilitated.

Both Malblanc (1961) and Vinay and Darbelnet (1965) produced a series of equivalent grammatical structures ('before arriving', *avant son arrivée, vor seiner Ankunft*) for French and German and French and English respectively, as well as lexical procedures such as transference ('bas-relief', *bas-relief, Bas-Relief*), literal translation, modulation ('shallow', *peu profond*) and adaptation ('hollow triumph', *'château de cartes'*), all of them rich in paired examples. Suzanne Guillemin-Flescher, Beverly Adab, Wolf Friederich and the brilliant John Desmond Gallagher have been notable successors.

It remains to list the philosophical/linguistic theories that have influenced this 'interdiscipline' and to give brief indications of their applications.

1. Functionalism

The most powerful influence on translation methods, since for so long the description rather than the purpose has dominated semantics and lexicology. In fact, function defines text-types (Bühler, Nida, Reiss, House, Halliday, me) and sentences (Firbas), whereas the downgrading (*Enthronung,* 'undermining' championed by Vermeer and Baker respectively) of the description or the essence of the original distorts a translation. The 'Lasswell formula' – who does what to whom and why (for what purpose? for what reason? on what grounds?) when? how? or what is/was/becomes/became what? – goes outside language to reality and helps the translator to visualise the real or imaginary situation.

2. Text linguistics

Cohesion links one sentence to another and coherence defines the logical thought or action of a text within a particular style. The various kinds of sentence connectives – pronouns, conjunction, familiar alternatives (*la Serenissima*), general or hold-all words (thingummybob) and other substitutions, enumerations, comparatives/superlatives, negatives/positives – are universal cohesive devices which are more frequently used in some languages (and discourses!) than in others and require a translator's special attention to secure a coherent flow.

Text linguists tend to ignore the significance of key words that have their own resonance which transcends context, as well as the deviations from standard discourses which concentrate meaning and emphasis.

3. Culturalism

When a text/language is regarded purely as the emanation of a peculiar culture and translation simply as intercultural communication, the universal elements of relevance, logic, intelligence, sensibility and feeling are ignored.

4. Reception theory

Here the translation is seen only as a text in the target language used to satisfy the requirements of its new readers, and its relation to the original text is seen as unimportant. Therefore the translation's accuracy and its quality are not worth studying.

5. Translation as a process

The translator's thought processes are recorded in 'thinking aloud protocols' and variations, after-thoughts and corrections are studied. Students and professional translators may be promising guinea-pigs. The techniques and procedures are considered without reference to the purpose of the translation.

6. Pragmatics

(Including Sperber and Wilson's relevance 'theory' and Grice's co-operative principles). These ideas have the merit of stressing the universal aspects of writing and translation, including the need to translate effectively, pertinently and elegantly. They bypass the pervasive difficulty of translating, which is how closely to translate, and how to translate closely.

7. Others

Other theories which have previously become current within psychology and linguistics such as prototype theory, scene and frames theory, functional sentence perspective, case grammar, componential analysis all have useful applications to translation. Too often they have been expounded (by linguists) in their own right, as though it were the translator's duty simply to follow their principles.

In fact there are many aspects of translation that still require treatment, starting off not from linguistic or literary ideas but from life or human behaviour, such as humour, irony, pauses, euphemisms and the talk of children. Translating period comedies and farces, one is faced with the difficulty, not only of puns and alliteration, but of physical handicaps such as stuttering, of mental illness, of practical jokes, of clumsiness (banana skins) and of drunkenness – all of which have been the source of nasty cultural merriment in the past and to some extent remain so. Given the partly cultural and partly universal nature of humour, the translator and the actormay attempt to preserve the laughs without giving offence to the moral susceptibilities of a modern audience not now amused by such 'comic' conditions or episodes, whose transformation may be justified provided they are on a farcical and superficial level.

Lastly, the critical analysis of translations is only at its beginning; it should lead mainly, not to the situating of the translation within the target language literature, or 'polysystem' useful as this may be as a minor chapter in the sociology of that literature, but to the more accurate retranslation of the original work, leading to a better assessment of its value as a comment on human behaviour and of its artistic qualities, its language and its formal balance.

Translation and education

For many years there has been confusion about the purpose and place of translation in the educational system. Traditionally, translation into English was regarded merely as an aid for enriching the pupil's knowledge of the foreign language by the use of variant synonyms and structures, not as an exercise in accurately rendering a foreign text into one's own language. Often the use of the source language word or a cognate word with similar form was, and is, approved of. Further, translation was mistrusted for its emphasis on the native language. Its nature was widely misunderstood; it was taught in language institutes rather than universities and not considered a subject suitable for academic study or research.

Now, in many countries, the great rush to learn English, sometimes involving a clash with and a rejection of French, often coincides with a rehabilitation of translation as an essential element in exporting, tourism and the business of international organisations. The university departments of translation, professionally run and concerned mainly with technical and business subjects, which started in Geneva in the inter-war years, began to appear in the 1970s in West and East Germany (Heidelberg, Saarbrücken, Mainz-Germersheim, Leipzig); in Finland, four institutes (Turku, Tampere, Savonlinna, Kouvala) became university departments; in the virtually plurilingual countries, translation courses have flourished: Belgium has Mons, Antwerp, Louvaine and Liege; the Netherlands Amsterdam and Maastricht. Enthusiasm for translation has swept over Spain (the Autònoma at Barcelona, Vitoria, Salamanca, Granada, Leon, Vigo, most of these with an impressive fan of languages). In Italy, two universities, Trieste and Bologna (Forli), specialise in translation and there is a large institute in Milan. Most courses on the Continent take four years. In Britain, there are one-year post-graduate courses at the Universities of Aston, Bath, Edinburgh, Heriot Watt, Kent, Luton, Salford, Surrey and Westminster, with a part-time course at Bristol (University of the South West of England). In almost all professional translator courses, students are trained to translate technological and business texts, to reduce foreign language texts to abstracts and summaries, to handle terminology, to use word-processors; they normally receive an introduction to machine translation and have a course in translation theory or principles and methods of translation that includes translation criticism; such courses 'apply' linguistics in varying degrees.

Literary translation is practised in special centres at Arles and Straalen. There are one-year MA courses at Warwick, Essex, Middlesex and East Anglia (British Centre of Literary Translation which offers bursaries of one month to translators with literary and scholarly projects), and a school of literary translation run by Magda Olivetti in Milan. As in schools of creative writing, the core of such courses is mutual comparison and collaboration and criticism of the versions in groups; lectures by visiting poets, writers, translation theorists, literary critics can be a creative stimulus.

The essence of translation

The user languages increase in number and change continuously, the readerships differentiate, situations vary, the purpose of translation extends to exposure as well as self-expression, to persuasion, and to information; the translator no longer instinctively identifies his readership with himself. Nevertheless, the basic process, the conversion of a statement or a message from one language into another for a different readership, is not going to change. A translation theorist can no more be avant-garde or state-of-the-art or progressive as can a translator, though, to advance professionally, society tries to compel her to be so. Computers can automate only the more routine and standardised translation procedures, and further progress, 'within the present state of our knowledge' – the phrase sounds modest, but suggests a promise which is unlikely to be realised, – is limited by the complexity of language. Translation will continue to straddle across the arts and the sciences, the humanities and the technologies, a universal conundrum which in fact nine times out of ten can be quite satisfactorily solved – not perfectly, but approximately like all important things.

Bibliography

(Abbreviations:

L	Literary translation
N	Mainly non-literary translation
L and N	Literary and non-literary translation)

English

Baker, M., In Other Words; A Course Book on Translation, Routledge, 1992. (N)

Bassnett, S., *Translation Studies*, (Revised), Methuen, 1993. (L and N)

Bell, R.T., *Translation and Translating*, Longman, 1993. (L and N)

Biguenet, J. and Schulte, R., *The Craft of Translation*, Chicago University Press, 1989. (L)

Brower, R.A. (ed), *On Translation*, Cambridge, Harvard University Press, 1959. (L and N)

Catford, J.C., *A Linguistic Theory of Translation*, Oxford University Press, 1965. (L and N)

Chesterman, A. (ed), *Readings in Translation Theory*, Helsinki, OY Finn Lectura AB, 1989. (L and N)

Chukovski, K., *A High Art; The Art of Translation*, Tr. L.G. Leighton, University of Tennessee, 1984. (L)

Duff, A., *The Third Language*, Pergamon, 1981. (N)

Gentzler, E., *Contemporary Theories of Translation*, Routledge, 1993. (L and N)

Gutt, E.A., *Translation and Relevance*, Blackwell, 1991. (L and N)

Hatim, B. and Mason I., *Discourse and the Translator*, Longman, 1990. (L and N)

Hermans, T. (ed), *The Manipulation of Literature*, Croom Helm, 1985. (L)

Hervey, S. and Higgins, I. etc., *Rethinking French/German/Spanish Translation*, Routledge, 1992-5. (N)

Hewson, L. and Martin, J., *Redefining Translation*, Routledge, 1991. (L and N)

House, J., *A Model for Translation Quality Assessment*, Tübingen, Narr, 1982. (L and N)

Kelly, L.G., *The True Interpreter*, Cambridge University Press, 1979. (L)

Kussmaul, P., *Training Translators*, Benjamins, 1995. (N)

Neubert, A. and Shreve, G., *Translation as Text*, Kent State University, Ohio, 1992. (N)

Newmark, P., *Approaches to Translation*, Prentice Hall, 1981. (L and N)

Newmark, P., *A Textbook of Translation*, Prentice Hall, 1995. (L and N)

Newmark, P., *About Translation*, Multilingual Matters, 1991. (L and N)

Newmark, P., *Paragraphs on Translation*, Multilingual Matters, 1994. (L)

Nida, E., *Towards a Science of Translation*, Leiden, E.J. Brill, 1964. (L and N)

Nida, E. and Taber, C., *The Theory and Practice of Translation*, Leiden, E.J. Brill, 1969. (L and N)

Nida, E., *Language, Structure and Translation*, (ed E.S. Dill), Stanford University Press, 1975. (L and N)

Nida, E. and Reyburn W.D., *Meaning across Cultures*, N.Y., Orbis, 1981. (N)

Nida, E. and Finchi, ??? *On Translation*, 1989.

Pym, A., *Translation and Text Transfer*, Frankfurt, Peter Lang, 1992. (L and N)

Robinson, D., *The Translator's Turn*, John Hopkins, 1990.

Savory, T.H., *The Art of Translation*, London, 1968.

Snell-Horney, M., *Translation Studies: an Integrated Approach*, Amsterdam, Benjamins, 1988. (L and N)

Seguinot, C. (ed), *The Translation Process*, Toronto University Press, 1989. (N)

Snelling, D., *Strategies for Simultaneous Interpretation; from Romance Languages to English*, Camponotto Udine, 1992. (N)

Smith, A.G. et al., *Aspects of Translation*, Secker and Warburg, 1958. (L and N)

Steiner, G., *After Babel*, OUP, 1975. (L)

Toury, G., *In Search of a Theory of Translation*, Tel-Aviv University, 1980. (L and N)

Toury, G., *Descriptive Translation Studies – and Beyond*, Amsterdam, Benjamins, 1995. (L and N)

Tytler, A.F., *Essay on the Principles of Translation*, Dent, 1912. (L)

Wilss W., *The Science of Translation*, Narr, 1982. (N)

French

Delisle, J., *L'Analyse du Discours comme Méthode de Traduction*, University of Ottawa, 1980. (N)

Delisle J., *La Traduction Raisonnée*, University of Ottawa, 1993. (N)

Guillemin-Fleschler S., *Syntax Comparée du Français et de L'Anglais*, Paris, 1988. (L and N)

Ladmiral, J.R., *Traduire: Théorèmes pour la Traduction*, Payot, 1979. (L)

Larose, R., *Théories Contemporaines de la Traduction*, Quebec, 1989. (N)

Maillot, J., *La Traduction Scientifique et Technique*, Paris, 1981. (N)

Mounin, G., *Les Problèmes Théoriques de la Traduction*, Gallimard, 1963. (L and N)

Seleskovic, D. and Lederer, M., *Interpréter pour Traduire*, Paris, 1992.

Vinay, J.P. and Darbelnet, J., *Stylistique Comparée du Français et de L'Anglais*, Didier, 1965. (N)

German

Honig, H. and Kussmaul, P., *Strategie der Übersetzung*, Narr, 1993. (N)

Koller, W., *Einführung in die Übersetzungswissenschaft*, (revised edition), UTB, Quelle und Meyer, 1991. (L and N)

Reiss, K., *Möglichkeiten und Grenzen der Übersetzung*, Munich, Heuber, 1971. (N)

Snell-Hornby, M., *Übersetzungswissenschaft; eine Neuorientierung*, Tübingen, Narr, 1986. (L and N)

Stolze, R., *Übersetzungstheorien; eine Einführung*, Narr, 1994. (L and N)

Vermeer, H.J. and Reiss, K., *Grundlegung einer allgemeinen Translationstheorie*, Tübingen, Narr, 1984. (L and N)

Translation Periodicals

Babel (FIT Journal) (Berlin)

Lebende Sprachen (Berlin)

Linguist, The (Institute of Linguists Journal) (London)

Meta (Montreal)

Parallèles (Geneva)

Rivista Internazionale della Tecnica della Traduzione(Trieste)

Target (Amsterdam)

Traduire (Paris)

Translator, The (Manchester)

Part II – Training and Development

2. Training

RACHEL OWENS

Do translators need training? And if so, what kind of training? Can they learn everything they need to know from vocational courses, practical experience, or do they need a mixture of both? These are the issues I will be looking at in this article while also taking the opportunity to examine whether there really is a case for one year postgraduate diplomas/MAs in translation.

Given my background of postgraduate qualification/inhouse translator/freelance translator/associate lecturer at the University of Surrey, I have a very real interest in training, particularly of young language graduates hoping to make a career in translation.

For the purposes of this article, I will be using three terms which I believe define the various stages of translator training: novice, apprentice and professional. A novice is someone who is new to translation (in all likelihood a modern languages graduate who has not worked in translation and indeed may not have worked full-time in any particular field. An apprentice is a fledgling translator who is likely to have completed a postgraduate qualification in translation (or acquired such skills) and who has little or no translation experience. A professional is a translator who has the qualities and skills I discuss below, who will often have been working in the field for some time and who can be relied upon to get it right and produce what the client wants.

I will start by examining in some detail the qualities and skills I consider necessary if someone is to make a good translator. With these in mind, I then go on to discuss training for novices (primarily students), apprentices (mainly inhouse translators) and professionals (inhouse or freelance translators).

What makes a good translator?

What indeed? I started planning this section by recalling the good (and not so good) students and translators I have known and listing their many qualities and skills. I eventually came to the conclusion that there are, in fact, several personal qualities without which a translator will ultimately remain mediocre. It may seem controversial and drastic to say 'Don't even consider a career in translation without them', but in my opinion the really outstanding translators are those with these qualities *and* the requisite skills. This is not quite so controversial given the increasing competition at apprentice level in the translation market.

As such, I have divided my wishlist of qualities and skills into 'innate' and 'acquirable' and have started by listing them (for ease of reference). I then go on to discuss each quality or skill and its relevance to working as a translator.

Innate

A good translator is:

Bright and quick on the uptake
To those in the know, this is something of a statement of the obvious. Translation is a very demanding job in that you need to have mastered at least one foreign language and have a good knowledge of several specialist areas. You also need to be able to develop these at apprentice level (whilst learning several new skills), maintain them at professional level, *and* deal with clients, administration, etc. Translation is a job for intelligent people!

Inquisitive and alert
Translators need an enquiring mind since they must fully understand what is going on in the source text – not just what is being said, but also the argument being put forward, the point being made, the reason why the text was written in the first place. A mediocre translator will translate what is there, not questioning the logic, maybe not noticing that a page has gone astray, and not thinking about the content – merely translating it.

Full of initiative
I can always spot a student with initiative – it's the very same student who tells me about a forthcoming dictionary, introduces me to a new service provided by the Computing Unit...in fact the selfsame student who (rightly) bothered to check and correct a 'fact' in the homework

'because it looked strange'. Initiative is doing things off your own bat, seeing that something is wrong, needs doing etc. and doing something about it yourself rather than waiting for someone else to point it out and tell you how to go about it. It's a very important quality in translation as it is the mark of someone who will ensure that something is right and will get things done.

Gifted with a flair with language

To my mind this is really what separates the wheat from the chaff. Flair is not just the ability to write beautiful flowing prose when translating a holiday brochure, but also to write concise, easy-to-read language for assembly manuals, instruction leaflets and so on. I have deliberately separated 'Flair' from 'Ability to write well in mother tongue' as the latter comprises several elements (such as grammar and punctuation) which can be acquired.

Flexible

This quality can be split into linguistic flexibility and flexibility of approach. The former is the ability to write in different styles for different clients and different texts, whereas the latter involves being flexible enough to accept different clients' requirements, to squeeze in a small job for an important client (despite working flat out on something else), and to be able to fill gaps between assignments with useful work such as glossary compilation. Inhouse translators will need to be able to jump from one assignment to another, drop everything to take on an urgent piece, or take time out from a long-term project to check someone else's work or take over from a colleague who is unwell.

Motivated

Translators have to enjoy translating! They need to be able to cope with what can be dull, monotonous work and do it well. They have to get a kick out of taking on a piece, getting on top of it and turning out a well-written translation. We don't call the shots, the client does, and most of us can't afford to be that picky that we turn down every piece of work which doesn't turn us on.

Acquirable

A good translator can acquire:

Stamina

Few of my students realise just how tiring it is to concentrate hard for a full working day – with a schedule of 17 or so taught hours a week (plus three assignments of 250 words of translation and theory-based assignments), they feel hard done by. I know that when I started working inhouse I was exhausted for the first three months at least. Stamina is one of those qualities which is gradually acquired – slowly I realised that I wasn't falling asleep on the train every day, and that I wasn't finding it such a struggle to get up in the morning. I think the important thing here is for apprentices to be aware of the fact that they will need stamina...and that they will acquire it with time.

A methodical approach

This is true of many aspects of translation right through from filing work properly and storing terminology so that it can be easily retrieved to maintaining consistency in both your use of terminology and your approach (e.g. consistently beginning someone's title with an upper case letter, or a lower case letter for that matter – it doesn't really matter which...as long as you're consistent!). Many companies will force apprentices to acquire a methodical approach by insisting upon adherence to procedures and systems (which have usually evolved over some time to ensure optimum efficiency).

Research skills

These can be acquired but to some extent also require a degree of initiative. Novices tend to stick to bilingual dictionaries (gradually progressing to using monolingual dictionaries where appropriate) and it is generally hard work pushing them towards background material in both the source and target languages, not to mention propelling them towards the CD-ROM and the periodicals section of the library. Apprentices should also get into the habit of obtaining help by posting messages in CompuServe forums (be it in the foreign language forum or in the specialist subject forums), networking and using the Yellow Pages as a resource (frequently the term you are looking for will be in the advert and you won't even have to ring the appropriate expert).

Computer literacy and touch-typing skills

Translators have to be computer literate. There is no room in the market for apprentices who have not mastered at least one of the major word processing packages. However, computer literacy goes beyond word processing – practising translators need to be able to use CompuServe and the World Wide Web, CD-ROM, databases, terminology management software and perhaps even machine translation software. Apprentices cannot afford to be scared or even shy of the computer. Furthermore, it is an enormous advantage for translators to be able to touch-type – not only because it is a skill which will ultimately determine their/their employer's earnings, but also because it eliminates one of the sources of error – their eyes never leave the source text page and, as such, there is less likely to be any omissions in their work.

The ability to work under pressure

Translation is a service industry where the client calls the shots. In these days of client awareness and client care, translators are under a great deal of pressure to do as much as possible, as well as possible, as fast as possible. This is a skill which, I feel, can be acquired only in a working environment. The only opportunity lecturers have to put students under pressure is 'timed translations' in class and, of course, end of year examinations. This is a great shame (especially as students' marks when working under pressure are invariably lower than for other assignments) as working under pressure is one of the most important aspects of translation – if apprentices can't manage it then they can't function as translators.

The ability to work quickly and absorb new information rapidly

I have included this as an acquired skill because, again, I think this is one area which novices cannot really experience in a course-based environment. Once they are working as apprentices in the real world they will have to speed up, and simply won't be afforded endless hours in which to research their work and acquire subject expertise (which isn't to say that their work shouldn't be well-researched). Clients generally dictate deadlines, and time is money. The much discussed figure of 2,000 words a day (completed, i.e. keyed in, checked, edited and read through) means very little to a novice...until they find themselves having to do it if they are to justify the expense of an employer taking them on and keeping them in employment.

An awareness of own capabilities and limitations

There are two aspects to this particular quality: an awareness of what to take on in terms of work; and an awareness of how you as a person function. The first is very important and is generally learned through error. I am the first to admit that as an apprentice I took on more than one text which I simply couldn't manage...and that it always ended in tears! However, I have come to the conclusion that this is an area where we have to make our own mistakes – I can only urge my students to turn down anything they are not capable of handling. They, meanwhile, are eager to impress their employer or, quite simply, are under pressure to be working rather than idle. It's a fine line but, at best, their supervisor will have to sort out the piece as a matter of urgency and, at worst, they may lose a client. As to the second type of awareness – make sure you are checking your work when you are at your most alert, and save mundane administrative tasks for the end of the day when you are not functioning at your best.

Time management and organisation skills

Again it's a case of sink or swim – constant time pressure and assignments mean that apprentices will be forced into prioritising their workload. Similarly, the amount of paper involved in translation will mean that they will have to get organised, file and document if they are to function effectively. While we're on the subject, every translator has to learn to make back-up copies of his work – better to learn it as part of a procedure rather than the hard way (you only have to lose an enormous file once!). The earlier apprentices start with the above, the better!

The ability to check their own and others' work

This is a vital skill particularly in these times of TQM (Total Quality Management), quality control, quality assurance and ISO 9000. It is also one of the most difficult to learn (particularly when checking your own work) as it involves checking not only for accuracy but also consistency. It may come as a surprise to novices to learn that checking others' work is also a very good form of training in itself as they will quickly come to distinguish the good from the bad, the consistent from the inconsistent and the outstanding from the mediocre – this is just one step away from incorporating what they have learnt into their own work. I will discuss checking at greater length under proofreading in the section on training novices.

The ability to write well in the mother tongue

Distinct from 'flair', this encompasses a good command of grammar, punctuation and collocations – all of which can be learned from textbooks (and, as such, can be self taught). These are features which every client has a right to expect in translated work, and should not be seen as anything other than mandatory.

Specialist subject knowledge

This is acquired over a long period (other than in instances where a specialist rather than a linguist has turned to translation). Translators should realise that it is extremely difficult to not only learn the terminology used in a specific area, but also to keep up to date with how it is used and how its usage changes. This is an area that requires a great deal of work in terms of reading around your subject and staying in touch with experts.

Proficiency in at least one foreign language

I have included this at the bottom of my list as novices should already be proficient in at least one foreign language. It is an obvious prerequisite to starting out in translation, though not quite so obvious is the need to have lived in the country concerned, know how its inhabitants think, have lived with the administrative system and be *au fait* with customs and practices. The latter three points are frequently the source of translation problems along the lines of how best to explain a concept or term which simply does not exist in the target language.

Training

1. Novice to apprentice

In the UK this training is usually undertaken by students at their own expense on postgraduate courses. Elsewhere in Europe it is possible to take an undergraduate qualification in translation, the length of such courses varying from country to country. However, it should be borne in mind that this is not the only route – an employer may well opt to take on a novice and turn him into an apprentice.

Rather than examine what is offered course by course, I have chosen to discuss what students should look for in a course if they want to work in translation. The views here are based not only on my opinions, but also those of various students who have passed through the University of Surrey.

One of the major benefits of vocational courses is that they tell students just what translation is. This may sound rather obvious, but the vast majority of my students are graduates from traditional language degree courses (how well I remember translating Evelyn Waugh into German without a dictionary!) and have very little idea of how translators work, what they translate and the kind of conditions they work under. This demystification is valuable in itself as it is not unusual for students to realise that translation isn't the career for them and that they would rather move on or return to a previous career.

That said, many students will stay in translation for the rest of their lives and, as such, have every right to expect a relevant and practical training. I would advise novices to look for the following (in some form or other, e.g. a series of lectures or a couple of seminars) in a course:

Practical translation classes using 'live' texts

By this I mean several hours every week where students work on a text which they are likely to encounter in the real world. They should also be given homework to translate other 'live' texts which may be a continuation of the text studied in class or a similar text on the same subject area. The importance of such texts cannot be overstated as they will give novices a clear idea of the type of material translated in the real world (rather than an academic environment), and the kind of standard expected.

Specialist subject classes

The practical translation classes should be supported by specialist subject classes – these may take the form of lectures in various areas of technology, economics, medicine, law or any other specialist subject which the university may be offering. As such, the practical translation classes and the specialist subject classes should be co-ordinated as far as possible to coincide so that students can gain maximum benefit from the terminology introduced in the specialist subject classes. Novices should be aware that one-year courses can do little more than give them a taster of various subject areas. Quite often students benefit from specialist subject classes in that they discover where their interests do and do not lie and, as such, narrow down the fields in which they will go on to specialise.

The opportunity to study translation from more than one language

This really is a must! Students need to be able to offer some degree of flexibility and will find that they are twice as marketable with two languages. Failing that, they should look for a course where they have the opportunity to learn a less common language *ab initio*.

Word processing classes

Each year of students that comes through is more computer literate than its predecessors, and more comfortable with computers and IT. However, novices who cannot word process when they start a translation course should take the opportunity to learn – an employer will be less than willing to foot the bill for similar courses and lost time.

*An introduction to machine translation, the Internet/
CompuServe, CD-ROM etc.*

These are vital tools which should not be overlooked by aspiring translators. In fact this is one area in which novices can gain the edge over older, less computer literate translators who may be reluctant to invest in, or use, such tools. Novices should be shown what is available in the way of terminology etc. on CD-ROM in their specific languages, and should expect to use these tools regularly in their homework assignments. Similarly, they should be shown how to compile glossaries and manage terminology using the most appropriate terminology software (see Klaus-Dirk Schmitz's article in this book).

Technical writing/copywriting classes

As Geoffrey Kingscott points out in his article, translators are writers and the type of translators graduating from translation courses should be excellent writers. The sad fact is that they aren't.

Many novices are blissfully unaware of how to write well – right from the very framework of sound grammar to the relevance of appropriate style. Every student can benefit from classes which outline the principles of good writing and provide an opportunity to put them into practice.

Proofreading

Given that students seem unable to check their work adequately, practical seminars explaining the basic proofreading symbols, how to use them and how to go about proofreading a text can only be a welcome element in translation courses. All of my students, past and present, will know that proofreading and checking are Rachel's hobbyhorses. It has bothered me for some time that students seem unable to master these skills even several months into the course. I have come to the conclusion that the problem is something of a mental block – I don't know a single translator who actually enjoys checking and, as such, it is very much a necessary evil. Students just don't seem to be able to leap the mental hurdle of accepting that they must allocate a great deal of time to checking, that they must be methodical in their approach and that they must go through a piece several times looking for different types of error. In the past I have tried (and failed) with the adult-to-adult 'You must find your own way of doing this, but this is mine...'. This year a colleague suggested that we introduce a 'Quality Control Sheet' (see below) in an attempt to push them a little harder towards thorough checking. Interestingly, this has met with a fair bit of resistance along the lines of students (wrongly) feeling patronised, and 'we find it very useful, but we'll do it our own way!'. As such, the problem stands. Novices find it very difficult to check their own work well enough to function in the real world and are unwilling to take advice and learn. It would seem to be a skill which they acquire with more practice and greater pressure and expertise (*and* when their livelihood depends on it).

Translation Quality Control Sheet

Accuracy
- Numbers checked?   Y/N
- Proper nouns checked?   Y/N

- Typography/punctuation checked?   Y/N
- Checked for omissions
  (paragraphs, words, sentences), extra words, etc.?   Y/N
- Grammar checked?   Y/N
  Final read-through for Target Language style?   Y/N
  Translation spell-checked after final edit?   Y/N

Research

I have consulted the following:

- General bilingual/monolingual dictionaries,
  BBI*, etc.   Y/N
  Which?
- Specialist bilingual dictionaries   Y/N
  Which?
- Specialist Source Language and/or Target Language
  monolingual dictionaries and encyclopaedias   Y/N
  Which?
- SL and/or TL reference materials
  (books, brochures, annual reports, etc.)   Y/N
  Which?
- CD-ROM and other sources   Y/N
  Which?

*Benson, Benson & Ilson, 1986, *The BBI Combinatory Diction-
ary of English. A Guide to Word Combinations*, John Benjamin's
Publishing Company.

Practising translators teaching practical translation classes

Many are the benefits to be derived from employing practising
translators to teach on translation courses. Firstly, they have direct
access to a variety of relevant and up-to-date texts of varying difficulty. Secondly, they are in touch with the market, know where
demand lies and can train students accordingly. Finally, they will
have a good idea of what is and isn't acceptable (and, by dint of
their professional role, will be trusted as having such), and will be
able to answer student questions about the workplace, profession,
life as a translator etc.

Practising translators visiting to give regular seminars

Again, students should look for as much exposure to practising translators as they can get. After all, this is their chance to benefit from someone else's experience and find out for themselves just what it's like to work as a freelance/inhouse translator/proofreader etc. A good course will have contacts in the form of previous years' students who have gone on to work as translators in any number of fields – this is both inspiring and useful for existing students.

Placements/visits to translation companies or agencies

As a lecturer, I know that these are a nightmare to organise, but I am still including them as I am convinced of their value. Translation courses simply cannot give novices any idea of how busy and pressured a job translation is. They need to be in the thick of it for a couple of weeks or, failing that, a day at the very least. They need to see sheet after sheet rolling off the fax, jobs coming in by modem for over-typing, jobs ten times as long as their homework assignments being turned around in less than a day, every day. They really need to have some idea of what they are letting themselves in for! I have always given my backing to students who have asked whether I know of Easter or summer work – if they've got the gumption to ask, then I will do my best to help them find something. I would urge all novices to get some kind of experience – ring or write to companies yourselves. If they can't afford to pay you, offer some of your time for free. Approach freelances who might be amenable to an extra pair of hands (don't expect to be given much in the way of translation, just soak up the atmosphere!). The important thing is to see for yourselves what goes on.

2. Apprentice to professional

Having completed a course and found work as a translator, the former novice will be embarking upon an apprenticeship and will be faced with the challenge of learning and developing most of the skills listed under the heading of 'acquirable'. Many of these will involve dealing with time pressure and working at speed. However, it doesn't stop there...apprentices need training and nurturing to build upon the skills they have acquired as novices. The real work starts here!

I have divided the types of training on offer at this level into three categories: training offered by the employer, training offered by external bodies, and training undertaken on the translator's own initiative.

Training offered by the employer

Again I have chosen to examine this from the point of view of apprentices, offering some ideas as to what they can expect from an employer. The first thing to note is that training will vary depending on the state of the market (training budgets are generally slashed in times of recession) and the size of the employer (it would be unreasonable to expect a freelance translator who has taken on an apprentice to foot the bill for a course in proofreading etc.). An employer will know how much work an apprentice needs to do each month to pay his way and, as such, the apprentice will have to achieve this target if he wants to keep his job.

Training offered by employers tends to divide into skills and qualities which can be taught, e.g. via courses and seminars, and those which can be nurtured. My own experience (and that of former students) is that apprentices are expected to adopt a very 'hands-on' approach i.e. they are thrown in at the deep end. Deadlines are set in stone and have to be met, come hell or high water. However, apprentices should expect to have their work checked and to be talked through any fundamental errors – this is one of the most basic and necessary forms of training. Similarly, systems should be explained, i.e. how jobs are numbered, the responsibility of the translator in terms of paperwork and so on. Larger organisations may have a per capita budget for training where it is up to translators to propose courses which they think will be useful. Employers may choose to wait until after the apprentice's trial period (or longer) before they invest in serious training (the commitment factor), and require that this investment be repaid if the translator leaves during the course or within one year of its conclusion (after all they will want to reap the rewards of their investment). Companies may choose to make the new apprentice the responsibility of a senior member of staff, or offer training through inhouse seminars on subjects such as checking, house style or style sheets. New apprentices may be given work to second-check or glossaries to compile so that they can familiarise themselves with specialist terminology and style. Some employers are happy to sponsor apprentices to maintain their language skills at evening classes or learn new languages.

It is at this level (i.e. during the apprenticeship) that I would expect the employer to have to nurture some of the skills outlined at the beginning of this article, most notably research skills, the apprentice's awareness of his capabilities and limitations, and initiative, inquisitiveness and alertness if the translator has them. As is the case at novice level, the individual may possess these skills but needs pointing in the right direction.

Apprentices should expect to be trained and should not be afraid to ask about training when being interviewed. The following is a list of some of the questions which apprentices should be able to answer after an interview (remember it's a two way process) either as a result of having quizzed the interviewer or existing employees of the company:

- Will all my work be checked?
- Will I have someone I can turn to for help?
- Will my performance be reviewed regularly (appraisals)?
- Does the company have a formal training policy?
- Does the company invest in training?...Is there a per capita training budget?
- How long will I have to work for the company before I am eligible for external training?

However, apprentices should remember that external training always involves a double cost to the employer in the form of the course fee as well as the income lost as a result of the apprentice having spent time away from his desk. As such, this type of training has to be justified in terms of the benefits the employer will reap.

Training offered by external bodies

These bodies are usually translation associations or institutes (or their various branches), universities and companies.

In the UK associations such as the Institute for Translation and Interpreting (ITI) and the Institute of Linguists (IoL) runs courses in everything from professional development to IT. It should be noted that the sub-groups of such organisations are frequently very active and may organise events of their own or merely provide translators with an opportunity to meet others who work in the same field.

Universities (particularly those which offer courses in translation) have also spotted this gap in the market and regularly hold workshops and courses. The following were taken at random from translation publications over the last two years: 'Translator's Workshop: Continuing education, banking, finance and related subjects' (Université de Genève), 'Law, business, finance and the translator' (University of Surrey), '3 in 1 – three workshops on terminology management, CD-ROM technology and modems' (City University) and 'Europe et Traduction' (Université d'Artois).

There is also a growing trend for companies (translation or otherwise) to run courses in areas in which they specialise. For example, one translation company based in central London regularly offers 'Medical and pharmaceutical workshops' covering such areas as laboratory techniques, statistics and sources of specialist information, and resources.

Own initiative

This is training to be undertaken in your own time and may include evening classes, correspondence courses (in proofreading and editing for example), or simply a conversation class in your languages or perhaps a new language. This is one way to really develop one or two specialist subject areas – one of the major challenges facing apprentices who find themselves thrust into a busy working environment. You may find that your employer recognises the benefits of such courses and is willing to contribute to their cost. It should not be forgotten that hobbies have been known to turn into specialist subject areas – what more of an excuse do you need to indulge in gourmet cooking!

3. Ongoing training

It is important for professional translators to realise that the world changes and they must make every effort to keep up-to-date with developments in their particular field and indeed changes taking place in the languages they work from. In addition to continuing with the type of training they have undertaken at apprentice level, this may be a matter of subscribing to specialist newspapers/periodicals (preferably in both source and target languages), taking one of the dailies in their source language two or three times a week, or subscribing to a particular specialist institute in order to receive their newsletters etc. Local chambers of commerce can prove a fruitful hunting ground for specialists who may be more than happy to answer queries and provide help where necessary. Professionals should also make a point of regularly spending time in the countries where their source languages are spoken to ensure that they really are up-to-date with current usage.

It is generally once they have reached professional level that translators choose to go freelance. Self-employment is a whole new ball game requiring that the translator develop such skills as marketing, dealing with clients and basic book-keeping. Again training is available, generally in the form of courses provided by institutes and associations, but also by specialist training companies.

Conclusion

Is there a case for university courses? Well, yes! Such courses will take translators from the novice to apprentice stage, give them a taste of what is involved and the expectations others will have of them, and provide them with some of the skills they will need during their working life. Furthermore, the value of such courses has been recognised by employers who are now stating them as a requirement for inhouse posts. It would be quite wrong, however, for graduates of such courses to consider themselves qualified professionals – the road is long and hard...and it's only just begun! As previously stated, this level of training need not necessarily be undertaken by a student at university – it can be offered in house by employers. However, such employers should note that these things take time, not only in terms of novice-time, but also employer-time (having to actively teach, supervise and monitor). Any employer plumping for this option (perhaps because novices come cheaper than apprentices) should be aware of the amount of handholding involved, the hidden costs of his own time lost and should expect to see a fair bit of bad work produced painfully slowly for several months. Bleaker still is the risk that a novice with little or no idea of what is involved in translation will leave, whereas an apprentice who has invested both time and money in a translation course is much more likely to be committed to his career.

Once in employment translators can, and should, expect ongoing training from their employer, be it in the form of all work being checked, appraisals, inhouse seminars or external courses. They can also expect to develop a number of skills which may not have been previously required e.g. working at speed, initiative etc. and to further their knowledge of their specialist areas.

Similarly, professional translators should be aware that it is all-too-easy to lose touch with a language and what is happening in their specialist field. Translation is, in many ways, a flexible job (have modem will travel) and many will stay in it all their working lives – a specialist field could develop beyond belief during that time (think of IT). Becoming a professional is not a matter of resting on your laurels, it's more a case of staying at the top. Faced with the challenge of staying up-to-date, professionals should continue to invest in training and may even find themselves looking to learn new skills if they intend to go freelance.

To return to my opening question of whether translators need training – the answer is a resounding YES! It is now widely accepted that there is much more to translation than the ability to speak a foreign language. Translation is a demanding job for bright people, and it doesn't stop there. They need to acquire and maintain any number of skills over a number of years if they are to be any good...and they need to realise it!

3. Careers and Career Development

CATRIONA PICKEN

Introduction

In this chapter I have attempted to give a picture of the actual and potential careers for translators and the development of these careers, as I see it. To help me with this I conducted a small and fairly random survey in mid-1995. I sent out about 75 questionnaires and received 20 responses, quite a good rate, I am told. In the questionnaire, I made a point of including sections relating to part-time staff and to short-term fixed contract staff as well as full-timers, since there is a clearly discernible trend towards less than full-time employment. After analysing the survey responses, I considered another source of information about current employment trends, the advertisements placed over the course of the year to mid-1995 in the ITI Bulletin. I gleaned further information about possible future trends from a report on graduate employment published by the National Institute of Economic and Social Research. Freelance translation is also a career for many linguists, for more and more of them, it would appear, and I have described the present-day translation scene for freelance translators, following it with a discussion of the financial aspects for both in-house and freelance translators. Translation as such is not the only possible career for someone trained as a linguist and specialising in translation, and I have briefly touched on a number of possibilities for those who are interested in pursuing what might be termed a 'para-translation' career. The chapter ends with a very brief look at the future – or a few of any number of possible futures.

Background

The following terms have something in common: streamlining, restructuring, downsizing, rationalisation, scaling-back, review, stripping out layers. Yes, they are all euphemisms for reducing staff numbers, whether by actual redundancies, early retirement programmes, or what is known as 'natural wastage' (i.e. not re-placing any members of staff who leave, for whatever reason). This is the somewhat depressing picture which emerges from a survey which I undertook earlier this year, with a view to writing the present chapter. The picture I have painted of diminishing, or even, in some cases, vanishing in-house translation units, applies first and foremost to the UK, which is where most of my respond-ents were located. The picture is very different on the other side of the Channel, where large numbers of translators are still employed, and still being recruited, especially in the mammoth translation services of the various European organisations in Brussels, Lux-embourg, etc.

While I make no claims that my survey is comprehensive (I lacked the time and resources to carry out a world-wide, or even Euro-pean-wide, investigation), it does seem to me to provide a snap-shot of the translation scene in the UK in the mid-1990s.

The questionnaire

I quote below, in condensed form, the text of the questionnaire I sent out.

Questionnaire on Careers and Career Development

A. FULL-TIME STAFF

1. What is the current number of full-time staff translators em-ployed in your unit?

2. Have you recruited any translators during the past 12 months?

    ☐ Yes
    ☐ No

2a. If no, please say why:

    ☐ Numbers already complete
    ☐ Staff leaving not being replaced

3. If yes, how many?

4. Did the recruit(s) possess translation qualifications?

    ☐ Undergraduatelevel
    ☐ Postgraduate level

5. Did the recruit(s) possess other qualifications?

    ☐ Yes
    ☐ No

    If so, in what areas? (e .g. chemistry, law etc.)

6. Did the recruit(s) come to your unit having already gained translation experience in some other job?

    ☐ Yes
    ☐ No

7. Does your organisation provide in-house training for the translators it employs?

    ☐ Yes
    ☐ No

8. If yes, what form does this training take?

    ☐ Learning on the job from experienced colleagues
    ☐ Formal courses on particular aspects of the work of your organisation
    ☐ Training in languages other than those originallyoffered by the recruit, or enhancement of a 'rusty' language
    ☐ Other

9. Is there a clear career structure for translators in your organisation?

    ☐ Yes

    ☐ No

10. If yes, please list the successive job titles (e.g. translator, senior translator/reviser, section head).

11. If no, is this because :

    a)there are too few staff?

    b) the problem has not been tackled?

    c) other reason?

12. Do you require your recruits to possess word-processing skills?

    ☐ Yes
    ☐ No

13. Do you require your recruits to have at least some knowledge of machine translation or machine assisted translation?

   ☐ Yes
   ☐ No

B. PART-TIME STAFF

i. Does your organisation employ part-time staff?

   ☐ Yes
   ☐ No

ii. If yes, why?

   ☐ organisational requirements
   ☐ at the request of the staff member(s) concerned

iii. Do part-time members of staff enjoy the same benefits as fulltimers, e.g. in opportunities for training, promotion etc.?

   ☐ Yes
   ☐ No

Please now answer Questions 1-13 for your part-time staff, omitting questions 7-11 if part-timers do not have the same benefits as full-timers.

1. What is the current number of part-time staff translators employed in your unit?

From here on, the questions were the same as questions A2-A13.

C. OTHER STAFF (Short-term contract, teleworking, etc.)

i. Does your organisation employ 'other' staff (short-term contract, teleworkers, etc.)?

   ☐ Yes
   ☐ No

ii. If yes, why?

   ☐ organisational requirements
   ☐ at the request of the staff member(s) concerned

iii. Do these members of staff enjoy the same benefits as full-tim-ers, e.g. in opportunities for training, promotion etc.?

   ☐ Yes
   ☐ No

Please now answer Questions 1-13 for your 'other' staff, omitting questions 7-11 if part-timers do not have the same benefits as full-timers.

1.   What is the current number of 'other' translators employed by your unit?

From here on, the questions were the same as questions A2-A13.

Analysis of response to individual questions

Full-time staff

Current numbers: The responses from translation units located in the UK revealed that the size of units varies between one and 23 full-time staff members, the average number being just under seven. In Europe, the range was from eight to 1,200 (the latter figure being the combined forces of all units of the Translation Service of the European Commission), giving an average of 436.

Recruitment trends: In the UK, one-third of the responding units had recruited new staff, while two-thirds had not. In the majority of the units which had not recruited, this was because the staff numbers were already complete. Only two respondents stated that members of staff who left were not being replaced. All but one of the European respondents had recruited staff during the previous 12 months, with once again the vast majority (115) going to the European Commission.

Qualifications of recruits: My question deliberately focused on the qualifications which were being looked for in new or potential recruits, not the qualifications of existing staff, some of whom might have been in post for so long that the possibility of pursuing translation studies, either at undergraduate or postgraduate level, did not even exist in their younger days. The number of respondents not requiring any kind of translation qualification was small, only two. However, one of these two respondents had recently recruited 50 translators, a figure described as 'much higher than the normal year's average' (for operational reasons). In this instance, a degree in a foreign language or languages was the basic requirement, though having said that, all the recruits were experienced translators. In all the other cases, the respondents either required or gave preference to candidates with translation qualifications, over three-quarters of them specifying postgraduate studies, as opposed to the quarter who would accept a first degree.

As far as 'other' qualifications are concerned, where this was mentioned, the type of qualifications ranged from fairly non-specific ('technical subjects, commercial subjects') to the highly specialised ('lexicology'). For massive translation units such as those in Brussels or Luxembourg, the 'other' qualifications listed were administration, law, finance, social affairs/sociology, informatics, education, politics, literature, foreign affairs, fine arts, medicine, philosophy, archaeology, advertising, marketing, statistics, chemistry, biochemistry, physics, music, and the theory of communications, clearly reflecting the wide range of topics the translators there are called upon to deal with.

Previous experience: Only two respondents stated that the recruits who joined them did not have previous translation experience in some other job. I deliberately did not specify 'in some other translation job', though it seems probable, in view of the high level of the requirement for translation qualifications, that this would in fact be the case. Here again, over three-quarters of the employers looked for previous experience, in particular the European organisations.

In-house training: Despite the requirements for translation qualifications, 'other' qualifications, and previous experience, here again over three-quarters of the respondents stated that in-house training was provided for recruits as compared with the quarter who said that no training was provided. The latter category were almost all small units, or in one case, an agency employing in-house translators. As far as the type of training provided was concerned, equal importance was attached to 'on-the-job' training, i.e. learning from experienced colleagues, and to formal courses on particular aspects of the work of the organisation. These formal courses would not necessarily be specifically organised for translators, and might possibly be provided for all new recruits to the organisation. Language training, as mentioned in the questionnaire, was slightly less popular, though still quite widely available to recruits, and there were a few instances of 'other' types of training.

Career structure: Turning now to the question of a formal career structure, it is not difficult to understand that such a thing is virtually impossible in very small units. Consequently, given the spread of large and small units responding, it was not surprising that one-third stated that there was no career structure, while the remainder replied in the affirmative. To deal first with those organisations without a career structure, about half of them maintained that their staff numbers were too few to permit a proper structure, although nearly as many cited 'other reasons' (not specified). Only one respondent stated that the problem had not been tackled.

As might be expected, the larger the translation unit, the more steps its career ladder provides. The category of 'translator' was the most numerous, with gradations rising up from this, via 'reviser' and 'senior translator' to 'head of section/unit/branch' (the title depended on the nomenclature used in the particular organisation). One respondent listed the job titles as 'administrative officer', 'controller' and 'senior controller', all titles I personally had never come across before, but presumably chosen to fit in with other strata in this particular organisation (motor industry).

Other skills: It came as no surprise to me that for every organisation which did not require recruits to possess word-processing skills (I deliberately did not describe them as 'qualifications') there were seven which did. Three of the respondents, one a very large organisation, said that word-processing skills were not a requirement, but that preference would be given to candidates who possessed them. One other large organisation stated that it did not require word-processing skills, but gave no reason for this. It may be that this particular unit has its own systems and prefers its recruits to come without preconceived ideas.

In contrast to the clear preference for word-processing ability, the picture was exactly the opposite when it came to knowledge of machine translation or machine-assisted translation. Only one respondent said that the single recruit who had been taken on had been required to have knowledge of machine translation or machine-assisted translation, and even in this case, it was merely stated that 'some' knowledge was desirable.

Part-time staff

Only one-third of the respondents stated that they employed part-time staff. For those who did, the balance was equally divided between those who employed part-timers for organisational reasons, and those who did so at the request of the staff members concerned. In one-third of the cases, part-timers did not enjoy the same benefits as full-time members of staff, though it must be borne in mind that we are here dealing with a very small sample. By far the largest contingent of part-timers (39) was to be found at the European Parliament in Luxembourg, but in this instance, as in all but one of the others, part-timers are not recruited. They are already on the staff, and change to part-time work for organisational reasons, or at their own request.

Other staff

This category was intended to cover any translators who did not form part of the two previous categories. About half the respondents did employ short-term fixed contract staff, teleworkers, etc. One respondent maintained that freelance translators were covered by this category, and it is true that unlike most organisations, this one did provide training for its freelances. Fewer than half the organisations employing 'other' staff stated that these people enjoyed the same benefits as their full-time employees. Another large employer of full-time and part-time translators was also contemplating launching a teleworking pilot scheme in the near future.

As far as the recruitment of this type of staff is concerned, the picture that emerges is that these people are experienced translators, who have either worked full-time for their organisation, or in some other employment, and can offer either intimate knowledge of the organisation as a result of having worked for it already, or qualifications over and above purely linguistic ones ('engineering' was specifically mentioned by two respondents). It was expected that all of these translators would have postgraduate level translation qualifications. Moreover, these translators were all expected to possess word-processing skills. In no instance was there any requirement for a knowledge of machine translation or machine assisted translation.

What does the survey tell us?

As far as aspiring translators are concerned, the main conclusion to be drawn from the survey is that the recruitment of novices, already on the decline, has almost dried up. It would appear to be an asset to be able to offer qualifications in a field other than translation, but the range of possibilities is so wide that on the basis of the results of this particular survey, it is impossible to say that aspiring translators should endeavour to acquire knowledge of one particular subject rather than another. The best solution would appear to be for potential translators to try to aim for an organisation offering the type of work in which they already have some experience or knowledge. Continuing with the theme of knowledge and skills offered by potential translators, it is clear that word-processing skills are virtually essential, or to put it in other words, since preference is almost always given to candidates possessing word-processing skills, there are very strong reasons for acquiring them. Speaking personally, I would say that these skills are likely to be of use in almost every field of endeavour, so there is no point in burying your head in the sand and trying to get away without them. Nowadays, there is nothing demeaning about sitting in front of a keyboard/0 everyone does it, and I get the impression that most young people learn keyboarding as a matter of course. All I can say is, that the higher the level of your skill, the greater is your ability to work fast and fluently, without having to spend time mastering the purely mechanical aspects of producing work.

It would appear that the sample covered by the present survey did not extend to those organisations in which machine translation (MT) or machine-assisted translation (MAT) is already a *fait accompli*. I know that such organisations exist, and their response to the question about having prior knowledge of the subject would be completely different from the answers I have reported on here. Nevertheless, it does seem that even in the large organisations in Europe, where MT or MAT is something which may very well be introduced sooner or later, recruits are not expected to offer any prior knowledge of this subject. This may come as a disappointment to those who have taken postgraduate diploma courses in translation in which MT or MAT forms part of the syllabus, but on the basis of the information presented here, it looks as though it might be preferable to devote less time to this topic and spend more on something else. My preferred option for this extra time would be enhancement of English language skills, or for those aspiring to a career in Europe, the acquisition of a good command of the spoken language of your target country – after all, you will have to reside there.

Let us assume that you have been recruited and joined one of the larger organisations. It appears highly likely that comprehensive and thorough training will be provided for you. This takes the form, first and foremost, of learning on the job, under the close supervision of more experienced colleagues – an absolutely vital stage of familiarisation with the subject-matter handled by the organisation you have joined, and its jargon, or to put it more tactfully, the terminology and phraseology it normally uses. You may also be required to go on what is sometimes known as an induction course, which is usually provided for all new employees, not just translators, and helps to ease all newcomers into their new surroundings. At a later stage, possibly depending on skills or inclinations displayed by the recruit, more specific courses may be organised with a view to providing greater knowledge of particular topics which are already, or are likely to be, useful to the translators. When we look at smaller organisations, however, formal training is far less likely to be provided.

Turning now to the question of careers for in-house translators, the overall picture would appear to be fairly predictable – the larger the organisation, the more clearly defined is the career structure, and, of course, the longer the ladder to be climbed in order to reach the top. The actual rate of progress through all the stages described by the various respondents must depend on a number of factors which are utterly unpredictable, such as staff turnover, the actual ability of individual translators (and their capabilities as supervisors or administrators, once they reach the higher echelons). In translation, just as in virtually every other field, those who reach the higher levels in the organisation usually find that they do less and less of what they started out doing – translation in the present case – and more and more administrative, supervisory and organisational work. It must be realised that this is not to everyone's taste.

Analysis of the advertisements in the ITI Bulletin

To round out the information gleaned from the survey above, I also scanned the advertisements for translators which have appeared in the ITI Bulletin between mid-1994 and mid-1995, i.e. covering the same period of time as in the questionnaire. I studied a total of 27 advertisements, mainly inviting applications for posts variously described as 'translator', 'staff translator', 'in-house translator', etc. Of these, no fewer than 23 specifically mentioned the word 'experienced' as an essential requirement. Interestingly enough, the qualifications aspect was rather different from the picture which emerged from the survey results.

The advertisements for posts which did not specify that candidates should be experienced mentioned a 'junior team member', or 'trainee translators' (the organisation which placed this latter advertisement was seeking several members of staff, and was looking for experienced candidates as well as trainees). The one which seemed to me to be the most challenging for an inexperienced candidate asked for a 'translator/bilingual secretary', a native English speaker with a good working knowledge of Russian and German, profound technical knowledge and a serious interest in translation (and occasional interpreting!) to work in Munich with a firm of patent agents.

Ten of the advertisements called for translation qualifications, 10 did not specify what qualifications were required, and the other seven mentioned a degree, but not necessarily in translation, or even modern languages. It seems reasonable to suppose, however, that a candidate with a translation qualification would have an advantage over candidates not possessing such a qualification, even though it was not specifically called for. Word-processing skills were actually named in 10 out of the 27 advertisements, and I must say that it would be surprising if the others did not regard at least some measure of ability in this area as a foregone conclusion.

Only four of the 27 advertisements were seeking short-term contract staff, whereas the half of organisations covered in the survey employed such people. It would appear that such opportunities do occur only rarely, and it is also possible, though I have no evidence to prove it, that some organisations may bring in former members of staff who have left to have a family, for instance, to provide short-term cover, rather than advertising for these translators. Speaking from personal experience, I would say that to recruit candidates with no previous knowledge of the organisation and its ways, for a period which might be as short as three months, could almost be counter-productive, because they require so much supervision in the early stages. On the other hand, if you are successful in being appointed to a post of this kind, it could provide valuable experience, and possibly give a 'foot in the door' (one of the short-term contract posts advertised mentioned the possibility of permanent employment once the contract had come to an end).

Throughout my analysis of the questionnaire responses and the ITI Bulletin advertisements, I have refrained from mentioning specific languages, nor have I gone into the question of whether the translators were being recruited to carry out work from or into English. In fact, quite a number of the ITI Bulletin advertisements were seeking native speakers of languages other than English, so that by extrapolation it can be assumed that openings for such translators must occur quite frequently. I know that this edition of The Translator's Handbook will be read not only in the UK but elsewhere, and I would strongly recommend all aspiring translators to scan the columns of the ITI Bulletin to see what possibilities are on offer. Although advertisements for translators do appear elsewhere, it means buying all the quality daily papers and ploughing through an enormous amount of irrelevant material. The ITI Bulletin, on the other hand, is targeted very specifically at existing and aspiring translators, and is almost bound, sooner or later, to produce an opening to match your requirements.

Report on the Graduate Employment in the UK, from the National Institute of Economic and Social Research, London

While I was preparing the groundwork for this chapter, I read an item in my daily paper with the rather alarming headline 'Menial jobs await many graduates'. The item summarised a report issued by the National Institute of Economic and Social Research, London, which was entitled 'The new graduate supply-shock: Recruitment and utilisation of graduates in British industry', by Geoff Mason (1995). The first sentence in the newspaper report ran as follows: 'Graduates with modest degrees in irrelevant subjects from undistinguished universities can look forward to little more than poorly-paid clerical jobs...' However, later on, I found the comforting statement that 'Managers of small and medium-sized firms preferred to recruit graduates with degrees in computing, languages and business or marketing, the Institute said'. The main thrust of the argument was that graduates without any 'vocational' element in their degrees might not achieve more than what were described as 'sub-graduate' jobs involving routine tasks traditionally assigned to school-leavers. Admittedly in some cases these menial jobs have been modified to suit the new level of recruit. Since by implication language degrees were regarded as 'vocational', something I had not previously thought possible, I acquired a copy of the report. It covered two principal areas of activity, the steel industry and the financial services sector, and was very positive about the prospects for language graduates in export departments in the steel industry, with linguists actually being recruited in order to 'help develop and process export sales', an area where a variety of linguistic skills is called for. The general conclusion reached was that 'the majority of graduate recruits in this branch of manufacturing (the steel industry) have gained degrees in vocational subjects – such as engineering and technology, foreign languages and business/financial studies – and are appointed to jobs appropriate to their level of education'. It is gratifying to find independent evidence of the fact that a language degree is not regarded as a 'soft' subject, and that because language graduates must by definition possess linguistic skills, coupled, one hopes, with the ability to communicate, their merits are at last being appreciated.

Freelance Translation as a Career

The orthodox career pattern for translators (by which I mean technical and specialised translators) has always been for them to learn their trade by taking a language degree (ideally one which includes the study of translation), and joining a large translation department. Then, after some time, they rise up the ladder until they can call themselves fully fledged translators. In the past, many translators, especially women who had worked in translation departments and had left to raise a family, then returned to the translation world as freelances. It has to be realised that in the really old days, maternity leave was virtually unknown and for a member of staff to leave and then rejoin the same department almost unheard of. This meant that there was a reasonably large pool of freelance translators who were, it must be admitted, of very variable standard as regards competence. Some of them took the trouble to keep up with their subject and allowed only a comparatively short time to elapse before resuming work, whereas others probably found that things had changed too much in the interim and that full-time freelance translation work, never an easy option, would be too much of a struggle for them. There were in those days, of course, also a good number of translators who for whatever reason had gone straight into freelance work – people who had previously had another career, in medicine or engineering for instance, but now felt that they could turn their language knowledge into good use as freelances. Such people are far less exposed to the risks of setting up as a freelance because they already know what the market requires of them. For a new graduate to embark on freelance work is tremendously risky, and not very lucrative either.

In the not-so-distant past, an important consideration for translators who wanted to pursue a really worthwhile freelance career was the problem of communications. It was essential not to be located at some remote spot where it would be difficult both to receive and to send out bulky documents. It was fairly common for documents to be delivered or collected by courier. This was certainly the case when I started freelancing about 10 years ago. Nowadays, this aspect of working as a freelance has completely changed. It is the exception rather than the rule to send finished work out in hard copy by post (I know this only too well, because the stack of one thousand A4-size envelopes I ordered has scarcely diminished, after several years). All freelance translators worth their salt have been equipped with fax machines for many years, primarily to receive work (or, initially, to give potential jobs a preliminary inspection by looking over sample pages and deciding whether the subject matter and deadline were feasible), and nowadays with modems as well. Modems really come into their own when work has to be sent abroad. They also mean that freelance translators can live just where they like – the remotest part of the North of Scotland, the Channel Islands, to name but two locations – and still remain in constant touch with the outside world, clients and colleagues. Unless freelance translators are lucky enough to have close links of co-operation with colleagues who work in the same fields or languages, and who are willing to provide mutual assistance, as a freelance one is very much on one's own. It is therefore essential for freelance translators to have acquired above-average competence in the languages and subjects they offer, or to have such good relations with their clients that the clients are prepared to send them work more or less on trust. Trust at this level inevitably takes some time, probably years, to build up. As far as the practical aspects of setting up as a freelance translator are concerned, I would recommend all those interested to read Geoffrey Samuelsson-Brown's A Practical Guide for Translators (1993), which covers in far greater detail than is possible here 'all aspects that are relevant to the would-be translator... intended mainly for those who wish to go freelance... Advice is given on how to set up as a translator, from the purchase of equipment to the acquisition of clients... Computer hardware and software are reviewed... [the book] covers most practical aspects of translation'. A second edition of this book has now been published, which covers a wide variety of new topics: Recruitment competitions; Marketing your services; Computer-aided translation (CAT); Production rates; Problems faced by the individual translator; Preemptive measures; Decision flowcharts; Electronic publishing; Setting up a budget; Fault analysis flowcharts - all this and more in 160 pages.

Financial aspects

It is perfectly legal in certain countries for the national association(s) of translators to publish tariffs of recommended rates for translation, graded according to type of language (basically Western European, and others), degree of difficulty, and in some cases the purpose for which the translation is required (information only, for instance, or publication standard). In the UK, the laws governing restrictive practices prohibit the publication of recommended rates. How, then, is it possible, especially for someone coming into the field for the first time, to determine what rate to charge for a given piece of work? The answer is that you can discover what rates are being charged through surveys compiled by organisations such as the Institute of Translation and Interpreting, and published from time to time in its journal, the ITI Bulletin. Issue no. 2, 1995, published in April 1995, gives the figures derived from a survey carried out in September 1994. I shall not reproduce the findings in any detail, but just remind readers that the figures are not necessarily representative, as they reflect the answers supplied by respondents to a questionnaire, and cannot therefore reflect the whole picture. As an indication, however, for a staff translator working in London, the salary varied between £18,600 a year for translators aged under 30 to £24,000 for translators over 45 (these are median salaries). Outside London, these figures were about £2,000 a year lower, reflecting the higher cost of living in south-east England. For translators working abroad, all but two of the sample of 23 were working in Europe, the majority in European Union countries; of these, four earned less than £25,000 a year, while at the top of the scale, three were earning over £50,000. If we draw a rough-and-ready conclusion from these figures, it would appear that to be a staff translator is not a highly lucrative career in the UK, though the picture looks rather more favourable overseas – the lowest salary figure mentioned is higher than the top earnings in the UK, though here again the cost of living abroad has to be taken into account.

What sort of income can one hope to earn as a freelance? Here again, the ITI survey is based on responses to a questionnaire. Of the people who claimed to work full-time as freelance translators (a lot of people would class themselves as part-time), 9 per cent earned less than £15,000. The largest single group, 28 per cent, stated that their income was between £15,000 and £20,000; one-third of the total sample, however, earned between £20,000 and £30,000 and almost one-third came into the £30,000 to 'over £40,000' bracket. If it is borne in mind that because freelances are self-employed and can therefore offset their expenses against income tax, it would look as though freelances are better off than staff translators. On the other hand, the staff translator has a measure of job security, a pension scheme, (usually) the morale-boosting environment of working with colleagues, and ready access to all the information resources of the organisation. Whether to try for a position as a staff translator or to go freelance is very much a question of individual preference (or circumstances), and there is certainly no definitive answer. Speaking personally, I have been a staff translator and a freelance, and have been equally happy in both roles.

Other careers for translators

A translation qualification leads to a job as a staff translator or freelance translator – or does it? There are other possibilities of employment, where a knowledge of languages is an asset and the discipline of translation studies makes it possible to contemplate work in which the ability to handle/organise/classify words is paramount. Even the far from comprehensive picture provided by the job advertisements in the ITI Bulletin over the past year reveals a small but steady demand for people with translation qualifications who can do 'other' jobs – a 'technical terminology specialist', 'language editors', 'foreign-language proof-readers', 'translation manager', 'copywriters/editors'. Lexicography is another possibility. Foreign language dictionaries are still being busily compiled, though when they are eventually published, they may not come out in the traditional print-on-paper form. In fact, the possibilities offered by dictionaries on CD-ROM of constant, instant updating must mean that there will be whole teams of people occupied in doing just that. The potential for employment in export sales, as described in the report of the National Institute of Economic and Social Research, is also worth exploring. In such cases, it goes without saying that the translator should also be able to offer a fluent command of the language(s) of the country or countries with which the employer organisation does business, and/ or be willing and able to visit such countries on business trips, as well as dealing with visitors who come from abroad. Such posts are well-suited to those who set store by the ability to communicate, to make good use of interpersonal skills, and to use their own initiative, as well as being good linguists. There is no denying that a measure of numeracy does not come amiss in today's business world. The current proliferation of broadcasting, whether by radio or television, means that there is an ever-growing market for translation connected with the media. Subtitling of cinema and TV programmes has been with us for a long time, but the demand for subtitling (and 'texting' of TV programmes to help the deaf) is bound to increase. It requires the ability to produce work rapidly to very tight limitations (of space and time on the screen), and at the same time, the translator has to have a command of the spoken language (both source and target) which far outstrips the need of the translator working with the written word alone. A knowledge of foreign languages in general can be of use in many careers which do not specifically call for translation skills as such – the travel trade, arts management, banking, the diplomatic corps are a few which spring to mind, but in such cases, linguists are not recruited on the basis of their language skills alone, and must have something else to offer their potential employers.

What of the future?

In the interests of covering all possible aspects of the work of the translator, I acquired The Daily Telegraph Guide to the Internet (1995). Having read it, and knowing that some of my colleagues are already hooked up to systems like CompuServe, I can see that the Internet could play a very large part in the future lives of translators. According to Sue Schofield, the author of the Guide to the Internet, 'the writing is certainly on the wall for providers who continue to lope along with character-based terminal interfaces'. I can foresee the day when someone who wants a translation done on a particular topic can post up on the Internet bulletin board all the details such as length, urgency, mode of delivery (by email, presumably), and freelance translators sitting in their homes can express their interest in doing the job – or if they are not free, can indicate a colleague who might be able to take it on. Freelance translators could be listed in a directory, which would enable clients to contact a particular translator who would be especially well suited to doing a particular job. And if a translator, having embarked on a translation, needed information on terminology, for instance, the bulletin board would again come into play, or a query could go out to a selected list of contacts who might be able to help. Anything which anyone writes about the Internet is of course doomed to be obsolete or at least outdated by the date of publication, and it may very well be that by the time this chapter is being read, further exciting developments have already been announced. For instance, a new book is to be published in February 1996 entitled The Coming Industry of Teletranslation. All I can do at present is quote from the publisher's description: 'This book is about 'Teletranslation' – a term the author uses to describe the offspring of the forthcoming marriage of the previously unrelated branches of the communication business: telecommunication and translation. It examines the need for telecommunications-based language services in response to the emerging communications environment and described how teletranslation services can be developed'. So there you have it: don't watch this space, watch other spaces, and keep abreast of the innovations such as those described in these two books. By the end of the present century, the work of a translator could very well be as different from what it is now, as the present-day scene is different from what it was in the early days of my own career – when some translators still wrote out translations in longhand. We have come a long way since then, but clearly we also have far to go.

References

1. Mason, G. (1995) *The new graduate supply-shock: Recruitment and utilisation of graduates in British industry.* National Institute of Economic and Social Research.London:(NIESR Report No. 9)

2. O'Hagan, M. (1996) *The coming industry of teletranslation: overcoming communication barriers through telecommunications.* Clevedon: Multilingual Matters.

3. Samuelsson-Brown, G. (1993) *A practical guide for translators.* 2nd edn, Clevedon: Multilingual Matters.

4. Schofield, S. (1995) *The Daily Telegraph guide to the Internet..* Addison-Wesley

4. Organisations for translators

CHRIS SCHRÖDER

The majority of those who earn a living from translation are affiliated to some form of translation organisation. Why?

This chapter looks at the roles played by translation organisations around the world, discussing not only the services they *aim* to provide but also the services they actually *do* provide and, rather more subjectively and contentiously, *should* provide.

Most of the facts and figures below are taken from the responses to a questionnaire (included at the end) which was sent out to 50 different national translation organisations in January 1996. I am grateful to all those who took time to complete and return the questionnaire along with often remarkable quantities of background information, brochures, journals and so on. I am also deeply indebted to many different translators and translation companies for their views on the subject.

Given the scope of the chapter, it has not been possible to provide exhaustive analyses and statistics for particular types of service etc, nor a comprehensive survey of translation organisations around the globe. However, I hope to give the uninitiated some idea of the potential benefits of membership of a translation organisation, and give the converted some food for thought in terms of whether their organisations really give them what they want and need.

What is a translation organisation?

Before looking in more detail at the nature of specific organisations and the services they offer, it might be a good idea to state the possibly-not-so-obvious and examine what a translation organisation actually is.

A basic definition of 'translation organisation' would of course be simply 'an organised body of translators' (association, institute, federation, guild, group, chapter, syndicate, committee, network...).

This covers an extremely wide range of different organisations, from the most informal local gatherings upwards, and so I have chosen to narrow the focus by concentrating chiefly on the *national* translation organisation, with special reference to some of the more interesting cases to be found in Europe.

For reasons of resources and logistics, the national organisation is generally best suited to playing the dual role of association *and* (professional) service provider which today's translator would appear to demand.

Nevertheless, it is important to remember that there are other types of translation organisation which may also have a good deal to offer. As a result, this section first runs through the main types of translation organisation before going on to discuss the national organisation in greater depth.

Size

The humblest translation organisations in terms of geographical scope and membership are the **local groups**. These are generally small informal gatherings of translators who work in the same area and meet periodically for essentially little more than a coffee and a chat. Owing to their small size, these groups may not be ideal for discussing the minutiae of a particular language pair or subject area and certainly lack the resources and clout to change the world; but they do offer plenty of scope for informal discussion about the latest software packages, sources of information or the merits of various local accountants. These groups can even be a good source of work for freelance translators, with members perhaps preferring to pass work on to someone they know well and trust.

Often equally small, in terms of membership if not in geographical coverage, are the **specialist groups**. The common factor here is specialisation (subject or language) rather than location. These groups often share the informal atmosphere of the local groups, but discussions will normally be oriented more towards the latest trends in a particular industry/country or the merits of a new specialist dictionary or termbank. Visits to factories or conversation evenings in relevant languages may also be arranged.

Next up are the **regional groups/associations**, ranging from larger-scale versions of the local groups to fully fledged translators' associations with full sets of bylaws, membership dues and the like. These are mostly set up or co-ordinated by national organisations, partly in recognition of the logistical problems of getting people to travel across a whole country to attend meetings: for instance, in the USA, where the average state is larger than most European countries, the regional organisations under the *American Translators' Association* (ATA) – the 'chapters' – have a vital role to play in bringing translators together. Nevertheless, some regional groups do retain full or partial independence (e.g. the *North West Translators' Network* in the UK or the *Landesverbände* under the national translation/interpreting organisation *Bundesverband der Dolmetscher und Übersetzer* (BDÜ) in Germany).

The advantage of these types of organisation is that their smaller size and often less formal atmosphere allow members to get to know each other better than is the case with a larger organisation. These organisations are also less heavily encumbered with the bureaucracy which threatens to overwhelm many of the larger national organisations.

However, their small size can also be a disadvantage. If you are thinking of joining one of these groups, it is important to bear in mind that members can only get out as much as they put in – these organisations simply do not have the resources to offer the services available from larger organisations. These are generally very much clubs or associations in the more traditional sense.

The largest organisations in terms of membership are of course the **national organisations**, of which most European countries, at least, have more than one. In general, these organisations coordinate the activities of a number of constituent local, regional and specialist groups/associations (see above) and, thanks to their larger membership, have the resources to offer a much wider range of services to their members and, in many ways, the profession as a whole.

Many of the national organisations are themselves members of the **international translation organisation** *Fédération Internationale des Traducteurs* (FIT) which seeks to represent the interests of translators at an international level. The main thing the FIT has to offer the individual translator is the opportunity to meet and debate with translators from other parts of the world at its triennial congress.

The only common feature of all these organisations is that in some way they aim to promote the interests of their members. This can mean anything from exchanging ideas on difficult terms or spilling the beans on clients with bad payment records, through organising professional indemnity insurance and pension schemes, to negotiating with national and international bodies.

Guise

There are of course numerous different ways of classifying translation organisations. Besides the differences in size outlined above, the most obvious distinction is perhaps whether an organisation aims to meet the needs of literary or non-literary translators; in line with the aims of the Handbook, this chapter concentrates on the latter. Other factors are the structure and origins of an organisation – is it independent or part of a larger organisation, was it set up by a group of translators, what are its main objectives, does it represent interpreters too? For the sake of brevity, I will restrict myself to a few key factors here.

One is the **maturity of the market** in which the organisation operates. In a highly mature market, a national translation organisation will generally have well-established links with industry and the public sector, maybe offering a wide range of professional services to members in the form of indemnity insurance or pension schemes. In the former Eastern Bloc countries and the former Yugoslavia, for instance, the translation market and its organisations are very young – at least in their current form – and often still finding their feet to some extent. Here the emphasis is more on securing a living wage for translators as opposed to, say, the niceties of regulation. Nevertheless, in this type of market there are likely to be fewer legislative obstacles for introducing fixed price tariffs for freelance translators or demanding copyright for members. Organisations are less restricted by their own traditions and bureaucracy and have perhaps greater scope to adopt a more idealistic and less resigned and world-weary approach than many Western organisations. Hence Slovenia's scientific/technical translation association *Društvo Znanstvenih in Tehniških Prevajalcev*

Slovenije (DZTPS) offers its freelance members a comprehensive invoicing service – to a fixed tariff – and looks after their tax needs! Mollycoddling or heaven, the choice is yours...

As the status of translators varies from country to country, so does the general nature of a translation organisation. Thus, in a country like Denmark where the profession is in some respects very closely regulated, the national translation organisation takes on many of the roles of a *professional organisation* like those for doctors, lawyers or accountants. National organisations in (established but) less developed markets are often more like *clubs* with the emphasis on informality and perhaps the social side of things.

Another factor is an organisation's **roots**. As was seen above, regional organisations are often affiliated to national organisations to give them more clout. Some translation organisations, such as the association of state authorised translators *Translatørforeningen* in Denmark, have adopted a similar approach and joined up with a larger, more general national professional organisation, in this case the association of business language graduates *Erhvervssprogligt Forbund* (ESF), which has a membership of 10,000 and the resources and reputation to match.

However, most national translation organisations remain stubbornly independent. Many were originally set up by a group of translator chums clubbing together and some have not really progressed beyond this stage despite the influx of many new members. Independence severely restricts what an organisation can do – all services have to be paid for somehow. Often subscription/membership fees are enough to cover little more than the production of a regular journal – with this generally comprising articles contributed free by members. As such, these organisations effectively remain clubs and struggle to embrace the role of service provider mentioned earlier. Where a body is run by volunteers, these volunteers can become very possessive of their 'baby' and frequently close ranks if challenged by new ideas – a situation which has beleaguered (and backfired on) many a translation organisation in the (sometimes very recent) past. The upper echelons of many translation organisations have often been perceived by the rank and file as an exclusive club to which they could progress only if they toed the line; fortunately new ideas and dynamism would now appear to be winning the day in most organisations.

Membership

Most national translation organisations operate more than one class of membership and in some way 'vet' applicants for membership. The most common classes are full, associate and student membership.

- **Full members** generally have to satisfy requirements which aim to ensure that only 'quality translators' get in: almost always some degree of experience, often a translation qualification, or occasionally a pass in the organisation's very own entrance examination. In return, full members enjoy a number of privileges not extended to associates and other lesser members, such as voting rights at the AGM or the use of the organisation's logo to 'certify' translations.

- **Associate members** are not generally required to be as experienced or well-qualified. They have fewer rights and in some ways get less from the organisation and so pay less for membership. Associate membership is very much a stepping stone towards full membership for recent entrants to the profession while they 'serve their dues'.

- **Student members** are generally offered cut-price membership and entrance fees to conferences etc in the hope that they will eventually subscribe as full members. The key benefit of membership is contact with real, live translators; in my experience many students of translation would otherwise seem to have little idea of what the job really involves.

- **Corporate members** are another interesting – but uncommon – class. These are largely specialist translation companies/agencies and the translation departments of (primarily) multinationals. In return for much inflated membership fees, these members get reduced rates for sending staff on training courses and publicity/PR benefits in the form of being able to use the organisation's logo, being listed in its directory or even having some free advertising in the organisation's journal.

Corporate membership has often aroused considerable controversy: most translation organisations serve primarily the freelance side of the profession, who can often view translation companies/agencies (their clients) as 'the enemy', and so there is clearly plenty of scope for a conflict of interests when representing both client and supplier. Nevertheless, there is also something to be said for promoting understanding and tolerance between these two parties.

Role

Earlier I suggested that today's translation organisation has to play the dual role of both association and service provider – it seems that members are demanding more out of their organisations than they are willing to put in. In place of the traditional barter-type system where each member contributes some of his or her know-how and experience in return for that of others (swapping glossaries etc.), nowadays translators appear to be more interested in simply buying in the services they need with hard cash. One might say that translation has grown up and become a true business.

Nevertheless, one key feature of translation organisations, as discussed above, is that they were founded by translators for translators and are still run largely by translators. How much the membership of a translation organisation gets out of the organisation depends on how much it puts in. Most of the current discontent with translation organisations has in reality as much to do with the apathy of their rank-and-file members as with the supposed shortcomings of the upper echelons of their hierarchies.

Due to the ever increasing emphasis on the services provided by the translation organisation, the rest of this chapter works with an expanded set of roles: four subsets of 'service' and, of course, the ever relevant 'association'. The role of any professional organisation will always be pretty much the same – a mixture of representation, regulation, information, qualification and association. Today's professional translation organisation should be no exception.

- **Representation** covers some of the services offered by trades unions, from wage bargaining through to pension schemes, plus more nebulous objectives such as raising the profile/status of the profession.
- **Regulation** may be de facto in the form of statutory fixed rates or qualifications for translators, or implicit where an organisation has the membership and power effectively to control the market.

- **Information** can be both for members (distributing a regular journal with news and articles) and for non-members (publishing directories of members or providing names of suitable translators).
- **Qualification** covers not only formal qualifications awarded or recognised by translation organisations but also training seminars and courses for members.
- **Association** is the traditional and still important role of the translation organisation in bringing translators together – be it for social or professional get-togethers.

Representation

The meaning of representation, as applied to the translation profession, varies from country to country, according in part to how the labour market is organised. Thus in some countries the representative function of a translation organisation is immediately akin to that of a trades union, while in others it is restricted to more nebulous aspirations such as 'raising the status of the profession'.

Most translation organisations offer at the very least some form of **arbitration** service. The scope of this is often determined by legislation but more often by general business/labour market practice. An organisation will for instance intervene or mediate in cases of disputes between freelances and their clients or between translation companies and their employees (though note the potential conflict of interests when representing both, as mentioned above!).

In some countries this is taken one step further. Take Denmark, with arguably the world's most highly developed translation market and the organisations to match. Having just 170 members (albeit highly-qualified 'state authorised translators' appointed by the Crown), the translation organisation *Translatørforeningen* is, as mentioned earlier, closely affiliated to the much larger organisation ESF which has a membership of over 10,000 language graduates – and so some clout in a country with a population of less than 5 million! ESF is heavily involved in **wage bargaining**; negotiates with government ministries on **official rates** for translators with different qualifications and in different circumstances; offers various forms of **insurance** to its members, including both professional indemnity and sickness insurance; runs a major **pension scheme**; has the resources to produce a wide range of **brochures and leaflets**; publishes a **glossy monthly journal**; has **close liaisons with higher education and industry**; the list really does go on. Quite simply, ESF is a heavyweight professional organisation in a well-organised labour market and so in an excellent position to represent and raise the profile of translators – and certainly in a better position than the tiny *Translatørforeningen* on its own.

Ultimately, with just 170 members and with all of those authorised to use an official seal on their work, it is clear that *Translatørforeningen*/ESF have a group of translators of some distinction to promote and represent. So, unlike the membership of many a translation organisation, the members of *Translatørforeningen* are clearly of the calibre to have their status raised.

Which leads us on to one of the loftier aspirations cited by the translation organisations in every country from Australia to Venezuela which replied to the questionnaire sent out: '**to raise the status of the profession**'. As most respondents replied that translators do *not* enjoy the status of true professionals like doctors and lawyers in each country, raising their status would appear to be a pressing issue. However, it would seem that most organisations are better at finding elegant formulations of their overall aims in this area (along the lines of 'forging closer ties with industry') than at actually coming up with specific policies and measures to realise them!

In many countries the translation organisations have established lines of communication with government authorities on rates of pay and the like, but, while the state remains a major translation buyer, in a global market industry is very much where it's at. So raising the status of the profession effectively means impressing industry; a translation organisation wanting to improve our sorry lot needs to raise the profile of translation in industry.

This is easier said than done. Of course, the major multinationals, with their huge translation/documentation budgets and often also their own translation departments, do normally take translation seriously and have some idea of the problems and time involved in the translation process. However, most trade is between smaller companies and, as the world opens up and international trade blos-soms, most translations are being commissioned by these smaller companies which have much less of an idea of what the job of a translator involves. I believe this is where translation organisa-tions have achieved the least and have the most work to do; of the translation organisations replying to my questionnaire, only 40% be-lieved that industry is generally aware of what translation involves.

To some extent this problem must be solved by translators and translation agencies themselves by **'educating the client'**. How-ever, I do not believe it entirely unfair to suggest that quite often it is only those clients who are already partly 'in-the-know' who are willing to be educated at all; many are unlikely to heed the words of a lone translator unless they already hold him or her in high regard.

So somebody – and who better than translation organisations? – has to get across to the world at large that someone who com-pleted a three-month correspondence course in French in the 1950s might not necessarily be the best person to translate manuals for a key safety component for the aerospace industry. Or, to take an example from my own career, that a translator willing to take on the financial/legal side of an invitation to tender might not be the best person to write translations of the names of electrical compo-nents directly onto the blueprints for a power station... (Oh, but *please*! Couldn't you just do it anyway...) – and this was a *transla-tion* company... (or does that say it all?!)

Question 21 of my survey, on liaisons with industry, produced some interesting results. In brief, 40% of the organisations re-sponding claim to liaise with industry, with 55% attending trade fairs and 45% advertising in trade journals etc. Only ESF in Den-mark and the translation/interpreting organisation *Österreichische Übersetzer- und Dolmetscherverband* (ÖÜDV) in Austria do all three. Why so few? What better way is there to raise the status of the profession?

Attending trade fairs – the right ones at least – is bound to raise industry's awareness of the organisation in question and, by associa-tion, of translation as a profession. **Advertising in trade journals** will achieve much the same, but is admittedly a rather expensive route to take and generally only the larger organisations with extensive re-sources and the literary organisations have adopted it.

There are of course more '**subliminal**' forms of advertising. For instance, the *Institute of Translation and Interpreting* (ITI) in the UK **scans the press** for mention of translation matters, quickly replying to authors etc to put them right or provide additional information.

Members of translation organisations are often approached to contribute **articles**, especially in Europe in the context of the European Union. Prominent mentions of an organisation's name may have a cumulative effect in raising awareness. In some ways this is akin to the '**product placement**' seen in the cinema and on TV. While spotting the name of a translation organisation might not offer the same level of excitement as, say, the various sports cars featured in the latest James Bond film, it is better than nothing...

Prizes for translation were also cited in this area. The ITI, again, has introduced annual awards for Best Translation Agency, among others. Awarded at the organisation's annual conference and voted for by members, it is doubtful whether these really have any impact on the world outside.

Some literary translation organisations award prizes for the year's best translation. The *Israel Translators Association* (ITA) insists on the **translator's name** being published not only in the book etc itself but also in related press articles and the like. This would not be easy to introduce for the non-literary side of the profession; nevertheless many translators cite having the name of the translator and the organisation(s) to which he or she belongs at the end of a translation as a good way of not only raising standards (making the translator accountable) and advertising (bringing in more work), but also raising the profile of the organisation(s) in question and so putting them in a stronger position when it comes to representing the profession. However, this presupposes that the translations in question are of a reasonably high quality and ignores the fact that many translations go through agents who would not want to risk their clients approaching their suppliers direct.

Another key factor when it comes to the representation of translators is the **number of organisations in a country**. Only 25% of the countries in the survey have only one translation organisation: 30% have two, 25% have three, 10% four and 10% at least five! Clearly, if each organisation is hell-bent on promoting the interests of its own members as well as (or over) the profession as a whole, at best the general public and industry will end up mightily confused. It is important for translators and their organisations to present a united profile; different organisations would do well to cooperate more closely in future.

Also important is the proportion of translators in a country who are members of an organisation – i.e. **how representative an organisation really is**. Again the figures from the survey are rather revealing. While not all were willing to hazard a guess at question 9, 'What proportion of full-time translators in your country are members [of your organisation]?', of those which did, only 40% claimed to cover over 40% of translators in their countries. With such low levels of representation, can these organisations really claim to represent the profession rather than just their members?

Still on the subject of how representative an organisation really is, 55% of organisations 'admitted' that their services are mainly **geared towards freelance members**. While this is in many ways natural (freelance translators stand alone, work alone etc), it would suggest that these organisations may largely be representing the interests of only a proportion of their members.

Notwithstanding all the above, the status of the profession can only ever be raised if its practitioners are of a sufficiently high quality. Otherwise, for every step we take up the ladder we will slip two rungs down as the world at large loses faith in our inflated claims of professionalism. There is little point in promoting the merits of a membership or profession which simply does not have what it takes to live up to the promises made. If we cannot promote the profession on the basis of quality, what else is left? And the only way to 'guarantee' the quality of the profession is to **regulate** it.

Regulation

Nearly 40% of the organisations replying to the questionnaire believe that translation is seen as a true profession in their countries. Two-thirds of these organisations operate in what they would term closely regulated translation markets (note, however, that these organisations operate predominantly in countries where the labour market tends to be far better organised than elsewhere in the world anyway – countries where even the most menial of jobs are carefully regulated and only ever carried out by fully-trained and qualified 'professionals'). Is there a link?

In the world at large, regulation appears to be making a comeback after the deregulatory dog-eat-dog free-for-all of the 1980s. True, the more you mollycoddle translators, the less free rein there is for the few entrepreneurs in the business. But many, if not most, translators seem to want to be closely regulated, with only the talented (qualified, tested) given a licence to practise and the 'cowboys' confined to trading their illicit wares in seedy back-streets. Translators would like to see themselves high-profile front-line professionals on a par with accountants or solicitors. But it just never seems to happen. Is regulation the answer?

The key reason why there is demand for regulation in the industry is clear: not all translators out there are very good – a widely recognised problem. It is a moot point whether the reason why the calls for closer regulation remain somewhat muted is because too few translators are sufficiently confident of their ability to meet the standards required in a really closely regulated market.

The bad eggs out there bring down standards as a whole. While of course in theory the quality translators can and will ultimately shine when clients realise just how good they are (a.k.a. leaving things to 'market forces'), the sheer volume of low-quality translation around the world means that many clients become so accustomed and resigned to inadequate translation work that they lower their expectations, they no longer care. There is undoubtedly a major market for low-quality translations, otherwise the bad eggs would not survive.

Of course it could be argued that the market for low-quality translation is only there at all because high-quality work might not be needed by every client for every purpose. It can also be argued that this is because demand for quality translation exceeds the supply of quality translators.

Whatever the case, it is important to distinguish between '**cheap and cheerful**' and '**cheap and nasty**'. A regulated market might hope to oust the latter, permit/tolerate the former and promote the category to which we probably all want to belong: the '**expensive but still good value**'.

Most translators prefer to see themselves to some extent as 'artists'; quite rightly so in my opinion. Translators must be copywriters and technical writers; they are not automatons with dictionaries. In some ways it would help the pro-regulation translators, the copywriters and technical writers, if MT could progress to the point where its output is vaguely acceptable; at least then customers wanting quick translation could use machines instead of the 'cheap and nasties', allowing the 'real translators' (craftsmen, artists) to receive at last the recognition they have always deserved and craved.

Many countries already have forms of **accreditation** or **certification** to mark out *proven* quality. These range from the accreditation certificates awarded by the ATA in the USA on the basis of one-off tests, to the more official 'state authorisation' found in, say, Sweden (based on a one-off test but must be renewed periodically) and Denmark (lasts for ever but normally based on a five-year degree course dedicated to translation).

In Scandinavia, **state authorisation** brings several very tangible benefits. One of the most obvious is that authorised translators have their own section in the Yellow Pages with everyone else in a separate section for 'Other translators'. Authorisation is a powerful marketing tool which really does mean something. The fact that the state recognises that translation is a job which requires skill and training means that others are likely to follow suit. In a country like the UK, where there are no meaningful qualifications at all for translators, most freelance translators have to work mainly for translation agencies which have the extra resources and skills needed to attract the end-client. In Scandinavia, those with state authorisation will normally find it much easier to work for companies direct – a company may well head straight for the authorised freelance translator and circumvent the twice-the-time-and-twice-the-price agency route.

So why doesn't the whole world have state authorised translators? And what has all this got to do with translation organisations? The short answer is that the state probably isn't interested (political reasons), which leaves the translation organisations as the only possible regulators.

There are also other points to be made here. While there is clearly no need for a translation organisation like *Sveriges Facköversättarföreningen* (SFÖ) in Sweden to work on regulation with the state appearing to have everything sewn up, it must be stressed that the examination procedure on which authorisation is based is extraordinarily tough. As a result, there are many perfectly good translators in the country who are not state authorised. Someone has to regulate these translators, help distinguish between 'cheap and nasty' and 'cheap and cheerful'. This in turn brings up the issue of price: authorised translators charge highly inflated rates. The principles of free market economics apply here; an authorised translator in Denmark will generally charge half as much again to translate a text as one who is not authorised, and nearly twice as much as a UK agency and three times as much as the average freelance translator in the UK. Clients are not always able or willing to stomach the inflated prices charged by even the acknowledged elite.

Moving swiftly along... Only 10% of organisations returning the questionnaire consider the profession to be closely regulated in their countries. If 40% of countries nevertheless consider translation to be a true profession, this might suggest that regulation is not essential for professional recognition. However, it is important to remember that there are different ways of interpreting 'closely regulated'. The BDÜ in Germany, for instance, did not consider the German market to be closely regulated – perhaps because its membership accounts for only 40-55% of translators in the country or because in such an export-oriented country many clients use translators in other (cheaper) EU countries. However, the German market is closely regulated in the sense that membership of the BDÜ generally does mean something – clients are aware of what the BDÜ is and that its members are well-qualified translators. Furthermore, many of the regional organisations within the BDÜ work on negotiating fixed tariffs for freelance translation with the governments of the different *Länder*.

The point here is that regulation can also take another form – **implicit regulation**. Some 80% of the translation organisations responded that membership of their organisation is intended to serve as at least an indication of quality (though only 45% believed that it does in practice!). This means two things: one is that the organisations try to restrict their membership to high-quality translators, the other is that most of them are not succeeding. Restricting membership to high-quality translators can only ever have one aim: to give an organisation the confidence to say that its members will provide a quality service. Assuming that the organisation and its aims are well-established and well-respected, the implication will be that those who are not members may – or will – not be as good. This is effectively a form of regulation.

Some 40% even allow members (generally full members as they are assumed to be of a higher calibre) to use **the organisation's logo to 'certify' translations**. This also plays a key role in these organisations' work on professional standards, which surely is an integral part of regulation.

Interestingly, only one organisation did not give **raising/maintaining professional standards** as one of its main objectives – the *Society of Translators and Interpreters* (STI) in New Zealand. Yet full membership of the STI is dependent on the applicant having a translation qualification; unlike most organisations which do claim to work on standards, there is no soft option with experience counting in an applicant's favour.

How can an organisation raise or maintain its professional standards other than by restricting membership and promoting it as an indication or guarantee of quality?

While most organisations offer a range of training courses and seminars, as discussed elsewhere in this chapter and book, these are optional and generally poorly attended. The only way to raise the standards of members is to make it pretty damn difficult to get in.

Of course, all translation organisations replying to the questionnaire have certain admission requirements, and these play some role in restricting membership, but there is one slight snag: the way in which translation organisations set these requirements. My survey came up with some revealing statistics here. Only one organisation requires that members pass its own **entrance examination** (Slovenia's DZTPS). Only around half require members to have a **translation qualification**. Which means that around half of the organisations are happy to accept members purely on the strength of a set period of **experience** – normally three to five years. The idea might appear sound in theory – time sorting the wheat from the chaff – but, as discussed above, there is plenty of room in the market (especially today's global market) for low-quality translators and so experience cannot necessarily be taken as a sign of quality. The other 50% of organisations are happy to accept members on the basis of a qualification, generally awarded by a university or similar. As discussed later, there are wide variations in the nature – and presumably standard – of these qualifications.

The upshot of all this is quite simply that as things stand most translation organisations are not in a position to raise or maintain professional standards, let alone regulate their members or the profession, because they do not have the means to restrict their membership properly.

There are also other types of regulation, the main one being **price regulation**. Official or unofficial prices for translation are found in over 50% of the countries covered by the questionnaire. In many cases (less mature markets) this is in an attempt to guarantee a *living wage* for members; in others it is more difficult to explain, but presumably an attempt to raise translators' income to the level of a 'true professional'.

It would appear that many organisations would be interested in introducing standard tariffs for members rather than guides, but are stopped by the laws applying in their country. In Europe, EU law prohibits *de facto* price regulation as the enemy of the free market and open competition, but there is nothing to stop an organisation providing guidelines and its members choosing to abide by them. Unfortunately, price is an important competitive parameter and getting members to adhere to such guidelines proves impossible.

The ideal world would nevertheless have proper price regulation; this would remove the option of competing on price and force translators to compete on *quality alone* – surely a good thing.

The snag – there always seems to be one – is that, assuming the legislature allowed the introduction of fixed rates, when translators in Germany can command three times the rates charged by translators in the UK, there is every chance that German clients will look to other countries for cheaper services. And if regulation was introduced by one translation organisation in a country, clients might look for cheaper services from members of other organisations. It is essential to remember that in an open market – today's global market is ultimately too large to be regulated properly – a supplier has to supply what the client wants. The regulation argument tends to assume that the client always wants top-quality translation and is willing to pay for it; as discussed earlier, this is patently not the case.

The UK serves as an interesting case study. The UK has what is generally regarded as a relatively immature translation market, where industry has little or no idea what translation involves (maybe because English is so much of a lingua franca around the world) and where there is little in the way of meaningful qualifications for translators. There are four different national translation organisations, but none try to regulate the market and most struggle to regulate their own membership. For instance, the *Institute of Linguists* (IoL) awards a diploma which commands more respect than any other UK translation qualification yet admits members on the strength of a language degree as it is not a pure translation organisation. As a result, the UK market is very much a free-for-all where anyone can set up as a translator – and it would appear that anyone does! There are massive variations in rates charged by freelance translators as they compete largely on price. The low profile of translation as a profession means that individual translators struggle to woo direct clients. The agencies which dominate the market can pay very low rates to their suppliers because there are so many 'cheap and nasty' cowboys out there; most of the quality translators have to look elsewhere if they want to command decent rates of pay. Take, for instance, translation from the Scandinavian languages to English – the market in which I work. Most of the good translators work directly with customers in the Scandinavian market where quality is better recognised and appreciated and where they can command at least twice the amount of money for the same amount of work. This leaves the UK market (agencies and others) with mainly just newcomers and the severely translationally-challenged. Only if the translation organisations were to club together to form a cartel and introduce high fixed rates would it be worthwhile for the quality translators to return and bring quality back to the UK market. If, as we have found, regulation is simply not feasible in today's world, then the outlook is bleak unless the translation organisations take the alternative route of raising awareness of translation as a job, and so the status of the profession and, in turn, the kind of rates translators can command. As translation prices are so low to start with in the UK, there is plenty of scope for the translation organisations to do something here.

Another interesting outcome of the survey is that some 30% of the organisations have no disciplinary procedures, such as the option of expelling members for misconduct/poor work. *Without disciplinary procedures or any meaningful admission requirements, it is difficult to see how they can hope to raise or maintain professional standards.*

Finally, only 50% of organisations keep statistics of any kind on translation prices (salaries and freelance/agency rates). Promoting the profession will surely always be an uphill battle without this elementary background information.

Information

Representation and regulation are perhaps rather wishy-washy and certainly highly complex areas, and any discussion of them will always stir up some degree of controversy. However, translation organisations also offer a range of more concrete services, and it is these which will be discussed now.

Information can be divided into two types: information for the outside world and information for members.

Information for the outside world falls into a number of different categories. The most important, perhaps, has been covered above – information or PR activities relating to raising the profile of members or translators as a whole. These include 'press response' services, actual and 'subliminal' advertising, presence at trade fairs and so on, as discussed above.

All of the organisations returning the questionnaire will **give names of suitable translators** to enquirers, while four even go so far as to act as agents and **place jobs with specific translators**. This is a valuable information service – not only for translation buyers but also for the translators who get to do the work. This type of service is tricky to operate because of the risk of favouritism, which is why most will simply produce a database print-out of all members working in the relevant languages and subject areas. In an ideal world, perhaps a translation organisation would have big ads in the Yellow Pages and act as an independent agent for its members that way. The snag here (besides the fact that it would be an administrative nightmare!) is that some organisations have corporate members (mainly translation agencies) who would clearly not be in favour of this! There are also various 'translators' cooperatives' which might stand to lose.

Virtually all organisations publish a **directory of members** (in one case – Austria's ÖÜDV – of qualified translators including non-members!). However, it should be noted that some 40% of the organisations do not distribute their directory free of charge. Surely sending out free directories to exporters or handing them out free at trade fairs would be a really useful service for members? It would raise the profile of the organisation and bring work direct to the freelance translators listed. I am convinced that the increase in annual membership subscriptions needed to fund these free directories would pay off immediately in direct approaches from potential clients.

When I worked freelance, I was listed in the directories of two translation organisations. In three years I received only two enquiries, one of which was from a translation company. While this is an abysmal hit rate, it is only to be expected. The directories in question are not marketed to the outside world and even when a company does show an interest both directories are only available at a cost (yet strangely they are distributed free to members... Can anyone enlighten me?!).

Both directories and telephone job placement services could play an important role in raising the status of the profession. The chances are that those approaching translation organisations rather than agencies are new translation buyers and looking for a quality/professional service; the impression given by the translation organisation will therefore be instrumental in determining how the enquirers go on to view translation as a whole. At the very least a translation organisation needs to provide a bright and professional interface with the outside world. If someone's first contact with the profession is an unhelpful and unfriendly receptionist or even an answering machine (yes, it does happen), this will rub off on not only members of that organisation but also the profession as a whole. If members want to be seen as professionals, they must ensure that their organisations act professionally too.

Information offered to members is mainly focused on the needs of freelance translators. 60% of the organisations operate black-lists of non-paying clients (how openly depends largely on national slander/libel laws!); 40% automatically distribute their directories to members; most have schemes to assist translators turning freelance, from information leaflets on the equipment needed or on how to set up a business (70%) to the guardian schemes operated by organisations like the ITI where an established freelance translator acts as 'mother hen' to the fledgling translator by offering guidance and advice (40%); information sheets are often provided for students of translation and prospective entrants into the profession; most have bylaws, mission statements and what have you which set out their aims and objectives for the perusal of both members and the outside world.

Every organisation publishes a regular **journal** (predominantly bimonthly) which contains a wide range of information, from reviews and adverts for new software or dictionaries, to dates of meetings, conferences and training events at home and abroad, to problem pages (business, IT and terminology), to changes of address and lists of new members, to more academic articles, to...

The quality of the content and presentation of these journals varies widely (not necessarily according to the size and resources of an organisation) as must the impression they give of the profession as a whole – from amateurish school-style newsletter through to scholarly journal, from smudged photocopies to professionally laid out glossy magazines.

Ultimately, most members of most translation organisations are members for one of three reasons: to get work, to make contacts or, probably the most common, to receive a journal so as to keep abreast of events in the translation world. As mentioned later, very few members take part in training courses/seminars or attend conferences; the journal is often their only contact with other translators.

Another source of information is the **conference**. Attendance figures are generally low as conferences are expensive to organise (though the French translation organisation *Société Française des Traducteurs* (SFT) still manages to hold two a year!) and so expensive to attend – yet they do have much to offer. Besides keynote speeches on trends in the industry, there are also workshops in specific specialist subject areas, presentations of new software and dictionaries, numerous discussion groups on aspects of translation as an art or as a business, and so on.

Finally, information is also provided by the **Internet and other on-line services**. Translation organisations have been rather slow to pick up on the benefits of the information superhighway, but are gradually coming to see it as a tool rather than a threat. Many organisations now have home pages on the World Wide Web, and at least one operates its own bulletin board service for members. I will return to this area in my thoughts about the future for translation organisations at the end of this chapter.

Qualification

I have used the term qualification as one of the roles of a translation organisation in the loose sense of anything which qualifies translators to do their jobs – i.e. not only formal qualifications (certificates of competence) but also subsequent training. It is fruitless to try to differentiate between the two anyway: some qualifications are themselves the end-result of a course of study, and some courses or seminars do not result in any kind of qualification – without being any less valid for that. It is important to remember that the point of training for a qualification is not to have as many letters after your name as in it but to have learnt something. Most translators need to be something of a jack of all trades; continuous training is vital if we are to avoid being master of none.

Formal qualifications generally fall into two categories according to whether they are the end-result of a course of study. The diplomas issued by government bodies, translation organisations and so on, plus the various forms of accreditation available around the world, are based on a one-off test. Those which follow a course of study (generally a degree or postgraduate qualification) often involve a degree of continuous assessment.

In theory, qualifications awarded following continuous assessment will be more revealing than exam-based qualifications in that the person concerned must consistently perform to the requisite standard. Continuous assessment covers both sides of the quality equation – not only the potential to do well but actually realising that potential. In practice, however, these courses are geared mainly to linguists who have not worked as professional translators and may not be able to cope under the pressure of exam conditions or a busy real-world environment.

The ideal qualification is therefore based on a mixture of continuous assessment and exams – the translator can perform under pressure and consistently. While working in the real world should serve as the ultimate test for any translator, as discussed earlier, this presupposes a translation market which demands quality.

Several countries also have qualifications based on one-off tests awarded by either state or translation organisations, but in general the qualifications for practising translators take the form of accreditation or state authorisation (see earlier).

Earlier I looked at the need to 'educate the client', 'raise the status of the profession' and 'raise professional standards' and found that these are all dependent on having a high-quality stock of translators in place to begin with. But when the translation organisations finally manage to convince the world at large that other countries too should have documentation to the standard of that produced by copywriters and technical writers in their own country, that quality does actually matter, how can people choose the right translation provider? With every one-man one-room agency in the world offering quality translation in all subjects to and from all languages, and most of them able to gain ISO 9000 accreditation without actually having to send out quality work, there is a real need for someone to promote translation qualifications as the route to finding quality translators. We all know that we produce better work if we have direct access to the end-client and/or the person who wrote the text in the first place; yet few countries operate any kind of system which would encourage companies to look for specific translators and allow them to get the consistent quality they need.

This is where translation organisations come into the equation. Very few actually award their own qualifications (10% of those replying). What they do instead is recognise qualifications awarded by universities at home and abroad and admit members on that basis; they then promote membership of their organisation as the qualification. This is reasonably valid as members of the organisation, unlike non-members with the same qualifications, have to abide by the rules, standards and procedures laid down by the organisation. However, of the organisations covered by the survey, only Slovenia's DZTPS and the UK's ITI have their own entrance examinations, and the latter is currently optional.

The questionnaire did not reveal any particularly surprising statistics on qualifications. 95% of countries offer full university degrees in translation lasting 3-5 years, 50% have university diplomas in translation lasting 1-2 years and one had a private course-based diploma lasting 3 years. In general the respondents did not differentiate between these types of qualification when assessing how useful they are in obtaining work. This is surprising because qualifications of such different duration surely cannot be of an equal standard/value? Indeed, all the organisations returning the questionnaire believe that qualifications from other countries are recognised in their country. With some countries happy with one-year wholly theory-based diplomas and others demanding five-year practical degree courses, it is clear that translation qualifications are far from universal in scope and standards. I personally have found huge differences in the quality of graduates of similar courses, even the same course! Perhaps this is an issue for the international organisation, FIT, to address: an international qualification standard, which accredits some university courses and qualifications and not others, thus helping universities to aspire to a defined international standard. As ever, logistics and resources are a problem, but it would perhaps help clients choose a good egg and make those with the qualifications a little more proud of their achievements and their work in general.

The other side of qualification is **training**. While qualifications help you find work, training helps you do it properly. Continuous training and refresher courses, seminars, evening classes and even simply research at the library are absolutely vital, especially in today's ever more rapidly changing world. This is widely recognised: 45% of the organisations offer full-time or part-time training courses and some 80% one-off training seminars. The emphasis on seminars rather than courses is natural considering the limited resources at the disposal of most translation organisations.

However, offers of training and actual attendance are two very different things! One third of organisations admitted that less than 10% of their members ever attend such courses and the highest level of attendance reported was a measly 30%... The implications of these statistics are clear.

Training for translators is covered in greater depth elsewhere in the Handbook, so I will limit myself to one closing observation: I am very surprised that I have yet to come across a translation training course offered by any translation organisation or university anywhere which contains elements of copywriting and technical writing, despite these being among the core skills of any translator. Why?

Association

By definition, translation organisations bring translators together. And translators need to be brought together.

This is not a profession which would naturally appeal to the more gregarious type. With work arriving and leaving by fax or modem and with all the reference material anyone could ever need readily available on the Internet, there is precious little need for the translator ever to venture outside his own home. Translation can be a lonely business – even in-house – and those not naturally equipped with social skills may find they need a little help. Hence virtually all translation organisations arrange **social events** for members.

However, these social events appeal only to a limited circle of members. Most translators do not seem to want to come together of their own accord – they are happy to work under the same banner as other translators, but they do not actually want to meet them! Hence the small numbers attending training courses, as mentioned above, are mirrored by the small numbers who actually attend regional group meetings and even conferences. This is not necessarily a purely anti-social tendency. For one thing, translation can be a tiring and sometimes monotonous job and so the last thing most translators want to do after work is go out with other translators and 'talk shop'. For another, one has to question whether organising sponsored fun-runs and picnics has a place in a 'professional' organisation.

A much more valid side of association is **networking**. In other words, translators getting together to discuss issues of relevance to the work they do. The social role can be *important* (a happy translator will be more enthusiastic and have a more positive attitude to his or her work, a translator who leaves the office once in a while will be more aware of what goes on in the world) but professional contact is *essential*. On one level there is much to be gained from simply sitting down and discussing difficult terms and how to translate them. On another, the more informal setting of a group meeting in someone's front room may give more than a seminar or lecture at a conference: for instance, a friend's experience of the latest software package may carry more weight than the claims of an official of a national organisation who was given the software on free trial in the first place.

Outings to factories and the like are one form of association-type service which is generally provided by local groups rather than national organisations. These serve both as social get-togethers and as a valuable learning and networking experience.

The Future?

As we have seen above, today's translation organisations play a number of very different roles and offer a wide range of services in order to meet very disparate needs. It is difficult to find a single common feature of all translation organisations – except maybe that everything is set to change.

As we near the end of the century, more and more translators seem to be looking to their professional organisations and demanding more. At the time of writing, many of the world's largest and most well-known translation organisations are in a state of turmoil – on the face of it for very different reasons, but ultimately all are struggling to overcome the same underlying obstacle: while the art (or science, if you like) of translation in its purest sense is much the same as ever, its application and practitioners are undergoing a rapid transformation.

Quite simply, the global village is in the process of revolutionising the translation industry. On the one hand, demand for translation has rocketed as trade (and physical) barriers continue to crumble and international trade booms. On the other, advances in telecommunications technology have allowed a truly global translation market to develop (after all, there can be no language barriers in this business).

So, as the translation market grows, the individual translator will continue to pale into insignificance relative to his environment. For many translators, it really is one man against the world, leading to a much more urgent need for **representation**. Today's translation organisations are generally too small and too ferociously independent to meet this need properly – they need to team up with other translation or labour market organisations to get the power and resources to supply what their members want.

The increased demand for translation has been met not by the much flaunted but ultimately disappointing MT but by the influx of large numbers of 'amateurs' – untrained and untested translators, bilingual secretaries and the like. These are naturally perceived as a threat by the 'professionals' who are now calling with renewed force for some element of **regulation**. Yet the global market would appear to make national regulation impossible. The FIT or maybe a new and more dynamic international translation organisation needs to take on board the needs of the professionals and see if it cannot launch some global initiative to allay the profession's fears and ensure that translation remains (becomes?) a real profession.

The global village has come hand in hand with the information society. Translation organisations and translators have generally been slow on the uptake so far, but things are beginning to snowball now. Rapid access to **information** is essential in all professions. Translation organisations need to embrace the information society and see how they can compete with other information providers. The electronic bulletin and constantly updated BBS must surely be no more than a stone's throw away now. After all, everyone and his dog seems to have a Web page already and they say things are only just *beginning* to take off!

The international market means international competition, and so there is a clear need for translators to acquire and update a high level of expertise if they are to survive, hence greater calls for **qualification**. The organisations need to have more than just vague liaisons with universities and the like. Perhaps international accreditation of translation courses and qualifications could be integrated with the international regulatory initiative mentioned above? Certainly regulation is impossible without qualification.

Freelance translators and even many staff translators are effectively teleworkers and in desperate need of contact with the outside world. With today's on-line communications, translators no longer need even to go to the library or Post Office, and so more and more may start looking to their organisations for **association**.

One major threat to the translation organisation which has emerged in the last few years is the **electronic service provider**. The breakthrough of the Internet and other on-line services in the translation sector has brought a number of electronic meeting places for translators, currently dominated by CompuServe's Foreign Language Forum (FLEFO). FLEFO serves as a forum for the exchange of views and ideas, where subscribers can seek and give advice on both business and translation matters, buy and sell translation services, and even make friends and arrange face-to-face meetings and get-togethers. This is at least as much as is offered by many a national organisation. Indeed, FLEFO even seems to offer many of the association-type services discussed above – it has a real club of regular users. Members of the ITI, BDÜ and ATA seem to be the keenest surfers, judging from recent traffic, and so FLEFO has almost become a separate electronic branch of these organisations! Certainly saves on petrol...

A number of organisations are aware of the threat posed by what is effectively the **international on-line translation organisation**. Sweden's SFÖ has long operated a bulletin board where members can post notices of forthcoming events and ask for help with tricky terms. The UK's ITI and others have set up home pages on the World Wide Web. However, to my knowledge, no translation organisation has yet set up any terminology database/query system for use by members; this would seem one of the more obvious applications of the latest technologies.

The information and communications revolution is at best making exacting demands of the dynamism of national translation organisations. At worst, it could bring their speedy demise.

Questionnaire on Professional Organisations and Qualifications for Translators

So as not to take up too much of your time, I have tried to make this questionnaire as straightforward as possible to complete.

Most questions require you only to tick a box or insert a number. Feel free to miss out questions - answers to most questions would be better than answers to none!

You may find some questions difficult to answer, but general impressions and rough estimates will still be useful to me - simply indicate your uncertainty by adding a question mark and I promise not to quote you!

A big thank you for your time!

Chris Schröder

Section A - Translation in your country

1. Is the profession closely regulated?
    Yes ❏   *No* ❏

    If so, by whom?
    Translation organisations ❏   *State* ❏   *Other* ❏

2. Is translation generally considered a "profession" like accountancy or law?
    Yes ❏   *No* ❏

3. Is most translation carried out by qualified translators?
    Yes ❏   *No* ❏

4. Do most full-time translators have a purely linguistic background rather than a technical/business background?
    Yes ❏   *No* ❏

5. Is most translation carried out into the mother tongue?
    Yes ❏   *No* ❏

6. Are there standard official or unofficial rates for freelance translation?
    Yes ❏   *No* ❏

7. How many other translation organisations are there?
    0 ❏   *1* ❏   *2* ❏   *3* ❏   *4+* ❏

Section B - Your organisation

1. Membership

8. How many members do you have?
   < 500 ❑   500-999 ❑   1-2000 ❑   2-3000 ❑   3-5000 ❑ >5000 ❑

9. Roughly what proportion of full-time translators in your country are members?
   < 10% ❑   10-25% ❑   25-40% ❑   40-55% ❑   55-70% ❑ > 70% ❑

10. What proportion of members come from overseas?
    < 5% ❑   5-10% ❑   10-20% ❑   20-30% ❑   > 30% ❑

11. Please complete the following table with the annual membership fee and membership requirements for all grades of membership (see examples):

Grade of membership	Annual membership fee	Requirements for membership		
		Translation qualification	Experience (years)	Entrance examination
Full	$ 200	Yes	3	Yes
Associate	$ 100	No	1	No

12. Is membership or any grade of membership intended to serve as a qualification or guarantee of quality?
    Yes ❑ No ❑

    Strictly off the record, does it in practice?
    Yes ❑ No ❑

2. Role and objectives

Status, standards, rates etc

13. Is raising the status of translators a main objective?
    Yes ❑ No ❑

    If so, how do you aim to do this?

    ....
    ....
    ....

14. Is raising/maintaining professional standards a main objective?
    Yes ❑ No ❑

    If so, how do you aim to do this?

    ....
    ....
    ....

15. Do you have disciplinary procedures for members?
Yes ❐ *No* ❐

Do you use them much?
Never ❐ *Almost never* ❐ *Rarely* ❐ *Regularly* ❐

16. Do you regulate (or issue guidelines on) the rates charged by members for freelance translation work?
Yes ❐ *No* ❐

Briefly, why (why not)?

....
....
....

Training, information, PR etc

17. Do you offer full-time or part-time training courses for translators?
Yes ❐ *No* ❐

18. Do you organise one-off training seminars for translators?
Yes ❐ *No* ❐

Roughly how many members ever attend such seminars?
< 10% ❐   *10-20%* ❐ *20-30%* ❐ *30-50%* ❐ *> 50%* ❐

19. Do you award your own qualifications (diplomas etc) or accreditation?
Yes ❐ *No* ❐

20. Do you liaise with universities and other translator training bodies?
Yes ❐ *No* ❐

If so, what form does this take?

....
....
....

21. Do you liaise with industry?
Yes ❐ *No* ❐

If so, what form does this take?

....
....
....

Do you attend trade fairs?
Yes ❐ *No* ❐

Do you ever advertise in trade journals, daily press etc?
Yes ❐ *No* ❐

Is industry generally aware of what translation involves?
Yes ❐ *No* ❐

Member services

22. Are your services mainly geared towards freelance members?
    Yes ❑ *No* ❑

23. Which of the following services do you offer freelance translators:
    ❑ *Giving companies names of suitable translators*
    ❑ *Placing specific translations with members*
    ❑ *Blacklist of non-paying customers*
    ❑ *Directory of members distributed free*
    ❑ *Directory of members distributed at a cost*
    ❑ *Schemes to assist those going freelance (guardian schemes etc)*
    ❑ *Information sheets etc for prospective freelance translators*
    ❑ *Allowing use of organisation's logo to "certify" translations*
    Any other services (please specify):
    ....
    ....
    ....

24. What do you offer staff translators?
    ....
    ....
    ....

25. What do you offer corporate members (if you have any)?
    ....
    ....
    ....

26. What do you offer student members (if you have any)?
    ....
    ....
    ....

3. Miscellaneous

27. Do you publish a regular journal?
    Yes ❑ *No* ❑

    If so, what does it contain?

    ❑ *academic articles*   ❑ *practical articles*
    ❑ *translation news*   ❑ *book reviews*
    ❑ *training news*   ❑ *conference news*
    ❑ *members' news*   ❑ *details of social events*
    ❑ *job vacancies*   ❑ *general interest articles*
    ❑ *members' letters*   ❑ *supplier advertisements*
    ❑ *quizzes/competitions*   ❑ *help pages - terms/words*
    ❑ *help pages - IT solutions* ❑ *help pages - translation as business*
    ❑ *ads*   ❑ *humorous items*

others (please specify):

....

....

....

28. Do you hold an annual conference?
Yes ❑   No ❑

29. Do you keep data on:
❑ *income of freelance translators*
❑ *salaries of staff translators*
❑ *national translation volumes/turnover*
❑ *freelance rates*
❑ *agency rates*

NB I would be grateful if you could forward any data you have in these areas!

30. Does your organisation arrange social events for members?
Yes ❑ *No* ❑

Section C - Qualifications and accreditation

31. Which of the following qualifications are available in your country?

Awarded following a course of study:

Full university degrees	courses last .... years
Diplomas etc from universities etc	courses last .... years
Diplomas etc from government bodies	courses last .... years
Diplomas etc from private institutes	courses last .... years
Diplomas etc from translation organisations	courses last .... years
Others (please specify):	courses last .... years

Awarded solely on the basis of examination:

Accreditation from the state	valid for .... years
Accreditation from translation organisations	valid for .... years
Diplomas etc from universities etc	
Diplomas etc from government bodies	
Diplomas etc from private institutes	
Diplomas etc from translation organisations	

Others (please specify): ....

32. Please indicate how much help these qualifications are to translators when looking for employment or freelance work by inserting the appropriate number(s):

Key: 1 = qualification widely unknown and therefore of no help
        2 = qualification of little help
        3 = qualification of great help
        4 = qualification effectively guarantees work will be found
        5 = qualification essential for finding any work at all

Awarded following a course of study:
Full university degrees ☐
Diplomas etc from universities etc ☐
Diplomas etc from government bodies ☐
Diplomas etc from private institutes ☐
Diplomas etc from translation organisations ☐
Others (please specify): ....

Awarded solely on the basis of examination:
Accreditation from the state ☐
Accreditation from translation organisations ☐
Diplomas etc from universities etc ☐
Diplomas etc from government bodies ☐
Diplomas etc from private institutes ☐
Diplomas etc from translation organisations ☐
Others (please specify): ....

33. Are overseas qualifications generally recognised in your country?
Yes ☐ *No* ☐

Finally, totally off the record... (honesty would be appreciated - and I won't quote you!)

34. In practice, which of the following is generally the most important when a translator is looking for work (first freelance commission or employment): Please tick only one box!

☐ membership of particular professional organisations
☐ qualifications
☐ experience
☐ good references (i.e. ability)

Part III – Quality

5. Working Procedures, Quality and Quality Assurance

GEOFFREY SAMUELSSON-BROWN

1. Introduction

When discussing the contents of this chapter with the editor, I was very happy to have the title already resolved for me. Though I have given a number of papers, I find deciding on the title the most daunting part of the task – once you've written the title, you're more or less committed. It's like many things in life; once you've made the initial step, you're on your way.

I have used the masculine form in my writing. This is purely a practical consideration and should not be interpreted as gender discrimination on my part. Similarly, I have referred to translation companies and translation agencies collectively as translation companies.

To understand procedures it is first necessary to define what is a procedure. In very simple language, a procedure is a set of steps to be gone through in a predetermined order. The purpose of a procedure is to ensure consistent treatment in the interest of a particular goal, and to improve operational efficiency by reducing the need for judgement and decision making. In large organisations procedures may, for example, be written to ensure compliance with policies. Once the steps of a procedure have been defined, it is then possible to define the skills that are necessary to implement that procedure.

I'll refer to several procedures a little later since I would like to look first at operations. The two are not unconnected since procedures form part of operations. Again, I'll attempt another definition. An operation is a process in which inputs are converted into outputs. Perhaps you are wondering what all this has got to do with translation. Don't worry – all will be revealed! The most fundamental operation in translation is to take an input text (in the source language), translate it, and produce an output text (in the target language). It would be naive of me to leave it at that since the number of inputs and outputs constitute a lot more than input and output text.

Some academics would look at this in terms of a systems model. To understand why, it's worth persevering with another definition. A system is defined by a number of attributes:

1. it is an assembly of components that are connected in an organised way,
2. the components of the system are affected by being in the system, and the system is affected if a component is taken out,
3. the assembly of components does perform some kind of operation,
4. the assembly is defined as being of particular interest.

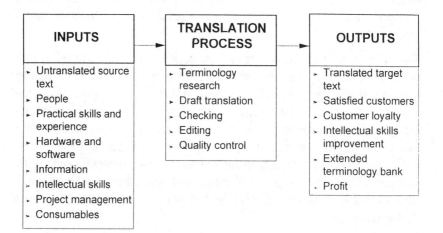

Figure 1. A transformation model for a translation operation

Systems are considered hard or soft depending on the level of emotional involvement and the degree of technology involved. Consider Figure 1, which shows a transformation model for translation operations, and it will become apparent how complex things can be. Since this chapter is also about quality and quality assurance, let's look at the different phases of the operations, how their various components are interrelated, and how they affect quality. Quality and quality assurance are not easy subjects since the mere suggestion that somebody's translation is of an unacceptable quality is such an emotive issue. After all, who likes their intellectual output challenged? In very simple terms, an operation comprises inputs, the transformation process, and the outputs.

2. Analysis Of The Translation Operation

2.1 Inputs

2.1.1 Untranslated source text

For the most part, you as the translator will have little influence on the source text – what you see is what you get! I know from experience that there have been many occasions when I would dearly have liked to rewrite the source text, or consult the originator, to clarify ambiguities and errors. Invariably, people know what they want to say but the intended cerebral output is not always matched by what appears on paper. Translators do perform a number of miracles on a daily basis but trying to make a silk purse from a sow's ear is always a difficult challenge. You should accept a translation assignment only if you are confident that you have the skills and the facilities to provide quality work in the time allocated.

How you approach a translation is a matter of personal preference. I tend to quickly scan through the text to ensure that I feel competent to do the work and then dive straight into it. If you know your subject areas well, you will be able to anticipate what the originator intended and can therefore make the necessary editorial changes as you work through your translation.

Offering constructive comments or criticising some other person's intellectual output is a delicate matter; but if you are to produce a text that makes sense in a target language, it is evident that the source text needs to make sense. A reasonable person will be grateful for anomalies having been brought to his attention. Regrettably, not everybody is reasonable. It is worth bearing in mind that the writer of any text seldom has the translator in mind and may not be able to appreciate the challenges you face. Put any questions about the source text in writing and fax them to the client. Telephone messages can get forgotten or disregarded whereas a fax or letter is less easy to ignore – there is clear and tangible evidence that you have submitted a query.

I know it sounds simplistic but make sure that you have received all the text to be translated and that it is legible. This is particularly the case with faxed documents since the source documents may, on rare occasions, skip a line or two when being transmitted.

2.1.2 People

The input to the translation process by people, or human resources, is still an essential component to the translation operation. In fact, there are few processes where there is not some human input at some stage. There is, of course, the vision of talking to your computer and the computer recognising your voice and doing the translation for you. But I would like to think that our profession will not become totally dehumanised. Would you like your working life regulated by a nasal, synthesized version of North American English?

Early in my career as a translator (mid-1970s) I used to dictate my translations for an audio typist to type. (The height of standard office technology at that time was an IBM typewriter that had the ability to physically erase characters printed on paper using a separate adhesive ribbon that lifted the ink from the paper if the erroneous character was typed again.) I used to imagine having a machine that would recognise my voice and would output my verbal input on paper. Such technology is now available so why do I not use it? There are several reasons. Firstly, I find dictating translations deadly boring. Secondly, if I am keying in the text myself, I am able to make changes as and when I want to. Thirdly, I enjoy producing translations that are, I would hope, visually pleasing as well as being accurate. No doubt my second objection will be overruled when I am able to give verbal commands to my box of electrickery.

A question that I get quite often is, "Won't your job be taken over by a computer soon?". There is no doubt that information technology allows us to do amazing things with text and graphics but I feel that there will be the need for creative human input for a long time to come. Make sure you are the master of the computer and not vice versa. If all translations were done by computer then individual style would be lost. And although style is often a very large bone of contention, such a development would be sad.

I find it difficult to imagine working in an environment where practical skills and experience gained over decades cannot be passed onto inexperienced fledgling translators who are straight from university. One of the disadvantages of our profession is that so many of its practitioners work in isolation, often from their own choosing. Translators seldom meet their clients and rarely know what happens to the fruits of their labours. Thus they develop in their own way with little feedback from their clients.

One of the difficulties I experience is getting new clients (i.e. clients who have never used translation services) to understand that translation requires a lot more than a knowledge of a foreign language. The translator needs the ability to offer thorough subject knowledge in addition to language skills. But more of this later on.

The bottom line is that good quality human resources are vital if good quality output is to be achieved.

2.1.3 Practical skills and experience

Practical skills and experience are essential inputs. It is heartening that fewer people use their PC as though it were a typewriter but are becoming computer literate as well as skilled wordsmiths. There are those who argue that translators should not be asked to word process documents or that they should be paid extra to do so. Since I work for a translation company, I know that preference is given to freelance translators who offer the following:

1. translations that are accurate and of a linguistic quality that is suitable for the intended purpose,
2. competence in the subject area,
3. delivery of translations on electronic media in the specified layout and in the required software package.

It goes without saying that delivery on time is expected.

How you gain your skills and experience is dealt with elsewhere in this book. If you are a staff translator, encourage your manager to arrange seminars on various aspects of translation – style sheets, proper checking procedures, specific aspects of word processing. You will have learned by experience and it is to the company's advantage if the skills acquired through experience can be passed onto others. One of the disadvantages of working as a freelance translator is the lack of contact with other colleagues. Having worked as a freelance and in a translation company, I can appreciate the viewpoints espoused on both sides of the divide.

2.1.4 Hardware and software

The pace of technological development is almost frightening and certainly very difficult to keep up with. I bought my first PC less than 10 years ago. It had a 16 bit processor (limited by an 8 bit data bus) and it ran at a clock speed of 4.77 MHz. It had a RAM of 256 KB and a low resolution mono screen. It had two floppy drives, each with a capacity of 360 KB on 5.25" disks. The software was not resident and needed to be loaded each time the machine was switched on. Only one software program could be loaded at any one time. Text files were stored on separate 5.25" floppy discs. The PC was connected to a dot matrix printer that had a limited range of fonts and took about 40 seconds to print a page. This neat little package cost well over £2,000 at the time! My daughter eventually inherited the system five years later when she started her university studies, by which time a 20 MB hard disk had been added. When I recently asked whether she still used it, the scathing reply was, "No, I've lost the handle to wind it up!".

The computer that now sits on my desk has a 32 bit processor running at 100 MHz and has a RAM of 16 MB. It has a high resolution 17" colour monitor that can be split into different windows. It has a storage capacity of 2 GB on its hard disk (equivalent to around 6,000 5.25" floppy disks each storing 316 KB!) and additional drives for reading, removable CD-ROM disks and read/writable optical disks – each of these drives alone has a capacity of 650 MB. All the software that I use is resident which means that I can do several tasks concurrently without having to reload. This PC is connected to either a high-speed laser mono printer that prints 12 pages a minute at a resolution of 600 x 600 dots per inch or to a slower ink-jet colour printer of much the same resolution. The latter allows me to produce more visually-attractive graphical presentations. This system cost a lot less in real terms than my first PC!

What has coloured printing got to do with translation you might ask. Without clients, you do not get translations and to win clients you need to present yourself in competition with others. Since many translation assignments may be awarded without the client and translator even meeting, the quality and impact of your visual presentation may provide you with the competitive advantage. What the future might hold is limited almost by what we are able to imagine. We will probably see convergence between all the IT systems we use – computer, video recorder, fax, modem so that all these functions will be available from the same piece of equipment. We will soon start talking to our computers and less to each other. (Come back Isaac Asimov – all is forgiven!)

We must not lose sight of the fact that IT should be used as a tool to facilitate our work. It is all too easy to become a slave to the computer and to lose sight of the essential element of translation – transferring a concept from one language to another language. The challenge is to get manufacturers to produce software that actually helps us to do our work. IT provides us with some of the tools that allow us to produce what the client wants. It is not possible to survive for long without satisfied clients.

2.1.5 Information

Different perceptions of the intended use and specification for a translation can lead to quality gaps. This is illustrated in the following (adapted from Paraswaman *et al.,* 1985). Though I have adapted this model for application in a translation company, parts of it are equally applicable to the work of individual translators.

Gap 1 is the difference between the client's expectations and the translation manager's perception of what the client wants

This arises when the translation manager does not understand what the client considers to be important in the translation process. The client may expect a perfectly-formatted and independently-checked and edited translation (although has not specifically stated so)

whereas the translation manager believes that the translation will be used only for information purposes and requires no special layout.

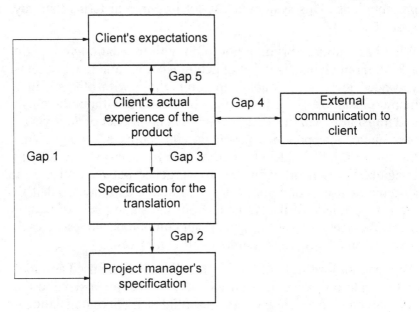

Figure 2. The quality gaps model for specifying the intended use for a translation

Gap 2 is the gap between the translation manager's perception of the client's expectation and the translation specification

This arises when the translation manager does not draw up a specification that is detailed enough to show clearly what is required. This may leave the translator who actually supplies the translation unsure about what is exactly intended. The gap may arise because the translation process may not be adequately specified – the client may expect the translation to be in a particular software format whereas the translator is not informed of this.

Gap 3 is the gap between the specification and the client's experience of the translation

This gap occurs when the translation is not delivered as specified. There may be many reasons for this. One example is the translation being longer than originally anticipated. It is the client's perception that counts and there is a number of intangible factors that come into play.

Gap 4 is the gap between the client's experience and external communication to the client

This arises when the translation provider cannot deliver what is promised in advertising or promotion. In other words, make sure you can deliver what you promise.

Gap 5 is the gap between the client's expectation and the client's experience

A client's experience is affected by his own experiences, the recommendations of others and the claims made by the translation supplier. You must bear in mind that the client's experience is determined by his perception of what is supplied, not by the perception held by the translation supplier.

Information from the client concerning the end-use of the translation is perhaps the most important. Many clients neglect to specify what the translation is going to be used for. In fact many translation agencies and other work providers may not be aware of the end-use themselves. It is vital to ask what the intended use is before accepting a translation assignment since this will determine the level of quality control that will need to be applied (and whether you are competent to do the work). The three principal uses for translation are: information, publication, and legal purposes. It should be obvious that the level of quality control required for a legal translation is likely to be much higher than that required for information purposes.

Your client has a perceived view of what he expects to be provided. If you sub-contract to a freelance translator, he in turn will have his perception of what is required. This is not the same as Chinese whispers but can have the same effect and introduce quality gaps. Each link in the chain between client and translation supplier must be correctly informed and properly aware of the exact requirements. The difficulty in many cases is getting a proper specification from the outset. Those of you who work as freelance translators are no doubt aware of the situation where you get a frantic call from an agency on a Friday afternoon with a request to take on some translation work. (I can play the devil's advocate here since I've worked as a freelance and now head a translation company!). You're informed that "it's technical, and I think it's something to do with cars" when in fact it may turn out to be a contract that is related to franchising. It is not until you get the work that it turns out to be other than you had expected. Of course, by the time you endeavour to get back to the client he will have left the office for the day. This is another good reason for not accepting an assignment without seeing at least a few sample pages.

2.1.6 Intellectual skills

The intellectual skills you need as a translator range from those you learn during your formal education to those you acquire during your day-to-day work as a practitioner. If you work for a translation company, there may be a formal skills development programme from which you can benefit. In my ignorance, I find it difficult to isolate what practical and intellectual skills you need as a translator but have endeavoured to illustrate the range of skills in a matrix.

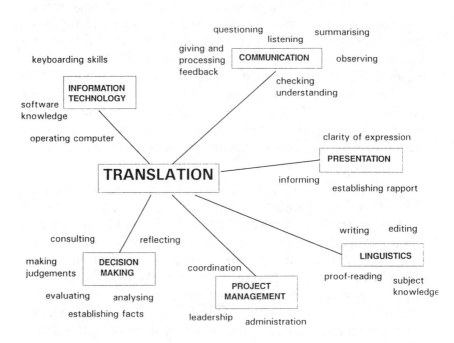

Figure 3. Matrix of fundamental skills used in translation

Whatever assignment you do, there will be some level of project management. This is an element of accountability which, in turn, forms part of quality management. Allow time and allocate overheads to project management. If a project is not managed properly, as sure as eggs is eggs, it will go off the rails. Try and anticipate what could go wrong and consider measures to prevent mishaps occurring.

The level of project management will depend, of course, on the scope of the project. Whatever the case, make sure that every stage is recorded and written down. As a minimum, you should have some form of job sheet that contains all the detail related to the task in hand.

If several translators are involved in a project it is necessary to have a co-ordinating editor to contribute to project management. The following lists typical responsibilities of this person:

1. To check and proofread the translations produced by the different translators and to ensure continuity and consistency throughout,
2. To coordinate the work of an editorial assistant who keys in the changes in the different software packages used – word processing and graphics, for example,
3. To despatch original glossaries and updated glossaries to the translators and the client's verifier (if the client is involved in the verification process),
4. To act as a central co-ordination point for queries from the translators and to resolve these queries with the client,
5. To ensure that the project schedule is maintained.

2.1.8 Consumables

Despite visions of the paperless office ten or so years ago, it seems that we use more paper than we ever used to. The probable reason for this is we print more draft translations than we ever used to simply because printers are so fast and efficient nowadays. Although very little can be said about the impact on quality by consumables, they are essential if we are to produce some tangible evidence of our mental endeavours.

From a purely practical point of view, the company I work for uses coloured paper in its plain paper fax machine. This is very useful since a large proportion of incoming translations received from clients arrive by fax. As a consequence, it is very easy to identify the client's original text even though you may make subsequent photocopies. The feasibility of using different coloured paper for various stages in the production process is being considered.

2.2 The translation process

2.2.1 Terminology research

I'll not say too much about this since reference material and resources are dealt with elsewhere in this book. I will assume, however, that you have access to the correct terminology to or to people who have the required expertise.

Nearly all translators are faced with the dilemma of being asked to translate all subjects. The difficulty is knowing when not to accept a translation assignment because you do not have the necessary competence. Quite often the client is aware that the text to be translated is in, say, German and it's "technical". It goes without saying that you should not accept an assignment without seeing at least some sample pages to see whether you are happy with the text and the complexity of the terminology it contains.

Terminology research is part of the learning curve of any translator. The important element of the process is to ensure that you record the results of your research in a manner that will allow you to retrieve the information at some later date if and when you do a similar translation.

2.2.2 Draft translation

Perhaps the term draft should be qualified in this context. The translation is at a draft stage when the translator has completed all his checks before passing the translated text and the original to the checker. Your draft translation should be as good as you can make it and should be complete and accurate.

"Accurate" is one of those weasel words that is hard to define – what one person may deem to be accurate may not be suitable in another person's eyes. I suppose the only way to determine whether a draft translation is of a suitable standard is to ask a number of fundamental questions:

1. Has all the text been translated?
2. Has a spell-check been carried out?
3. Are proper names and numerical data correct?
4. Does the target text read like a piece of original text in that language? Or can you recognise the source language in the structure and syntax?
5. Has terminology been properly researched?
6. Is the style of the translation suitable for the intended purpose?

If you can truthfully answer Yes to these questions then the draft translation can go for checking.

It is very important to keep track of the translation so you know the state it has reached. I work primarily in Word for Windows and I have set up a document template and a style sheet for my translation work. The document template contains fields to identify a number of attributes which include:

- Source language
- Page number
- Number of pages in the document
- File name
- Date and time when file was last saved
- Number of words in the translation
- What stage the translation has reached, i.e. draft, copy for checking or editing, checked and corrected translation.

Any of these fields can, of course, be deleted before the final version of the translation is sent to the client.

2.2.3 Checking

There is the temptation, when you know that somebody else is going to check your translation, to be less than 100 per cent conscientious with your own checking. Checking is as important as the actual translation process. The important thing to establish is who is responsible for the various stages of checking and what is going to happen with the draft translation that you have produced.

The difficulty facing most freelance translators is that they cannot pass their work over to a colleague for checking. It has to be said, as well, that translators do not take kindly to having their work commented upon by other translators. I am fortunate since I work for a translation company that has a number of staff translators. We are able to check each other's work and benefit from the skills that each of us has developed. I have to confess that I would feel very unsure about sending a translation to a client without having it checked by a colleague even after having worked as a translator for over twenty years.

Of course, it's the easiest thing in the world to comment on what somebody else has written. Such comment, however, usually relates to style. Whenever I check a colleague's translation, or a translation produced by one of the company's freelance translators, I do not comment on style unless it is patently unsuitable for the intended purpose.

There are two principal levels of checking – full checking and scan checking. When carrying out a complete check, a translation checker should repeat the checks made by the original translator and mark the text up accordingly. Any queries must be raised with the original translator and resolved.

In the case of scan-checking, the checker looks through the text to ensure that all the text has been translated and that it reads well. Sample paragraphs are fully checked and, if these are considered to be accurate, the rest of the check is assumed to be accurate. If not, a full translation check must be performed.

We now come to a couple of procedures, one for full checking and one for scan checking These procedures are adapted from notes produced for an internal seminar at Aardvark Translations Ltd by Siân Marlow. They are designed for use in a translation company that employs translators and checkers but parts of the procedures are equally applicable to individual freelances who check their own work.

Procedure for full checking

You will need a ruler, a red pen, a copy of the source text and a copy of the target text.

- Place the source text on your left. Place the target text to the right of the source.
- Place the ruler at the beginning of the source text.
- Begin checking by moving the ruler down one sentence at a time. Do not move the ruler on until you have checked the sentence for correctness, all your corrections/notes have been made, and you are satisfied that the sentence is now complete and correct.
- When making notes, use the proofreading marks shown in 'Copy preparation and proof correction', BS 6261 : Part 2 : 1976 so that whoever is correcting the checked translation knows exactly what is to be changed and how. (See also the Appendix to *'A Practical Guide for Translators'*, G Samuelsson-Brown, 2nd Ed. 1995, for a fully-worked example.)
- Make all notes in the <u>left-hand margin</u> where possible. If this is not possible, put a note here to the effect that you have made notes elsewhere (in the right-hand margin, on the reverse, etc.). This ensures that nothing is missed out at the correction stage.
- The right-hand margin should be used only for notes which do not need to be incorporated into the translation, e.g. page/ line references for source document, CONSISTENCY or STET marks.
- If the left-hand margin of a document is too small, ask the translator for a double-spaced copy of the text so that corrections can be made in the line directly above the translation. (Do not make corrections in the line below!).
- If you do not have space to insert a correction (e.g. if an entire paragraph needs to be rewritten), put an insertion symbol into the left-hand margin, followed by a reference letter (e.g. A). Then rewrite the paragraph wherever there is space to do so (the reverse of the page is usually good for this), labelling the rewrite 'A'.
- Sometimes you will find that a document contains several sections that are identical or similar. If the sections are identical (and you know this to be a fact because you've compared both sections in the source text!), check that the trans-

lator has used the same translation twice (i.e. copied it over). However, you may find that the translator has not checked carefully enough and used an identical translation when the source text varies slightly. If you find this happens frequently within a translation (or over a number of translations), mention to him that simply copying over text without checking for similarity is not acceptable.

- Although the translator should have spell-checked his translation, do not take it for granted that this is the case. It may be that words which are spelt correctly but are incorrect in the context (e.g. 'he' instead of 'the') have crept in, so the spellchecker will not pick these up. Also, double-check that company names, names of people, etc. are spelt correctly!

- Check that the layout of the document is exactly what the client has requested or, if no specific requests have been made, that the layout follows the original (where possible) or is at least consistent (where not). Ensure that the correct font has been used throughout, and be careful to check that the font has not varied even slightly (e.g. the translator may start the text in Times Roman 12 pt. and then go on to use New Century Schoolbook 12 pt. – these are very similar, but not identical!).

- If you find yourself changing the same word more than three times, check this with the translator before making any changes – do not just assume that the translator was having an off-day. He may have had a good reason for using an 'incorrect' word.

- If a word is obviously wrong and crops up several times in the text, specify a Global Search and Replace ('GSR' or 'Global') so that the corrector does not have to change it every time it appears. However, do specify all possible instances of the word so that nothing is overlooked. For example:

does > makes
    doing > making
    done > made
    do > make
    or:
    firms > companies
    firm > company

Make sure that you define the global replace operation uniquely. One easy way to do this is to enter a space after the search word, and a corresponding space after the replace word. Just consider what would happen in the first example if you simply instructed the computer to replace all occurrences of 'do' with 'make'. You will be surprised at the result.

Do not forget to let the corrector know when confirmation of a Global is required: for example, in the latter case, the corrector should choose to confirm the word 'firm' before changing it to 'company' – suppose the word 'firm' is used as an adjective instead (e.g. 'a firm commitment')?!

- Be careful when checking paragraph numbers. Bear in mind that you may find an out-of-sequence number, but do remember to check against the original document before changing it – it is possible and, in fact, quite likely, that the numbering is incorrect in the original. (This is where a translator's note is warranted.)

- If you change anything at all in a sentence, do not forget to re-read that sentence before going on. One simple change may necessitate changes further down the line. For example:

  The quick brown fox jumps over the lazy dog
  > The quick brown foxes jump over the lazy dog.

- If the client has provided a glossary, check that this has been used to produce the translation. It is equally important to offer feedback to the client if you consider that the terminology in the glossary is inappropriate or incorrect.

- Do not be too concerned with the style a translator uses, unless you know it to be inappropriate (too formal/informal, for example). Contact the translator before checking the text if you suspect the style is unsuitable. If the overall style is good, do not alter any small points you feel would 'improve' the translation: it is the job of the translator, not the checker, to produce a translation which reads well, and selection of style is largely subjective.

- Point out any sections of the translation which you think may be ambiguous in the translation. If possible, suggest a less ambiguous (or, better still, a completely unambiguous) alternative.

- Report to your section leader or manager any text which you think has been poorly translated or contains many errors. This will ensure that the performance of the translator in question is monitored carefully in the future, and continued poor performance will result in the deletion of the errant translator from the database (or have a quiet word with the in-house translator!).

- If you find a translation is full of errors, do not waste time checking the whole text. Inform your section leader or manager of this fact as soon as possible and await further instructions.

- Keep going until you reach the end. Do note however that beginnings and ends of paragraphs, the end of the document, headings and subheadings, and headers and footers often do not receive the same attention from the translator as the main text, so do be aware of this and check these bits extra carefully.

- Finally, do not rush checking. Be thorough when you check a text, but take occasional breaks if you feel you are concentrating less effectively than before. Bear in mind the fact that you will check more quickly and less thoroughly as the day wears on, so try to make a conscious effort to slow down if you feel you are checking too quickly.

Scan-checking is an equally important operation though less extensive than full checking. The operation is simply a check to confirm completeness of a text and accuracy of vital formulae, etc.

Procedure for scan-checking

As before, you will need a ruler, a red pen, a copy of the source text and a copy of the target text.

- Place the source text on your left. Place the target text to the right of the source.

- Place the ruler on the source text at the top.

- Check the beginning and end of each paragraph, this should be possible even if you do not speak either of the languages you are checking. If any paragraphs seem a lot shorter or longer than they should, consult the translator.

- If any paragraphs are missing, consult the translator. Check this carefully though since Swedes, for example, are fond of writing single sentence paragraphs and the translator may combine several to make a coherent paragraph. Conversely, some people have a penchant for writing page-long paragraphs (or longer) which the translator may have split to enhance readability.

- In the event of problems arising, you should consult another translator only when the original translator of the text is unavailable or unable to answer your queries.

- Check all numbers, formulae, company names, etc. very carefully. Inform the client of any errors you may find in the original text.

- Do not bother reading through the text unless specifically instructed to do so. Do not change anything in the text unless it is grammatically incorrect or misspelt.

- If you think a translation is poor, advise your section leader or manager of this fact as soon as possible and, if possible, carry out a full check of, say, the first page of text to establish whether a scan-check is going to be sufficient for the purposes of the document in question.

- You may occasionally be asked to spot-check some documents. This involves checking random paragraphs fully while scan-checking most of the rest of the document. This is most useful when checking work by new translators which does not necessarily have to undergo a full check.

- When filling in the 'Checked by' section in the quality control documentation, do not forget to add the word 'Scanned' so that it is clear that the translation has not been checked fully.

The checking process may need to be iterative to achieve a desired level of quality. The arrows in Figure 4 show parts of the loop where discussion is bidirectional.

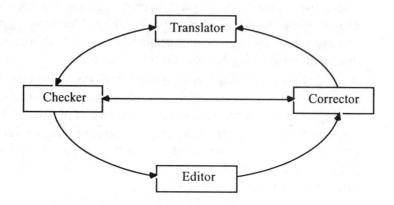

Figure 4. A control loop illustrating staff categories involved

2.2.4 Statistics

I have monitored production statistics of translators where I work. Not for any sinister motive but to provide an assessment of performance and an accurate means of quoting for translation work. These statistics show that an experienced staff translator should be able to produce around 30,000 words in a month, based on a seven hour working day. Factors such as type of text, purpose of the translation and layout all have an effect on production capacity. This works out to be around 1,350 words a day. I know this does not sound much since a competent translator with average keyboarding skills can easily complete a draft translation of this length in two hours. What you must consider is the time you need to spend on terminology research, skills development, expertise improvement, checking, and other attributes that are necessary as part of the job.

In addition to producing translations, our translators also assist in the checking of translations produced by colleagues. Again, statistics compiled at our office show that a translation checker should be able to complete a full check at the rate of around 1,200 words an hour. A check is probably not being done thoroughly if it is done at a faster rate. Of course, this needs to be qualified according to the accuracy of the translation and the amount of marking up that needs to be done. The job of checking is very under-rated and not at all easy.

2.2.5 Editing

Although a translation may be linguistically accurate, it may need the attention of an editor so that it meets certain criteria. Quite often, this work may be done by the client's overseas office to ensure that the text complies with legal, marketing, or stylistic criteria about which the translator may not be fully informed. The operation is also known as 'localisation'.

A case also arises where several translators may be working independently at different locations, even in different countries, on the same project and a co-ordinating editor needs to work on the text to harmonise terminology and style.

2.2.6 Quality control

I suppose the obvious question here is, 'What is quality control?'. I have endeavoured to answer this in more detail later in the chapter. For the purpose of this model I will restrict discussion at this juncture to those elements of quality control required for the model

QUALITY CONTROL MATRIX

Check \ Purpose	Information or abstract	Publication	Legal, notarisation or certification
• Pre-translation edit	✓	✓	✓
• Terminology check	✓	✓	✓
• Compile/update glossary	✓	✓	✓
• Resolve queries with client	✓	✓	✓
• Checked for completeness by translator	✓	✓	✓
• Spellcheck by translator	✓	✓	✓
• Grammar check by translator	✓	✓	✓
• Figures checked by translator	✓	✓	✓
• Checked for completeness by checker	✓	✓	✓
• Syntax checked by checker	✓	✓	✓
• Grammar checked by checker	✓	✓	✓
• Figures checked by checker	✓	✓	✓
• Changes incorporated by translator	✓	✓	✓
• Repeat spellcheck by translator	✓	✓	✓
• Harmonisation by coordinating editor		✓	
• Copy editing and localisation		✓	
• Source code verification and harmonisation		✓	
• Submit to client for approval		✓	✓
• Incorporate client's amendments		✓	✓
• Check remaining legal queries		✓	✓
• Check layout		✓	✓

Figure 5. Quality control matrix

I have chosen to illustrate this as a matrix that shows what needs to be included according to the end-use of the translation. We will return to the subject of quality control in Section 3.

2.3 Outputs

2.3.1 Translated target text

If what you have done so far in the operation is satisfactory then the translated target text should be suitable for the intended purpose. You will have done all that can be reasonably expected of you in terms of inputs and the translation process.

2.3.2 Satisfied clients

There are many important goals in business, one of which is satisfying your clients. If you do not achieve this goal you will quickly run out of clients and you will be out of business. It is important to determine any possible reason for satisfaction since, if you get no feedback, it is nigh impossible to know how you might make improvements.

2.3.3 Intellectual skills improvement

It is fashionable among management gurus to talk of 'the learning organisation', in other words an organisation that understands change and how to learn from that change. Most people are homeostatic, that is to say they are comfortable with the way things are at the moment and tend to resist change. While I do not advocate change just for the sake of it, there are obvious benefits if changes in your approach can be bettered by implementing the practical skills improvements you learn. Being aware of the changes that clients are likely to demand, say using Word for Windows instead of WordPerfect, also allows you to maintain a competitive advantage.

2.3.4 Extended terminology bank

Updating your terminology bank is a continuous process. The important consideration is the management of the information you have gained as a result of the operation. Again, since this subject is dealt with in detail elsewhere in this book, I will not dwell on the matter.

Proper management of information is an important aspect of quality management. Do you have a proper procedure for storing the terminology you have researched as part of the translation process? Can this be readily accessed at any time in the future?

2.3.5 Profit

I mentioned above the important goal of having satisfied clients. The principal reason for working as a translator is to earn a living, although some people may translate purely as a matter of interest or for altruistic motives. Make sure that you structure your pricing so that it reflects the amount of work you do. If you provide quality and good value for money you will be able to demand higher fees since the end-user of your translation output will recognise added value and will not need to devote resources to bridging quality gaps.

3. What Is Quality Control?

To control something, you need some way of measuring it. Measuring the physical property of a tangible object rarely presents a problem since there is usually some formal agreement of what can be measured, as laid down in a British Standard, for example. A kilogram of salt always weighs a kilogram, no more – no less. General engineering steel may have the following composition which can be measured accurately using instruments or other tangible means:

Composition
Iron	*98.45%*
Carbon	*0.25%*
Silicon	*0.40%*
Manganese	*0.80%*
Phosphorous	*0.05%*
Sulphur	*0.05%*

Because there is precious little agreement on what constitutes quality in translation, there is no generally accepted means of controlling that quality. Life would be a lot simpler if you could quantify a translation in terms of physical properties. Just imagine how much simpler life would be if you could weigh a translation and say 'That translation weighs 6.2 grammes and has an average text density of 370 words per page' knowing that nobody could dispute that measure of quality.

Translations cannot be stored for sale at some later date like spares. This makes inspection of translation output difficult unless somebody carries out an inspection at the point of delivery. The dilemma is even more acute for interpreters unless the spoken words are recorded and analysed at some later time.

A common denominator of all service industries is the need to take into account the perceptions of quality made by the translator and the client. Remember the quality gap concept? The translator needs to consider what attributes the client deems to be important and measure performance and quality against those attributes. Berry *et al.* (1985).

Normally there are three sets of criteria used as appropriate measures – those that relate to translation operations, those that relate to financial matters, and those that are determined by your clients.

3.1 Translation operations

I would like to think that the easiest to quantify are criteria applied to the translation operation. These could determine 'conformance to specification' which I've tried to list as follows:

- Have the checks listed under the 'Translation Process' (2.2) been satisfactorily completed?
- Is the translation delivered in the correct software format and laid out according to the client's instructions?
- Has the agreed verification procedure been applied? For example, you may be responsible for providing a linguistically-correct translation whereas your client may be responsible for verifying style via his in-country agent.
- Has the translation been delivered on time?

3.2 Financial considerations

Quality does not come cheap. I remember when I first tried to introduce formal quality control in my fledgling translation company, there was immediate opposition from the person who was responsible for doing the accounts on the basis of what it would cost. I am pleased to say that the self same person is now very careful to ensure that, wherever feasible, no translation is despatched to a client without having gone through some form of checking procedure. We inform a client if we are unable to check a translation, either through lack of resources, time or competence. The client is then aware of the fact and can accept or reject the situation. I suppose the strongest argument in favour of quality control is the cost of not exercising the option. Let's look at the different costs.

3.2.1 The cost of checking

These include costs for proofreading and checking by a second translator to ensure linguistic accuracy. These costs also extend to assessing and approving suppliers i.e. freelances in the case of a translation agency, and auditing the quality system that is applied to the translation operation.

3.2.2 Cost of preventive measures

These are the overall costs of structuring, exercising and maintaining a quality management system to prevent problems of non-conformance occurring. These costs include implementing the translation operation model referred to in Figure 1, planning for quality, training translators and other staff. They also extend to creating and maintaining a quality assurance system. All these costs are invested in an endeavour to 'do things right first time'.

3.2.3 Internal rectification costs

These are the costs of bringing the work up to the standard of quality required by the client. These include the amount of correction work, possible re-checking after correction or, even worse, rejection of the output and the need for re-translation. Added to these costs is the additional administration work, plus the time and effort expended in analysing the source and reason for non-conformance.

3.2.4 External non-acceptance costs

These are the most devastating costs since they arise as a result of the client detecting non-conformance. They include re-working or re-translation, time taken up in dealing with the client's complaint, investigation into the source of the complaint, possible liability claims resulting from non-conformance, delays in payment of invoices (or reduction of invoice amount) and, worst of all, loss of reputation and future sales. The latter are the most difficult to quantify.

3.3 Client considerations

The client's perception of quality is difficult to assess since in many cases, the translator seldom meets the client. It is regrettable that very little tangible feedback is given to the translator – response or the lack of it is usually manifested in four ways:

- The client rejects the translation for some reason or another.
- The client praises the work you have done – a rare occurrence even though you regularly produce good quality work.
- The client continues to use your services.
- The client goes to another supplier without telling you why. Even a negative response can be constructive since unless you know why the client is not happy you will be unaware of the need to make the changes.

It is only by conducting a client satisfaction survey that you can gain some idea of the client's perception of the quality you provide. A client survey is not a bad thing bearing in mind the intangible nature of services such as translation.

3.4 Quality assurance

Most translators tend to be reactive to the demands of clients rather than looking at what problems could occur so that preventive measures can be considered. The purpose of any quality assurance system is not to point a wagging finger and lay blame since that approach does not resolve any underlying problem. The intention should, instead, be to isolate where non-conformance with agreed practices lies and to rectify what is wrong. If there is true accountability it is possible to isolate faults and take the appropriate measures.

Rather than discussing non-conformance in detail, I would instead recommend reading Chapter 8 'What to do if things goes wrong' in 'A Practical Guide for Translators'. This chapter concludes with a number of flow charts that consider common reasons for dispute between translator and client, and how these disputes might be resolved.

I have endeavoured in the following to identify the various stages between an enquiry being received and a translation being delivered, and the elements that require quality management in those stages.

Receipt of enquiry and submission of quotation:

Ask the following questions to ensure quality of information and that you have a proper understanding of what the client wants:

- What is the translation going to be used for?
- What is the volume of the work?
- What are the software requirements?
- How is the translation to be delivered?
- Is reference material available where applicable?
- Are sample pages available?
- Do I have adequate and competent resources?

If you have a full understanding of the requirements, and you can comply with them, give a quotation to be confirmed on sight of the complete text to be translated.

Receipt of quotation by the client

Has the client fully understood your quotation and accepted any reservations you may have in relation to delivery time, responsibility for validation, etc?

Issue of firm order by the client

- Does the order comply with what was agreed with the client?
- Does the material submitted for translation agree with what was originally discussed?

Contact the client to resolve any variance. If appropriate, hold a project meeting with those involved in the translation production.

Allocation of work

Give the work to the appropriate translator(s) and advise others involved, i.e. checkers, coordinating editor, corrector, that their services will be required. Advise them of the schedule that needs to be followed.

Make sure that those working to produce the completed translation fully understand what the client requires.

Monitoring while work is in progress

Ensure that the work is progressing as scheduled. Contact the client immediately if there are any problems to be resolved, particularly if there is any likelihood that the delivery date could be exceeded. Problems seldom go away if they are ignored and, if you do not talk to the client, there is no possibility that he might be able to help.

Pre-delivery checks on the completed translation
- Does the translation comply with the client's requirements?
- Have the original text and reference material, the completed translation, and the disk file been stored in a manner that will facilitate retrieval at a later date?
- Has the disaster recovery procedure been followed?
  (See below)

Receipt of the translation by the client
Note any feedback from the client.

- Did the client perceive what he has received to be what he expected to receive?
- Do you have a client dispute procedure in place? The mere fact that you do is evidence that you have considered what could go wrong and introduced the necessary measures to ensure that things do not go wrong.

There is mention of disaster recovery in the table. This is used as a generic term to cover a number of situations. A large part of quality assurance and its management stems from proper accountability. Part of your quality assurance is to ensure that you are properly prepared if anything should go wrong. Consider how you might be prepared to deal with the following contingencies:

- Your client phones you and says that he wants to make some amendments to a job you did, say, nine months ago and has lost his disk copy of the work. Can you easily locate the documentation for the original job – including the file in electronic format? What system do you have for identifying your client's files?
- Do you have a client dispute procedure? If you feel you are in the right but cannot provide documentation (both as hard copy and on disk) to support your viewpoint then your position is severely weakened.

- What would happen if your office were broken into and your equipment stolen? Do you have copies of essential disk files stored in a separate location? Hardware and software can be replaced and reinstalled providing you have appropriate insurance and software licences. But what about all the files that contain irreplaceable information? How long would it take to recover from such an episode?

3.5 Formal accreditation

This is a thorny issue and guaranteed to provoke strong feelings among translators. The Institute of Translation and Interpreting formed a BS 5750 sub-committee in an endeavour to introduce some form of structured quality management for individual translators. The efforts of the committee ran out into the sand because of the perception that translations were inviolate and formal quality management was unnecessary.

I find this a 'head in the sand' attitude. Nobody is that brilliant that they cannot learn from the experiences of others. Again I come back to the observation that most translators work on their own. Unfortunately some become so entrenched in their own ways of working and feel affronted, and sorely wounded, if any form of criticism is levelled at them. I am indeed fortunate to have worked as part of translation teams on various projects and I have been very grateful to receive the comments and observations of my colleagues. But I could also take the attitude that I'm qualified (*FIL, FITI, MTA, DipTrans IoL, DipMgmt(Open), SFÖ*), I've worked as a translator for twenty years so why should I accept criticism?

BS 5750, or BS EN ISO 9000 to give the proper designation, identifies the basic disciplines and specifies the procedures and criteria to ensure that products and services meet the client's requirements. To be accredited, an organisation's quality system must be assessed and approved. This is undertaken by independent assessors who need to be satisfied that documentation drawn up for the quality system, and its procedures and related instructions, comply with the requirements of the standard. Likewise, they need to be assured that what is done in the organisation conforms to what is specified in the documentation.

Let's bring this back into perspective and take a look at some of the criticisms levelled against it and what formal accreditation offers in terms of benefits. First the criticisms.

Perhaps the strongest criticism is that it does not guarantee the quality of the product since you can specify any standard of quality you wish. As long as you maintain that standard you will achieve accreditation. The argument against this attitude is that you are unlikely to survive in business if you do not provide the level of quality your clients demand. The system does identify deficiencies in quality performance and it would be a cynical organisation that did not use this as an opportunity for resolving problems.

Introducing a quality system does cost money and there is a level of bureaucracy in producing the necessary quality manual and other documentation. Do not let the operation of the system become an end in itself – apply it as a way of managing quality. Costs will depend on the size of your organisation and should be viewed in the context of what failure can cost. Think of them as prevention costs that will eventually result in your investment being paid back.

There is the argument that the system is suitable neither for service organisations nor small businesses. I have a measure of sympathy for the first argument since BS 5750 was originally devised for manufacturing organisations. Part 8 was added to the standard in 1991 in response to this criticism. It may also be difficult for a small organisation to justify the costs of seeking formal accreditation and then paying continued registration fees. The counter-argument in this case is that you do not have to be formally accredited to adopt the principles of the system.

Enough of doom and gloom – let's consider the benefits. Both the client and the supplier know exactly what they are agreeing to. Consequently, the client knows that the supplier performs specific quality checks and does not need to repeat them. A common standard means that the supplier should not need to conform to a plethora of different standards. It also constitutes a quality benchmark for comparison with other suppliers.

It is worth quoting the Department of Trade and Industry (DTI). 'The benefits of BS 5750 are real: it will save you money – because your procedures will be more soundly based and more efficient: it will ensure satisfied clients – because you will have built in quality at every stage. It will reduce waste and time-consuming reworking of designs and procedures.'

Having formal accreditation is a powerful marketing tool. It enhances the company's image since it demonstrates to potential clients that you take quality seriously. You are also listed in the DTI's National Register of Quality Assured Companies and other directories.

3.6 Timetable for achieving accreditation

If you have decided to introduce a formal accreditation system, you should be aware that it is not something that can be done overnight. Quality management is a system of continuous improvement since you learn as you progress. You should be prepared to accept that it will probably take around two years from setting out on the long road towards accreditation to reaching your goal. It will probably take you a year to write your quality manual and the related procedures. You will need to implement them, and amend and revise them on the basis of experience. It may then be advisable to talk to an independent assessor to draw up a formal timetable.

I will not go into detail since there are several books that offer wise guidance. Suggestions for further reading are offered in the references below. It is useful to have a copy of the relevant British Standard, BS EN ISO 9002 : 1994, since Part 8 of this publication shows the elements of the standard that apply to services. Your will need to comply with these requirements to gain accreditation. The following is an example.

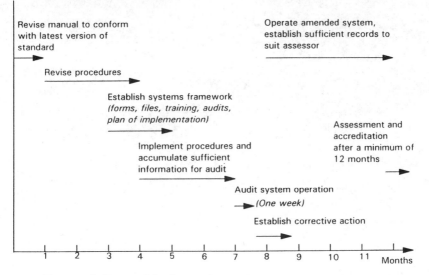

Figure 6. Timetable for seeking ISO 9002 accreditation

4. Conclusion

Trying to qualify what is meant by quality in translations is, and will continue to be, a divisive issue because of the intangible nature of the service. The only true benchmark if you are translating for a living is whether you provide what your client wants. The fact that you may not agree with your client's perception of quality is another matter since you might feel that your client needs educating.

Now that is an entirely different kettle of fish!

References

1.   Berry, L. *et al.* (1985) Quality counts in service too. *Business Horizons*, May-June, pp. 44-52.

2.   Paraswaman, A. *et al.* (1985) A conceptual model of service quality and its implication for further research. *Journal of Marketing,* Fall.

3.   Samuelsson-Brown, G. (1995) A Practical Guide for Translators, *Multilingual Matters*, 160 pp, ISBN 1-85359-303-6.

4.   British Standard (BS EN ISO 9002 : 1994,) *Quality systems,* ISBN 0 580 23440 1.

5.   Byrnes, David (1995) *Managing Resources for the Market,* (Block 4 – Managing Operations), Milton Keynes: The Open University, 139pp, ISBN 0 7492 7100 0.

6. Providing quality and value

GEOFFREY KINGSCOTT

How good should a professional translation be? How do we determine quality in translation? Is the customer getting value for money from the translation industry as at present constituted? These are the questions which this article will try to answer.

'Try to answer' is the operative phrase here. There can be no definitive answer to these questions, for translation is a fluid activity, with no set boundaries and no universally accepted parameters. The answers which this article puts forward should therefore be regarded as merely tentative.

For decades now translators have dreamed of making translation a closed profession, with 'licences to practise' issued only to certified practitioners, as is the case with architecture, medicine or law.

This is an idle dream, a vain hope. Here again the problem is that of the fluidity of translation activity. In this world of instant global communication, there are thousands of individuals, even in Britain, who operate in more than one language, and who might do something akin to translation in the course of their daily duties.

Also, we are seeing the growing integration of all documentation processes, so that translation is seen less and less of a discrete activity. Any attempt to set up our own separate little garden is doomed; there will be more and more people trampling over our flower beds.

In the same way it is difficult to define a 'professional' translator. Is it someone who makes his or her principal living from translation, or is it someone who translates to a particular level of quality? If the former criterion is used, then there is the problem that there are many people in Britain translating for a living who are deluded about their own ability and who are turning out translations which are quite disgraceful. If the latter criterion is used, there is the problem that some of the best translations are produced by subject specialists who normally do other work but occasionally have to turn their hand to a translation in their domain.

Having made these reservations we can actually accept that there is a body of professional translators in the UK (many, but not all, members of the Institute of Translation and Interpreting) who both make their principal living from translation, and who try to be responsible in the way they produce translation work.

Most of them would define an acceptable translation as one that rendered accurately the message of the source text into the target language, and which was written in an idiom natural to the target language. The latter requirement normally presupposes that one is writing in one's mother tongue, which is why the 'mother tongue rule' is usually considered de rigueur for professional translation.

Having established this definition so early in my article, I could end here, or just go on to amplify the concepts of accuracy and natural idiom.

But this traditional definition misses a crucial factor – what exactly is it that the customer wants?

For far too long the translation profession has assumed that what the customer must want, and certainly ought to want, is the accurate, idiomatic translation. The profession has also maintained that the customer must be prepared to pay the cost of such a translation, and to allow time for such a translation to be produced. The profession, insofar as it is organised to promote itself, and with the lamented absence of the 'regulation of the profession,' has therefore concentrated on promoting 'professional translation' to the customer.

The problem is that the customer often has a different perspective to the translator. A poor-quality translation, provided it does not positively mislead, which is ready for a businessman on Tuesday before he catches his plane to Tokyo, is far preferable than the accurate + natural idiom translation which is not ready till Friday of the same week; in fact, in such circumstances, the latter translation is worthless. This is where raw-output machine translation can be useful; it is cheap, it is quick, and it can provide a level of information which the customer requires.

Here, then, is the first point to be established, and one difficult for established translators to grasp: Quality is relative.

In one way this is fortunate, for no language-based activity can be an exact science. The use of language is as individual as a person's physiognomy. Every translator knows that many complaints are unjustified, in that they relate to personal stylistic preferences. In translators' circles this is sometimes known as the IDTISIC Syndrome, IDTISIC being an acronym for – if you will forgive the indelicacy – 'I didn't translate it so it's crap'. The trouble here is that the customer – or his busybody reviser – often does not understand that there can be more than one way to translate a text. Many non-linguists think of a foreign language as being a mirror reflection of their own, with direct word-for-word or phrase-for-phrase correspondence. The notion that each language encapsulates a different way of looking at the world is far too sophisticated a concept to convey easily.

Nevertheless, the raising of customer awareness must be the first priority of the translation profession if we are ever to enhance its status and create an appreciation of quality in translation.

And the way to achieve this is to insist, wherever possible, on a customer specification. Often asking for such a specification will mystify the customer – 'But I just want you to type it up in French!'.

This is where some simple explanations of what language differences actually involve are necessary. Many years ago J. G. Weightman, a well-known writer on the French language, took the apparently simplest of English sentences, "The cat sat on the mat", and showed in a full-length article that it was impossible to translate it into French unless extra-textual knowledge was available (le *chat, la chatte,* sitting as single action (perfect tense) or continuing state (imperfect tense), nature of the way it sat (*se poser, s'allonger*) etc., the need to know what type of mat it was, etc. etc.). And this involves translation between two closely related languages, which do have similar ways of looking at the world. Translation between English and Japanese requires a far greater number of intellectual leaps.

Everyone who has contact with customers should have some well-rehearsed examples of the difficulty of translation, to show that it is not straightforward word-mapping. An example from the technical sphere is the English word 'bolt', which can be translated into German as *Schraube*, *Bolzen* or *Stift*, according to the type of 'bolt' it is. Similarly 'valve' in French could be *soupape*, *clapet*, *valve*, *vanne*, *robinet* etc. In both these cases the terms in the target language are not usually interchangeable, and to put the wrong one would be incorrect and misleading. The world is seen in different ways in different languages, and the fact that the Germans and the French differentiate between different bolts or valves is not bloody-mindedness or finickiness on their part, they actually consider the differentiated items to be different objects.

In the same way many English learners of foreign languages have great difficulty comprehending the differentiation of the verb to know, which is found in practically every other language (the *kennen/wissen* or *connaître/savoir* distinction). Other peoples see the distinction as crucial.

The customer must therefore supply the context to any translation. If illustrations are available, they must be given to the translator (in patent translation, the illustrations play such an essential role that translators should simply refuse to translate patents unless they are given sight of the illustrations). Any previously translated text upstream or downstream of the piece to be translated should also be provided, if only for the sake of consistency. Truly ignorant customers have been known to cut out new sentences (and even isolated words) from a revised text and give them to a translator, so that the translation can be pasted in without 'troubling' the translator with the previously translated material. No professional translator should accept being kept at arm's length in this way.

Translators have got to become more proactive and less reactive in their relations with customers. The problem here is that many translators are rather timid creatures, and however much they complain at translator gatherings or in translation magazines, never like to say 'Boo' to a domineering customer. This has got to change if we are ever to establish quality and value in translation.

The customer must also be asked to state what the translation is to be used for. There is a big difference between different types of application: for example, raw information needed urgently for an important meeting, a technical manual intended for skilled and knowledgeable operators, instructions for laypersons (users without specialist knowledge), a text used to support an important application in the target country, a text which will have legal status, and advertising text which is written to persuade.

A customer specification will also cover matters of procedure and delivery, but here we enter the realm of formal quality assurance and the procedures covered by my colleague, Geoffrey Samuelsson-Brown, in another chapter of this book.

But once the principle of customer specification is established, it will be realised, by users and suppliers of translation alike, that it is a question of 'horses for courses'. There are times when fast, cheap, raw machine translation will be appropriate; there will be other times when the need is for a carefully crafted translation produced by a subject specialist.

The supplier of translation services must always be asking himself or herself (or itself in the case of a translation company) 'What exactly am I offering?' It will be immediately apparent that 'professional translations' is not a very meaningful reply.

For this reason I consider it important that the translation profession get away from the theoretical notion of 'professional translation' and move towards the concept of 'added value'. 'What exactly am I offering?' could be re-phrased as 'What added value am I giving the customer?'

For example, an English customer has received a very large document in Spanish, the specifications for building and equipping a sugar cane processing plant in South America. The customer wants a quick, rough translation of the contents; he simply wants to know what the specifications contain. Almost certainly, because deadlines in tendering are crucial, the speed with which the translation can be prepared is more important than 'polish'. The documentation is quite voluminous, and until the customer has obtained a broad idea of what the documentation contains he does not know whether he will want to tender. The customer therefore will not want to pay what some translators would call a 'professional' price for the translation at this stage.

The added value which in other circumstances would be represented by a well-crafted translation as compared with a rough-and-ready translation has in this context only a negligible significance. If 'professional translator' X charges £20,000 and takes two months to do the translation, while 'robotic translator' (whether human or machine) Y charges £5,000 and produces a translation in five days, then the customer will prefer Y, and rightly so. The translation profession has no right to complain about, or attempt to bar from practice, the translators Y of this world.

The point needs making, since the universities which are training the translators of the future are training translators who are geared to hand-crafting translations to a high standard. There are still work opportunities for such translators (if and when they later acquire some specialist knowledge), but not as many as in the past. There is a definite demand for translators who can produce translation-for-information quickly and in volume, but no-one is training such people. Once, deliberately trying to provoke, I told an audience of translation teachers that no-one should be given any form of translation diploma unless and until they had shown, on continuous repetitive text, they could use translation aids to produce in excess of 10,000 words a day (and the 10,000 words a day is just for starters).

Here again, even for high-volume translation-for-information, one must insert the proviso that a translation must never be so bad that it positively misleads the customer into making serious erroneous judgements.

Every translator supplier, therefore, identifies the 'added value' which is being offered. This should make translator suppliers think hard of where their expertise lies. The days of the translator-who-would-tackle-anything (and I was once one myself) are definitely numbered.

Some may feel that what I am advocating is a two-standard form of translation, like first-class and second-class post. It is not as simple as that. What I am trying to say is that there is nearly always, in translation, a trade-off between translation performance and other factors, such as time and price. Sometimes these other factors are of more value than the 'quality' of the translation itself, and this must be recognised, by both customers and suppliers, before any progress can be made in raising standards generally.

Of course one of the reasons why the translation profession resists the idea that there are different forms of translation is the fear that the bad may drive out the good. Customers do seem to be, by and large, undiscriminating. What if they became accustomed to accepting over-literal unidiomatic texts?

The answer to this is, customers do so already. The professional associations have simply not succeeded in controlling translation supply, and now, with the rapid expansion of all forms of documentation and information, they never will. Promotion of the added-value approach is the only way to move forward (see also Tristam Carrington-Windo's chapter in this book).

And in fact, even with heavy reliance on translation aids, and using machine translation itself, it is possible to produce texts which are reasonably intelligible. The standard of computer-produced and computer-aided translations is improving all the time, and will go on improving. The use of aids can also improve the performance of even the translators producing work of the highest quality.

And the advances in language engineering do mean that translators who offer the added-value of well-crafted, accurate, translations using correct terminology and idiom, must look to their laurels – the work they produce must be worthy of their pretensions. If the customer is paying for this added-value he must not be cheated by failure to research the correct terminology, or by translators taking on work in a specialist domain not covered by their expertise.

The most common complaint among users of translation services is the poor quality of the writing. The ability to write in the mother tongue is too often taken for granted, both in translation training, and by practising translators. Translators must realise that they are, by exercising their profession, professional writers. As 90% of translation work involves commercial, scientific or technical texts, translators have to exercise a skill akin to that of technical writers.

The guiding principle these days for technical authors is 'reader-oriented writing', and this principle must also be adopted by translators. In technical texts there should never be a deterioration in communication from source text to translated target text; on the contrary, the target text, because it has gone through the hands of a professional writer (the translator), should be clearer than the original text, because the translator has exercised all his skill to enhance the message-conveying role of the source-text. It would be as well for all technical translators (and this should certainly be part of their university training) to study technical writing techniques and theories. Obscurities and ambiguities in the source text must be cleared up, and if necessary the text re-structured to meet the pattern usually found in target-language technical documents. The old adage of 'garbage in, garbage out' should no longer provide an excuse for poor target texts produced by 'professional' translators. The added value here is that the message has been clearly conveyed, because the customer has had the sense to use the services of a 'professional'.

In the future literal-type translations will be provided by machines. The professional translator must provide added value, a form of 'translation-plus'.

This approach reinforces the need for customer specification of the application of a translation.

Clarity of exposition will usually be required. In certain cases, however, it may not be the main purpose. For example, it can be argued that patents, though they are technical documents, are not designed at all for clear exposition of an invention. The aim of patent agents the world over is to seek to obtain the widest possible scope for the invention, while giving away as little as possible. The translator's customer will often be another patent agent. This is a case where fairly close adherence to the source text may be appropriate.

Traditionally translators come from a text-bound culture, and this is certainly true of those teaching translation, because of the generation factor. In future more and more texts will be 'multi-media', using illustrations, pictures, sound and even moving image (the sociologists refer to it as a shift in the icon/alphabet ratio). A different 'mix' may be appropriate in some cultures. The translator of the future will need to be acquainted with the techniques of communication – comprehensibility ratings, the language of pictograms, etc. – if he is to help to make the text work in the target culture. Technical writers in the UK call themselves 'communicators', and their professional association is the Institute of Scientific and Technical Communicators. Translators are also communicators, but communicators with a difference, because they are able to work between languages. But in the last resort communication is what it is all about.

So, to return to the questions posed at the start of this article, we can re-examine, firstly, how good should a professional translation be? The answer can be found in the criterion used in quality assurance procedures, that of suitability for purpose.

It therefore follows that quality in translation is relative to the purpose of the translation.

Is the customer getting value for money from the translation industry as at present constituted? Here there is a marked difference of opinion, between those who translate for a living, who feel, for the most part, under-valued and underpaid, and the customer, who finds translation costs far too high.

From time to time it occurs to gatherings of translators that they ought to invite users along to discuss matters of common interest. My experience is that firstly, users are difficult to identify and even more difficult to persuade that they should take an interest in the translation process, and, secondly, that wherever users have come together (as in the Localisation Industry Standards Association, for example), one of the first things they start discussing is how translation costs (and delivery times) can be reduced.

If all the material that might be worth translating were to be translated, then at present rates of translation output, the whole educated population of Europe would have to become translators. This is obviously impossible. But we must recognise there is a demand for cheaper and more accessible translation, if only it could be satisfied.

The number one challenge for the future for the translation profession is not to raise the said profession to the status of a highly respected guild pursuing a mystic craft, but to find ways of making translation cheaper and more accessible while preserving an acceptable level of intelligibility and the individual constructions and nuances of natural language.

Part IV – The Personal Touch

7. Educating the client

LUCAS WESCHKE

Introduction

The primary objective of educating the client is mutual business benefit. The translator is working to earn a living, and as long as the client remains in business and is benefiting from the translator's services, then the relationship is mutually beneficial. However, there are a number of obstacles which have to be overcome before this ideal situation can be established, and unless the translator educates the client correctly the relationship could fail to benefit anybody. A number of scenarios can be imagined:

Translator wins, client wins	Translator wins, client loses
Translator and client do business. They understand and agree to each other's expectations and conditions. The relationship is mutually beneficial and long-term.	Translator and client do business in the short term, but client is unlikely to use the translator's services again because the client's expectations were not satisfied.
Translator loses, client wins	Translator loses, client loses
Translator and client do business in the short term, but translator will avoid working for client again if possible because the translator's expectations were not satisfied.	Translator and client either find no common ground, or are both dissatisfied with the outcome of a translation assignment. They therefore do not remain in contact.

There is really no point in being anywhere other than in the translator wins / client wins box. You can get into the win/win box only if the client understands your expectations and conditions, and if you have made the effort to understand theirs. Whilst this section is about educating the client to ensure that this happens, the process of educating the client is inextricably linked with the translator's awareness of his or her own role.

Of course, there is a difference between what the client must understand about translation, and what it would be nice for the client to know, and I shall attempt to distinguish between the two. In outline however, there are four main areas in which clients frequently have a number of misconceptions:

1. What the translator does
2. Selecting the right translator
3. Agreeing the terms of business
4. The role of the client

Each of the above areas will be examined in this chapter, and followed by action plans for the translator to implement. I am assuming a readership of full-time translators (either freelances or employees), though part-timers and hobbyists may find my proposals useful, and it is probably worth listing the various types of client and translator at this point:

Clients regular and sporadic:	Translators full-time and part-time:
Public administration	Freelance self-employed
Company	Staff company/public
Translation agency	administration
Private individual	Staff translation agency
	Language student or hobbyist

There are many clients who understand the translation business very well, and who have a genuine commitment to quality. It is these clients who understand the importance of establishing and maintaining good working relationships with a team of well-qualified translators. This type of relationship is the basis for successful translation projects, and should therefore be the primary objective of both translators and clients.

Whilst different clients may have different expectations, different translation requirements, and different procedures for using translators, they should all be aware of certain ground rules, and this is where the translator can be ready to offer guidance if necessary.

1. What The Translator Does

Many clients are not familiar with the process of translation, and nor should one expect them to be: they specialise in what they do, and we specialise in what we do. In the same way as most of us cannot imagine the complexity involved in making an animated film, for example, many clients have misconceptions concerning the work of a translator. Clients may vary in their perception of what we do, categorising us as:

Interpreters, tour guides or public relations agents

It is often clear that many people do not understand the difference between translation and interpreting or liaising, and it is only because we work in the field of languages that it seems so obvious to us.

Someone with the relevant GCSE/A level or someone with a hobby

In a country where few people speak a second language, the language student or hobbyist is often regarded as the most effective solution. Some clients may have the impression that translation is a sort of sideline practised by people with spare time (a Civil Servant I know occasionally drops in and asks me to tell him the meaning of a single-line memo he has received in German). Whilst it must be remembered that some translators do translate for pleasure, that there is always a role for the language student or hobbyist, and that use of such translators is certainly cheaper and less of a threat to the client's ego, (bearing in mind our traditional wariness of things foreign); the majority of clients will nonetheless require the skills of a professionally qualified translator.

A bilingual secretary or other office services provider

Bilingual secretaries are often expected to act as translators (and are sometimes paid more than translators), but their occupation is not solely devoted to the activity of translation, and they do not normally have a specialist subject area beyond that of general correspondence.

A stop-gap solution until computers get a bit better

Given the widespread ignorance of the complexity of translation, a growing faith in the ability of computers, the occasional media focus on machine translation, advertisements for machine translation software priced at £99, and electronic dictionaries on CD-ROM, etc., it is not surprising that some clients genuinely feel that the translator simply has to press a button on his or her computer before sending off the completed job together with invoice. There are unfortunately a number of significant obstacles to machine translation becoming a viable option for most translators (e.g. quality of source text in terms of authoring and legibility, quality of translation software, quality and applicability of specialist electronic references used, problems posed by diagrams, tables, text attributes, etc). I have spent many days correcting translations produced by some of the best systems in the business, and it is always uppermost in my mind that the task of translation is more complex than we appreciate. And whilst advances are made in the computerised processing of language, the use of language itself is evolving, e.g. specialist terminology and neologisms, word processing features such as embedded objects, tables, indices, footers, etc.

An intellectual, artistic person or writer

Some clients who use the services of a translator have vague and woolly ideas about 'the feel' and 'personal touches'. Whilst some translators do work in literary, philosophical or 'creative' areas, the majority of translation is required in the scientific, technical, commercial or administrative domain, where not much kissing of muses goes on.

Action Plan: Make Sure Your Clients Understand The Service You Provide

Whilst it is unrealistic to expect clients to fully appreciate the complexities of translation, it is nonetheless essential for them to appreciate certain facts:

- There is a difference between translation and interpreting.
- Translators normally translate only into their mother tongue, since this is the first step towards guaranteeing the linguistic quality of a translation (I frequently receive enquiries for work from English into a foreign language).
- The daily throughput of a translator can be estimated fairly accurately (2,000 words or 8 average pages per day is a good rule of thumb), and the translator will produce better work given adequate time. The client should be clear that they pay for words rather than time in most cases.
- A qualified and experienced professional with the right specialist knowledge will always produce the best results.
- A computer cannot generally translate anything more than the simplest of text without requiring considerable post-editing. It is often faster for the translator to start again than to correct the computer output.
- The translator's objective is 100 per cent accuracy. No gists or inferior imitations, but an identical text in a different language, with the same referential and pragmatic effect as the source text. There is a huge difference between a good and a bad translation, and the consequences of a bad translation on the client's business could be very serious.

2. Selecting The Right Translator

It often appears that clients do not appreciate the wide range of translator profiles available to them on the market. Your personal profile is important from the client's point of view in establishing whether you are the right person to the job. It is therefore essential that clients are aware of a) the importance of selecting the right translator, and b) your own areas of expertise. The translator's profile includes:

Professional qualifications

This may be the client's only indication that the translator has followed an approved course of study, and is therefore in a position to provide a more professional service than someone who merely dabbles in translation. Another indicator of a translator's profile is membership of professional bodies such as the ITI (Institute of Translation and Interpreting) or IoL (Institute of Linguists). Some clients will offer work only to translators with the appropriate qualifications and professional affiliations.

Experience and specialist knowledge

Clients sometimes fail to grasp the importance of subject expertise, and of course they cannot be expected to know a translator's areas of expertise when making an initial contact. Some clients may feel that a text is straightforward because of their own familiarity with that area; others may feel that the translator should be able to adapt using the correct reference sources. However, it is essential to direct a client requiring a legal translation for instance to someone who specialises in that field (whether or not the client feels this is unduly pedantic). I say that this is essential for two reasons:

a. the translator cannot guarantee 100% accuracy in an unfamiliar subject area;

b. the translator's throughput will otherwise be so slow that the job will not be financially viable.

Resources

The resources used by a professional translator will reflect his or her qualifications and experience, areas of expertise, and level of commitment. A professional translator will be well aware of the computer resources required in terms of hardware and software, the specialist reference material required to ensure 100% accuracy, and the communications resources required to optimise customer contact.

Use of the latest tools and technology optimises both the speed and the quality of a translator's output. Such technology includes not only modem connections and electronic publishing facilities, but also software translation tools such as on-line glossaries, electronic dictionaries, etc., that are designed to increase the translator's consistency and productivity. A professional translator will always be ready to invest in the appropriate resources, since the earlier the investment is made, the sooner the translator and the client will benefit from the investment. Clients will be influenced by services which reduce their total number of suppliers and facilitate their project management task.

The translator's target market and client base

These are governed to some extent by the translator's area of expertise, and also by the amount of time they can spare looking for and working on juicy apples. I would love to work on the remaining Tintin translations, or on the many articles about his creator, but it is unlikely that anyone would pay me to do so.

Attitude

The translator's attitude can influence a client's perception of them. For example, I have heard clients complain of translators with a pompous attitude which puts them off using the translators concerned. The translator should avoid thinking: 'I am a creative intellectual, with a remarkable talent: admire and reward me', since the client does not often want this, or a jumble of excuses and translator's notes explaining linguistic and terminological problems or niceties. The client simply wants an accurate translation within timescales and to budget. It is easy for the translator to feel frustrated due to lack of recognition, or because the client does not appreciate the effort made or the difficulty of job. However, clients cannot always be expected to appreciate the intricacies of the service you provide, it's your job – not theirs.

Professional indemnity insurance

Some clients feel that a freelance translator should be covered by professional indemnity insurance, and may make this a precondition of working for them. Professional indemnity insurance shows that a translator is prepared to invest in his or her business, and ensures that the translator concerned will be insured should the client wish to take legal action against them. Some translation agencies have professional indemnity insurance which covers any freelance translators working for them.

Working as an agency

Some translators subcontract work to other translators, effectively operating as a sort of translation agency. In the case of large translation projects, your clients are entitled to expect a dedicated project manager; a manager who has experience of handling their type of project. In addition, your commitment to speed and quality should match that of the client. Discuss the procedures you will work to when managing their project, in order to satisfy them that they can expect an efficient service, free of unpleasant surprises, from start to finish. Ensure that your translation agency has an effective infrastructure that will enable it to cope with a potential growth in the client's requirement, either in terms of additional languages or in terms of pure volume. Furthermore, the client will expect some evidence that you are in good financial health. In this way, they will know that they are not investing in a short-term relationship and that when they are ready to move into bigger or different markets, you will be able to support them.

Action Plan: Establish Your Profile

It is essential for clients to understand the importance of a translator having the appropriate professional qualifications and specialist knowledge, and they must be satisfied that they have selected the right translator for the job. The translator's profile should be made clear to clients as follows:

- Ensure that your clients are aware of your professional qualifications and the relevance of any professional bodies of which you are a member. The client must be aware that you are not simply a typist with a dictionary, and that it is your bread and butter to turn out polished translations in the required format every day, using a wide range of specialist tools and resources. Headed notepaper, compliments slips or business cards can document your qualifications simply and effectively.

- As a translator, you offer very finely tuned skills. Ensure that your clients are clear about your experience and expertise in specialist areas and the use of specialist terminology, including the language combinations you offer.

- Ensure that your clients are aware of the resources you use as a professional. These include computer hardware and software resources (exotic input/output devices, different word processing packages, etc.), specialist reference sources (your knowledge of, access to, and compilation of specialist electronic and paper dictionaries and terminologies, databases, reference works, personal contacts, organisations, etc.), and communications facilities (answerphone, separate telephone lines, fax, modem, electronic mail addresses, dictation equipment, etc.).

- Get your attitude right, and strike a balance with yourself about what you do. As a translator, you are a professional language processor, with special skills, qualifications and expertise, and you should be proud of the work you produce. However, you must understand and accept the client's expectations to arrive at the win/win box. Do not become emotionally attached to translations: they are the client's property, and you have simply provided a service by converting the language. In seeking to maintain a consistent and positive attitude in terms of flexibility and availability, do not commit yourself to something you cannot deliver, and demonstrate reliability at all times. If you act like a professional, then you will be treated like a professional.

- If you are unable to accept a translation commission for some reason, always try to give the client a realistic contact point. This may be a personal recommendation you feel able to make, the name and telephone number of the ITI or IoL (both of which publish directories of corporate and individual members, or even a business directory).

- Let your client know if you subcontract work to other translators, and ensure that they are satisfied with the procedures you have in place to guarantee the level of service they expect from you.

157

3. Agreeing The Terms Of Business

There are two areas where agreement is essential to ensure that both translator and client get what they expect. The first is the translation requirement itself, and this will vary from assignment to assignment. The second defines the translator's terms and conditions, and these will generally remain constant for each client.

The purchase order is an important document in that it can be used to specify both the translation requirement and the terms and conditions which apply to a specific job. It is issued by the client, and represents a contract between client and the translator. From the client's point of view, it is important to ensure that the translator understands and reserves time for the job concerned (I often receive offers of work whilst awaiting confirmation of a job agreed only hours before on the telephone – this is particularly annoying if the second offer is more interesting than the first!). From the translator's point of view, the purchase order should provide an accurate record of the translation requirement and the terms and conditions agreed.

The translation requirement

It is surprising how often the translation requirement is not fully documented, and certain details are assumed or not even considered. The client may be unaware of some of the services which a translator can provide (e.g. sending computer files via modem), and the translator may not be familiar with some of the requirements specified by the client (e.g. computerised generation of subject indices). Some or all of the following details must be agreed for every translation job:

Text format

The format of the source text provided to the translator, and the format of the target text to be returned to the client. This could be paper, fax copy, computer file (in which case the word processing software format must also be specified), camera-ready copy, etc.

Text transfer

It must be agreed how the source text will be delivered to the translator, and how the target text will be delivered to the client (and the address or phone number for delivery). This could be by post for text held on paper or diskette (internal, external, registered, insured, courier), fax, or modem.

Start and finish dates

It must be agreed when the source text will arrive and when the target text must be delivered to the client. It may be necessary to specify a time as well as a date, since 21 June could mean 9 a.m., before lunch, before 5 p.m., etc. In the case of large jobs, clients often prefer to receive work in batches as you go along, so that they can manage the validation process more efficiently.

Estimated size of job

This may be estimated in pages, lines, words, days, hours, etc. The important thing is that the estimate is as accurate as possible. The size of any anticipated updates must also be estimated, as well as the dates these will be made available for incorporation into the text.

Language pairs and direction

This may appear unnecessary, but a misunderstanding would be unfortunate.

List of items requiring translation

This may include manuals, instruction cards, labels, spine inserts, screen messages, etc.

Status of source text

The client must specify whether the source text will be frozen or at draft stage when handed over.

Special instructions

The client may have special requirements for certain jobs, e.g. translate only certain sections, whether to retain column layouts, how to deal with headers, diagrams, indices, tables of contents, embedded objects, handwritten notes, etc.

House style guidelines

Certain clients will have established conventions governing page layout, use of company logos, spelling conventions, heading formats, etc. Specific conventions often apply in the context of large translation projects, particularly when a number of different translators are involved.

Preferred reference sources

These may be glossaries, dictionaries, previous versions of target text, or other reference materials. Reference sources may be supplied by the client or already in use by the translator.

Return of materials

It must be specified whether the client expects the return of materials other than the target translation, e.g. the source text, supporting reference materials supplied by the client, glossaries compiled during the translation process, etc.

Confidentiality and copyright

Whilst clients are entitled to expect a translator to exercise due care in the storage or disposal of reference materials supplied and assignments once complete, they may require an additional safeguard in the form of a confidentiality agreement, either for a specific job or for all work done on their behalf. Clients will normally own the copyright in any translation work produced, together with exclusive usage rights.

Client satisfaction

The client will generally include a clause in the purchase order to specify the consequences of unsatisfactory work on the part of the translator, usually in terms of missed deadlines or poor quality presentation/content. This may consist of refusing to accept the work, having the work corrected at the expense of the translator, withholding part or all payment, or even legal action.

The translator's terms and conditions

Your terms and conditions for accepting work are entirely your own choice. However, since you normally expect to achieve certain rewards from your translation activities, your terms and conditions must correspond largely to the expectations of your target market. If it has always been your ambition to translate one of the Dead Sea Scrolls for example, and there is a client who requires this, you may well be competing with many other academics for the honour of performing this particular translation, and your reward may be rather small in monetary terms. A translator's terms and conditions include:

Rates of pay

Whether the translator is paid by the word, line or hour, may be decided in advance by the client or left up to the translator. The translator should be flexible in this respect, since the important thing is to get paid the right amount. Both the ITI and the IoL publish average rates for translation work, based on surveys conducted amongst their members, and these are a useful starting point. However rates of pay do vary widely, and are often affected by the subject area, the translator's profile, internal client regulations, translator location, etc. Many first-time clients will not have any idea about rates of pay (my least interesting offer of work has been 'it's gotta be worth a fiver').

If you are being paid by the word or line, then it is important to decide the method used to count the number of words or lines, since different word processing packages produce different document statistics. Some translators add or subtract percentages to compensate for different languages requiring different numbers of words to say the same thing. Some translators always count the source text, others the target text. For the sake of simplicity, I would advocate counting your target text with the word processing software you have used to produce it, and leave it at that. If the client prefers a different method, then it should be clearly explained,and acceptable to the translator.

If you are being paid by the hour, then you must be meticulous about keeping a record of the time you spend working on the job concerned. Personally, I have found the best method here is to use a stopwatch, switching it off whenever I leave the workplace, (however, it is surprising how long it takes to work seven hours using this method!).

Special rates

This includes rates for e.g. work performed during unsociable hours, on-site work, minimum charges, cancellation charges, proof reading, etc.

Incidental expenses

These include travelling expenses, packing and postage, diskettes, telephone expenses, etc. My personal philosophy on the cost of sundry items is that it all comes out in the wash, e.g. diskettes travel back and forth numerous times, and it is generally simpler for all concerned to charge a flat rate you feel happy with for your translation work, and forget about minor expenses, e.g. anything under £10.

Terms of payment

Many clients already have an accounting system which it may be unrealistic to expect them to change on your behalf. However, 30 days from receipt of invoice is a good starting point. Where a translation project is likely to run for more than a month, you may wish to come to an agreement with the client whereby you submit a number of invoices to cover different parts of the job.

Throughput

This refers to the amount of work you can comfortably take on, and is an important parameter in calculating your initial response to the client's inevitable first question, i.e. what is your best date for completing this translation. Different translators work at different speeds (without there necessarily being any impact on quality) and you should be aware of your own limits, e.g. are you prepared to work flat out for more than a week? Some people are as fresh as a daisy on Monday after working all weekend, but most of us are not, and throughput (not to mention quality), suffers badly when you are not feeling your best. If a job looks like a marathon, treat it as such and pace yourself accordingly. Remember that your family and social life can be severely disrupted if you over-commit yourself.

Availability

The nature of translation is such that translation jobs are processed consecutively by the translator, and the client generally wants the job completed as soon as possible. The client may not be aware that there are a number of associated tasks which must be fitted in to ensure that the translation machine continues to run smoothly, just like a car needs oil occasionally. Remember that you are running a business over the long term, and schedule time for the administrative side of your affairs, such as preparing accounts, updating glossaries, buying dictionaries, equipment maintenance and upgrades, performing backups, ordering stationery, etc.

Contingency measures

Translation projects sometimes go wrong. A client may underestimate the size of a job, or it may contain diagrams, tables or specialist sections which significantly slow down the translation process, or the client may submit changes to the source text as you are translating (this requires particular care if it becomes clear that elements in the already translated text have to be changed in the light of new information received). These examples show the importance of accurately assessing a job from the outset. It is important to quantify problems when they arise, and apportion responsibility for the consequences.

Action Plan: Establish Your Terms Of Business

The client's translation requirement and the translator's terms and conditions form the basis on which both parties hope to achieve mutual business benefit. They must therefore be documented accurately. The many details which define the translation assignment can prevent confusion, misunderstandings and acrimony, (not to mention the waste of time and money). So:

- Decide on your terms and conditions in advance. The best way is to write them down. You may decide to apply different terms and conditions for different clients, or you may agree a special rate for a special occasion, but you must keep a record of these details, so that clients can always be clear about your terms and conditions.
- Do not be embarrassed about discussing terms and conditions in advance, and do it early. Always be polite, firm, and professional. Do not be confrontational.
- Let the client know that you expect a purchase order to confirm a proposed job as quickly as possible. Unless you know a client well, you should not start work on a translation until you receive a purchase order, a faxed copy is okay until the post arrives. If your prospective client has problems produc-

ing a purchase order quickly, there is a good chance they will also have problems when it comes to payment.

- Ask the client to specify all the necessary details about the translation requirement. These details may be documented on the purchase order or on a separate translation requirement form. The most essential thing to check is that the job described in the purchase order corresponds to the full text to be translated, since deadlines are often agreed before the translator has had sight of the full text. Clarify any unresolved issues immediately, e.g. if the client has promised to provide a glossary or style-guide, make sure that it arrives.

- Ensure that your purchase order contains all of the relevant details about terms and conditions, e.g. rates of pay, terms of payment.

- With regard to your own availability, remember to schedule time for administration purposes, and to give your clients advance notification of your intended holiday dates so that they can arrange their schedules accordingly.

- If you feel that you have been unfairly treated by a client, e.g. non-payment of invoices, then simply refuse to work for them again, notify the ITI and the IoL, and send a letter from your solicitor. This
  a. will make you feel better so you can turn your mind to other tasks (feeling bad reduces throughput);
  b. might result in corrective action by the client;
  c. may warn others via the ITI/IoL black list;
  d. will leave your legal options open.
  If a client does not treat you fairly, then do not waste time with second chances unless you are truly desperate for work (it is your choice at the end of the day).

4. The Role Of The Client

The role of the client is often underestimated, both by translators and by clients themselves. At the end of the project, the translation provided to the client will be evaluated by the target readership. The quality of the translation may have a significant impact on the client's image. So how can the client help to ensure the quality of a translation?

Adopt the right attitude

In order to achieve quality, the first decision your client must make is to take translation seriously. Translation must not be viewed as a necessary evil, but as another process in the development of a product or service; a process that will enable clients to offer their products or services in markets from which they had previously been excluded. So translation is not something that will cost the client a lot of money with very little return; it is in fact the contrary: a good investment. In order to be effective, this attitude must be shared throughout the client organisation by all departments concerned, for example, marketing, development, and sales channels abroad must all learn and agree to co-operate.

Invest in technology

Over the last few years, more and more companies have started to take advantage of the technology available to speed up and facilitate the translation process. It is gradually becoming standard practice nowadays to send the source document to a translation agency or translator in the form of data files on diskette, as opposed to paper copy only. In the same way, translation agencies nowadays often offer an electronic publishing service, which means that the translations can be handed back to the client as formatted data files, ready to be printed. This means that the client can avoid the costly and time-intensive step of typesetting. Speed can be further improved by establishing an electronic modem connection between the client organisation and the translator or agency. This enables the client to transfer data files either way in a matter of minutes as soon as they are ready, thereby reducing timescales significantly.

Designate a translation manager

Too often, documents requiring translation are handed over as an afterthought to an overworked secretary, with no advice other than to find an agency in the business directory – a procedure that usually leads to disastrous results. In fact, to assess the suitability of any agency or translator, the client organisation needs a certain degree of expertise in that particular field of activity. It is therefore beneficial for the client to appoint someone as officially in charge of translation. This is a very important step; one that will enhance the client's credibility both with local staff and with sales offices or representatives abroad – who often feel cheated by the quality of the documentation they are supplied with. Furthermore, the client's translation agency or translators will get the message that the client means business.

Work to procedures

In order to control the translation process and ensure realistic timescales, it is necessary for the client to work within an estab-lished framework of procedures. These procedures should ideally be documented in the form of a procedures manual, and cover at least the following areas:

- Planning a translation
- Specifying the requirement
- Sending source text for translation
- Monitoring progress
- Incorporating updates
- Quality control

Anticipate problems

In addition to quality control, which normally takes place after the translation has been completed, clients are sometimes obliged to become involved during the translation process itself, although they may not originally have expected this. There are a number of areas in every translation project, where problems are likely to occur. The secret is to identify and resolve them at the earliest possible stage in the translation cycle in order to avoid compro-mising quality or timescales. It must be borne in mind that in most cases the client simply wants a translation, not a lesson in transla-tion complexities, and I am referring here to issues which must be resolved if the translation is to be correct, for example:

- Specialist terminology particular to the client organisation, e.g. acronyms and proper names, that might remain untranslated.
- Cross-references to other publications that might or might not be available in the target language – what are the correct titles?

- References to country-specific products or institutions, e.g. British Telecom – what is the equivalent organisation in other countries and is it appropriate?
- Illustrations needing adaptation, e.g. keyboards, power cables and plugs
- Software messages that might not have been translated – how will they be dealt with in the documentation?
- Errors in the source text.
- Tables arranged in alphabetical order in the source text.

Quality control

On one level, clients are responsible for the quality of the target text, in that they supply the source text (garbage in – garbage out). However, assuming that a client has provided the translator with quality source text, and he or she is satisfied with the result in terms of budget and timescales, how can he or she assess the quality of the target text? It may look very nice, but is it right?

Although quality control should be applied in various forms throughout the entire translation process by the translator or agency responsible for carrying out the work, there are two procedures designed to give the client a final guarantee of quality. Firstly validation, which is usually performed by employees of the client organisation working in the country for which the documentation is destined. This validation should cover both the technical and the linguistic accuracy of the translation. Secondly, thorough in-house quality checks which should always be performed prior to sending a camera-ready copy to the printers. Some obvious examples of these checks would be:

- Checking that the formatting matches the original documentation.
- Checking that all updates and validation comments have been incorporated in the final text.
- Checking that no illustrations are missing and that they are all in the appropriate language.
- Checking that the contents table and the index reflect any updates that have been made, and that the page number references are correct.

Project analysis

Once a project is completed, the client has the opportunity to learn from experience, and to gather feedback from a number of sources. One of these is the target readership in the country for which the documentation was translated. Clients can also take the opportunity to review the project with their translator or agency.

Supplier relations

Finally, clients can be expected to go some way to nurturing their relationship with the translator.

Action Plan: Ensure That Your Clients Consider The Role They Have To Play

Clients should be made aware of the importance to their business of considerations such as image (the client's image will be damaged by unsatisfactory translations), quality (a good definition of quality is 'zero defects'), and consistency (use of glossaries, formats, versions). In other words, the results of the translation process are very important and very visible (unlike the mess a plumber may leave under your floorboards). These guidelines will help your clients to approach translation in a professional manner by creating an environment where quality can be achieved. In doing so, clients will have the best possible chance of ensuring language variant documentation that enhances the value of their products or services

- Make your client aware that translation is a good investment, and organisational commitment to the translation process is the quickest way to ensure a rapid return on this investment.
- Let clients know when you make new investments in hardware, software, dictionaries, etc. (particularly if the investments are made in the context of a project which is for them). At the same time, there will be occasions where clients might consider making appropriate investments at their end to improve the efficiency of their procedures and ensure long-term cost benefits, e.g. purchase of a high-speed modem. Such opportunities should be pointed out to the client.

- Encourage the client to nominate a translation manager (and a deputy). This person should be in a position to deal with any queries you may have, and pass these queries on within the client company if necessary.

- Ask the client if they have fixed procedures or a procedures manual. This will give them the opportunity to reflect upon the fact that they should. Make your client aware that the translation stage of any project should be given adequate priority and planned accordingly. For example, a client may wish to incorporate all updates as a translation is progressing, or leave them until the end. A client may want all translations sent directly to their marketing branch for validation.

- Establish whether the client anticipates any problems in the text concerned. Also ask whether they would prefer to deal with problems as you work through the text, or in the form of a page containing translator's notes at the end of the job, (appended to the text or in a separate document). It should be made clear that if the latter option is selected and deadlines are tight, then it may not be easy to resolve outstanding issues satisfactorily.

- Ask the client whether the translation process is subject to any in-house quality control procedures, and how you are expected to interface with these procedures e.g. the validation process.

- Let your clients know that you welcome feedback from them (if you do not ask for feedback, you will rarely get it). Ensure for example that any terminological queries are definitively resolved for use in subsequent jobs. At the end of a translation project, make sure that you and your client identify any areas where improvements could be introduced, thereby enabling you both to do a faster and better job next time. For example, the client may be able to offer suggestions on how your working methods could be streamlined.

- Treat your clients as individuals. As in any profession, translators tend to get so involved in their work that they see the world in a certain way (how does your doctor see you?). Make your clients appreciate the full range of skills you offer, for example the compilation of specialised glossaries for them, the development of tailored procedures for them, (e.g. designing macros to insert their preferred headers/footers), conducting relevant research to resolve translation issues (e.g. contacting the British Standards Institute to establish the latest version of a given standard). The client should be made to feel that you are an asset to them personally.

Conclusion

It is always worthwhile imagining yourself in the position of your clients, and the following quiz may give you an idea of issues they have not properly considered.

Translation Quiz For Clients

The service provided by translators

- Do you know the difference between translation and interpreting?
- Can a translator translate in both directions, e.g. to and from Japanese?
- How many words/pages would you expect a translator to translate per day?
- How many words do you think are on an average page of A4?
- Do you think translators will soon be replaced by computers?
- Would you expect a translation to be 100 per cent accurate?

Selecting the right translator

- Would you expect a translator to have professional qualifications?
- Would you expect a translator to have specialist knowledge for the job concerned?
- How many dictionaries do you think a specialist translator may need?
- What would you do if a translator told you the job was too long for the time available?

- How would you go about finding the right translator to do the job?

Terms of business

- Does your company have a house style for its documentation?
- Would you expect confidentiality from a translator?
- Would you expect a translator to be paid by the hour or by the word?
- Would you expect a translator to charge for floppy disks, fax usage, postage, etc.?
- Would you be prepared to take legal action if a serious translation error occurred?

The role of the client

- What would be the consequences of a bad translation on your business?
- Do you have written procedures in place for assigning translation jobs?
- Do your planning procedures provide for the translation stage of a project?
- Who is ultimately responsible for the quality of a translation?
- How can 100 per cent accuracy be ensured?
- What should the translator do with an error in the source text?

This quiz once again identifies four main areas in which clients may have misconceptions or misunderstandings about translation, namely:

1. What the translator does.
2. Selecting the right translator.
3. Agreeing the terms of business.
4. The role of the client.

The series of action plans in the preceding sections will help clients to understand the ground rules. These action plans should ensure that your clients gain a positive impression of the service you provide. We do not want to tell them our lives, or bore them with personal grumps, nor can we expect them necessarily to understand the processes and problems inherent in translation. So if a client has misunderstood something which you consider elementary, e.g. the difference between translation and interpreting, then you should be diplomatic in your efforts to divest them of their ignorance. You cannot afford to lose clients by making them feel stupid.

Always remember that you are providing a service. Some people clearly feel that there is something ignominious about the role of a service provider, and we can all quote examples of poor service we may have received. On average, dissatisfied clients tell ten to 12 other people, so remember your own resolve to steer clear of unsatisfactory service providers, and remember the pleasure you gained from having a service provided efficiently and courteously. Your clients should always feel welcome, and confident that they were right to contact you.

Remember that the primary objective of educating the client is mutual business benefit. In order to achieve a win/win solution, you must establish and maintain long-term, mutually beneficial, business relationships with your clients, based on a clear understanding of each other's expectations, terms and conditions, and this should be your objective every time you communicate with your clients. It is your attitude as a professional which will both influence and educate the client, and allow these relationships to develop.

8. Raising the profile of translation and translators: Britain

EYVOR FOGARTY

Though the concept of profile or public standing can be rather vague and subjective, it is a subject on which there is usually a general consensus at any gathering of translators: "The market doesn't value us according to our skills and expertise". Is this the case? What skills and expertise, anyway? And what can be done about it?

It used to be commonly held that if you had a second language, it was easy to find a job translating. Skills and expertise were of secondary importance. The situation now is very different. Translation, as a career, is serviced by good vocational university degrees, post-graduate studies and continuing training. The amount of investment required to set up as a translator has greatly increased. There have been huge changes in the standard and format of presentation expected from translators, and even, on occasion, in the willingness to seek legal remedy from translators. There is a growing need for specialism, as well as breadth of general knowledge. Translation is no longer 'a market it is easy to get into'.

What are Translators in Britain Like?

A traditional and widespread view of translators is that they are usually professional/highly educated people who share the problems such people have all around the world, for they often find that the conditions under which they work are dictated by people of a different educational background and perspective. Translators want to translate, but it is a rare society that has the surplus in its economy to keep translators free of the chore of earning their bread on a daily basis. Translators are not usually aggressive, but are often pushed into situations where they have to fight for their money. They tend to avoid open conflict, as they know they have to maintain a presence in the market for many years and cannot be seen to be curt and bad-tempered. They are often a distant, disembodied entity waiting at the end of an electronic wire.

Yet translators are not weak – they take a tough decision every time they write down a word; they know that the written word lingers and has a habit of rebounding several years later, with a string of conditions attached which were not mentioned at the time the particular job was commissioned. They are aware of the legal force of their every word and its long-lasting liability. They are also aware of the need to seek out customers, keep them happy and yet remain faithful to the document entrusted to them. In this way they lead the life of a funambulist, walking a professional tightrope every day. They like to be praised and to have their worth recognised. They like feedback. They would prefer to be paid a decent rate for the work they do without having to renegotiate every time, but renegotiation is something every person who works for himself in a free market has to do. Even for those in full-time employment, the situation has changed. There are fewer jobs and more people after them, with a greater diversity of qualifications. Job specifications have become wider, to take in more than pure translation, or, if translation pure and simple is required, then there is little in the way of a career structure on offer as a translator reaches the height of her/his organisational or management powers. Most people who emerge from university as a translator could quite easily have been accountants, doctors, biologists, priests, lawyers or whatever; they just happen to have chosen languages as their specialisation. For many translators, though, specialisation came first, through careers in chemistry, pharmacy, journalism, exporting etc, with a language as a bolt-on skill. Whatever their route into translation, they all belong to what has been a largely unrecognised profession, with unrecognised social status, never mentioned as suitable for signing passport photographs or writing references for other professionals.

The situation, however, is changing. Having remained determinedly professional, translators are now better armed in terms of qualifications than before. Translation *is* becoming recognised. It is mentioned more and more in the press, translated literature is discussed on the radio, and subtitles are quite common in documentaries. The general public is more aware of translation as a career option, universities offer more vocational courses, and in business, the need to incorporate translation at an early stage in any contract or project is recognised. Translators and their associations, like the ITI (Institute of Translation and Interpreting), have worked hard to achieve this success.

The Translation Environment in Britain

In Britain's market environment, there is a strange mix between free enterprise and regulation. For instance, a plumber can no longer repair a domestic gas water heater unless he is registered. The regulation exists to protect the public from 'just anyone' starting up as a plumber, and the terms of the insurance cover ensure that the regulation works. Almost anyone, however, can be a Member of Parliament or a translator. If you can get the work and be paid for it, for a reasonable length of time, then you are a translator. This is still the case even though there are so many more vocational courses now than there were fifteen years ago, and despite translators' own efforts to improve both the demand for, and availability of, qualifications. Translation is still a profession which encompasses the supremely qualified and the opportunistic, the polymath and the poorly educated. The demand for high quality information is increasing, however, and this demand can and must be used by translators to improve their position as information providers and as professionals. (One problem here is the word 'professional' itself, which seems to be acquiring the meaning of 'earning a living from translation' rather than 'belonging to a professional group'.)

What translators do and how the profession of translation is perceived are still, however, two completely separate things. As the need for translation has become accepted, and the need to keep costs down remains a dominant requirement, so translation hovers between quality and price. Resolving this is crucial to the esteem in which the translation profession is held; if translators do not earn enough to invest back in themselves, to be able to keep all their skills in peak condition and their technology up-to-date, the benefit they can offer their customers is diminished, their image is tarnished and their fees go down, leaving them no margin to re-invest and improve the quality of the service they offer. On the other hand, translators are very fortunate in that they do not have to make radical changes to their basic product – translation – as the world changes, only to the image people have of them. The image of translation is the reality of our lifestyle. If translators perform well, if their product is good, but the image ('The market doesn't value us according to our skills and expertise') is wrong, then the fault lies with translators for being bad communicators. If the image is correct and translators' skills and expertise are not of the standard required, then translators are again at fault for being bad managers.

Within Britain, there is a growing internal translation requirement for the languages of recent immigration, widely used in Town Hall literature, documents for local government, taxation, health and so on. Translators in these fields also find it difficult to achieve status, let alone recognised pay, often for the same reasons as those affecting the translators of major European languages. Language is viewed as a gift from God, a talent one is born with, like a gift for music or art, and is generally not perceived as something one works at, to be developed and maintained. Bilingualism is often seen as the only requirement for a translation job, and the skills involved and the development of professional attitudes are not given much stress. This devalues the translation produced and affects the market value of the job before it is ever costed. Concerned linguists will of course not be able to stand to one side and watch while people cannot cope without language help; they will produce the work for a very low rate or for nothing. Much is being done now to train people in the skills required in this area of translation work, but there no reason to believe that in the immediate future there will be any change in the usual quality-dedication-pay scenario.

Another major factor in the translation market place in Britain has been incoming labour, people who are new to the country and who initially have only their language skills to offer. It is a common perception that they undertake translations part-time or only for a short time, and that they may not want to invest in this business or in ways to develop their skills in it. This presents certain difficulties in the short term, for the number of players in the field affects the fees paid. This is a different factor from the influx of other professionals, from other jobs, who though they increase the numbers of practitioners, can enhance the profession with their own skills and expertise.

While the need for translation can be promoted, translations are not often sold off the shelf. While some translators may find a niche in the world of patents and scientific papers, making abstracts or full translations available for databases and CD-ROM libraries, or in multi-national or pan-European organisations where daily translation is necessary or mandatory, most translation requirements arise in response to some external need – marketing a new model of car, maintenance in a paper mill, laying a pipeline, launching new software and so on. Given the rather erratic nature of the market, it can be difficult for translators either to keep themselves up-to-date professionally or to maintain themselves in a business-ready mode. When a request comes in from out of the blue for a quote, a translator may not have a realistic idea of the current market value of his/her work, or of other market conditions like presentation and terms of business. Caught on the hop like this, the translator can become pressurised into accepting a commission without working out the basic details of the contract, and the customer may perceive the woolly-minded response of the translator as a mark of unprofessionalism or unworldiness. In such cases, the blame for any reduction in professional esteem must lie with the translator.

Estimating the number of translators in Britain is not easy; various guesses have been made, with figures ranging from 3,000 to 6,000. Statistics are difficult to come by, for the profession is not regulated and it is not easy to identify translators. For example, some people (scientists, journalists, sales executives, departmental managers etc) happen to translate or interpret at work; some qualified translators (with their names in many directories and databases) may translate professionally just once or twice a year; university staff may translate for colleagues in other departments or for publishers. Publicly available lists are not comprehensive as not all translators feel able to join a professional association or subscribe to a database. One worrying report is the decrease in the number of full-time employed (in-house) translators – a distressing situation from the point of view of giving practical training (as a form of apprenticeship) to new translators.

A well-established part of the translation environment in Britain is the translation company. In general, the old 'all-singing, all-dancing en-velope-changing' translation agency is dying out, or being forced out of the market place, and the new type of translation company brings a new attitude to the end-product, driven as it is by the rigours of the market, the terms of insurance cover and a more ethical approach. Translation companies fall into four general categories: sole traders, often translators, with a substantial proportion of their income com-ing from sub-contracting translation; family businesses – husband/wife teams etc., perhaps with extra administrative staff; large compa-nies, with one or two in-house translators, but mainly contracting out; and large companies often with several offices, sometimes with an in-house MT system. Other types of organisations (eg law compa-nies, construction firms, banks) often have their own translation de-partments which may both outsource their own work and act inde-pendently as translation agencies.

Some of these will have a niche market, like patents or chemical engineering or Arabic. Many will coordinate large, multi-lingual projects. While many translators will view them as rather large competitors in a small pool, there is no doubt that good translation companies are interested in improving standards and the reputa-tion of translation as a quality product. They invest in the effi-ciency of their business and the reputation of translation, and they give promotional hype by offering prizes and sponsorship in the translation world.

One perceived disadvantage of the possible predominance of com-panies rather than sole traders is that translators run the risk of being too far removed from the end-product. In a world where it is added value that is paid, not the original commodity, the practice of using a 'middleman' can encourage the view that translation is a bit like a cash crop – the translator grows the produce and some-one else processes it for the market place. This throws the transla-tor further away from the polished end-product and diminishes the translator's importance and status.

On the whole, Britain is a relatively 'safe' place in which to work. It is still generally the case that if you accept a verbal commission and submit an invoice, you will be paid. That translators tend to remember exact details of cases of non-payment or of mistreatment is a reflection of how seldom the environment of trust is found wanting. In any business environment, where there are punters who do not scrutinise the deal on offer, there are bound to be people waiting to rip them off. It is up to translators to monitor their own environment.

On a more sombre note, translators in this country have not been attacked or killed because of what they have translated; remember the translators of Salmon Rushdie's Satanic Verses – one translator seriously wounded, one translator murdered. This thought brings us away from the rather narcissistic view translators often have of themselves and their product, and out to the wider world, of human error, legal unawareness and ownership of rights. Working with translation is not for the faint-hearted or the intellectually lazy.

Copyright

One of the tools available to translators to keep their profession in the public eye, and to enhance it, is proper and constant use of the law of copyright. Under the Berne Convention and the Universal Copyright Convention authors (including translators) should be able to have their work protected in over 130 countries. The Berne Convention provides for a translation to be protected 'as an original work'. In Britain, under the 1988 Copyright Act, translators have a right of paternity, but have to assert it in writing. They should also remind the producer or publisher of a translation of their legal duty to ensure that when it is disseminated it always carries the translator's name.

Simple mention of course does not give financial reward, but it does give profile, and it is a right, under law. Translators should not be too anxious to divest themselves of their rights. Another of their rights is that their work should not be subject to derogatory treatment. Think of the consternation translators feel when someone interferes with their product. They are usually only too keen to protect their rights and reputation when that happens.

As more information is accessed through the information superhighways, so copyright will become more and more important to translators. The sudden availability of information electronically nowadays is not really so different from the wider availability of information which accompanied the invention of the printing press. Eventually and inevitably there was copying on a large scale without permission and without payment of a fee, with the authorities no longer able to control the ownership and dissemination of books. The Information Superhighway, like the printing press, makes copyright protection both important and necessary.

Once a work is created, copyright immediately protects it. Much has been said and written about imminent breakdown in the way in which authors and publishers are recognised and remunerated for the use of their material. Society, as the media constantly reminds us, is coming to terms with the conflict of interests between the desire to have information freely available and the need to sell information – as information is a commodity like any other representing money and of course power. Stakes in the world's wealth, we are told, will depend on information, and ownership of information, and this will require strong international protection of intellectual property. Translation in electronic form makes this information freely available, too, across linguistic and cultural boundaries – but it represents time, investment and research and should be both recognised and remunerated.

One example of how this can work has been put forward by CISAC which 'is presenting a plan for a Common Information System ... to prepare for copyright administration in the new information superhighways environment. Once these uniform numbers, codes, standards and tools are implemented, a global virtual database with an open sub-system in each of the member Societies of the common network will have been created. This will greatly increase the speed and accuracy of copyright administration.' Collecting societies can act effectively only if authors and translators identify their work.

Translation on the Internet/Copuserve

According to Bloomberg and Reuters (as reported in the International Herald Tribune) CompuServe has more than four million customers worldwide, with 200 000 new ones signing on each month and America Online Inc. has more than four million customers, with an annual growth rate of 27%. CompuServe has 500 000 European customers and America Online is aiming for one million European subscribers by the year 2000. No one knows exactly how many people connect to the Internet. What is important to the translator's professional profile here is that translation is now available through electronic information systems and the results in any one country will be discussed worldwide. According to a CompuServe representative, the company offers a translation service into Spanish, German, French and English. A 48-hour turnaround, from message to reply, is usually anticipated, and users have an option of an unedited, cheaper machine translation, or a version edited by a professional translator. It is also reported that there will soon be a Japanese /English translation service on the Internet. This is certainly exposure for translation.

Legal Unawareness

A representative of a company offering professional indemnity insurance reported recently that one of the recurring themes in the British translation market was a lack of precision in the terms of reference for a commission. The lack of clear instructions and clear understanding by both parties often led to problems later – and a call to the insurance company. The golden rule, he pointed out, was always to protect one's reputation. This is a very particular case where individual translators have control over the way in which customers and the public at large view their professional skills and expertise. In Britain's business environment the freelance translator has to learn how to handle disclaimers and exemptions, indemnity, competition, deadlines and penalties, price variations, fair dealing, confidentiality, licensing, non-payment etc. Failure to do so only reinforces the opinion that translators are 'not quite professional'.

Regulation

A common cry in the media nowadays is 'if they cannot regulate themselves, they will have to have an authority to do it for them'. This has been said, inter alia, of the financial sector, the utilities and the

Press. There is a constant debate between the desire for regulation as a prerequisite to improvements in standards, and the pressure for deregulation to allow progress and freedom of movement.

Britain is not the only country where this is a subject of debate. In France, the Chambre Nationale des Entreprises de Traduction, CNET, has been acting as a lobby for regulatory control. At a recent conference, its president reported, "As predicted in the early 1990s, opening up European borders has caused an influx of unemployed persons who are willing to 'translate' at very low rates. Natural selection is no longer taking place fast enough to eliminate 'sweatshops' that exploit this cheap labour: for every 50 'shady' outfits that disappear, another 200 spring up. Such competition is unfair to both legitimate companies and their suppliers, who invest large sums in *high-tech* word-processing systems and spend years acquiring specialised qualifications. It is very probable that unless the French translation community sets its own standards, its fate will ultimately be sealed by Brussels, without consideration for local needs.'

Translation is a cross-border activity. A job can originate in Sweden, be commissioned through Belgium, outsourced in Britain and performed in France. For the translation community in Britain, challenges to the volume of work available and its quality (and therefore profile) do not just come from within Britain but from abroad, either from well-established translation environments or from countries where running costs and therefore translation are cheaper. Anyone placing a translation is going to look at many factors, balancing the ease with which the job can be farmed out (including time zone and telecommunications) against the need for post-translation processing in addition to the basic translation costs (which will also be affected by exchange rates).

Translators in Britain also face the common European challenge of regulation from Brussels. The tool here available to them is the solidarity their professional associations have with other translation associations in the Community, most of whom are coordinating their efforts through the International Federation of Translators (FIT). A particular effort, on a European scale, is being made at the present time to define the job of a translator, the product produced, remuneration, professional status and training.

The Future

For the profession to progress, it has, as a body, to address certain fundamental issues such as quality assurance, training, professional status and duty to the public. This requires a solidarity of purpose and concerted effort. Like all professionals, translators need to belong to their own sectoral associations and pressure groups. At the individual level, translators need a good product, control over that product, confidence, a professional approach, and a living wage. At the corporate level, associations and pressure groups can offer professional solidarity and maintenance of a national voice and global presence. Yet the individual translator remains the most significant factor in the process of profile enhancement and any evaluation of the profession cannot ignore the general perception of a translator's skill, expertise, judgment and bargaining ability.

In conclusion, I would quote clause 9 of the Translator's Charter. For me, this simple statement is the ultimate test of recognition.

"In general, the translator shall neither seek nor accept work under conditions humiliating to himself or his profession."

Bibliography

Language International, 7/4, 1995.

The Importance of Copyright for Translators, by Gordon Fielden, the Translators Association.

IBC (International Book Committee). *Copyright: Our Once and Future Strength*, by Ralf Oman. IBC News 3/94.

CISAC (Confédération Internationale des Sociétés d'Auteurs et Compositeurs). *CISAC News* Dec 95.

International Herald Tribune, Dec 26 1995.

Translators' Associations

Institute of Translation and Interpreting (ITI), 377 City Road, London EC1V 1NA Tel: +44 (0) 171 713 7600 Fax: +44 (0) 171 713 7650

Technical Translation Group, Aslib, The Association for Information Management, Information House, 20-24 Old Street, London EC1V 9AP. Tel: +44 (0) 171 253 4488, Fax: +44 (0) 171 430 0514

The Translators Association, Society of Authors, Drayton Gardens, London SW7 Tel: +44 (0) 171 373 6642

Translating Division, The Institute of Linguists (IoL), 24a Highbury Grove, London N5 2EA Tel: +44 (0) 171 359 7445

9. Operating in a mature market: Translation in 'Standort Deutschland'

TRISTAM CARRINGTON-WINDO

Germany is a country where, according to the *Statistisches Bundesamt*, (Federal Statistics Office), translation turnover in 1992 was around DM 600,000,000 a year and there were an estimated 20,000 professional translators and interpreters in 1993, with over 2,000 translators being trained at the Germersheim school of translation alone at any one time. Statistics from the ever-willing *Statistisches Bundesamt* indicate that the number of translation agencies has doubled roughly every three years. Translation is charged by the line in Germany (50/55 keystrokes) with rates varying from around DM 1.50 at the lower end of the scale for literary translation and agencies to in excess of DM 5.00 a line for specialist corporate translation to publication standard. These figures translate into roughly £66 per 1,000 words and £222 per 1,000 words. The bulk of translation work handled by independent translators is charged at between DM 2.50 and DM 3.50 per line, i.e. between about £110 and £155 for 1,000 words.

Translators who study translation at university level come out with a degree in translation (*Dipl.-Übers.*).In order to certify a translation, a translator has to pass an additional examination to become a *staatlich geprüfter Übersetzer* (state-accredited translator). This examination varies from *Land* to *Land* in accordance with the educational sovereignty of Germany's *Länder*. The *Bundesverband der Dolmetscher und Übersetzer* (BDÜ) represents the interests of translators and interpreters and has affiliated associations in all the *Länder*. The BDÜ has recently upgraded entry requirements requiring all prospective members to have a degree.

Germany can be considered a 'mature' market. A mature market is one where the profession is well-established and respected, and – most important – has a degree of control over the fees it charges. The profession as a whole is concerned with creating opportunities and developing the services offered, with the translation provider actually driving the market and shaping the business structure. In order to be able to operate successfully in such a market it is necessary to understand the way the market works and the mentality behind the business ethos. The corporate identity of *'Standort Deutschland'* offers the key to understanding how the translation profession has matured and become an important factor in German business.

Business in Germany was founded on the *Wirtschaftswunder*, or economic miracle. This miracle involved hard work, an eye for detail, and attention to training. For several years Germany was the world's top exporter and it still ranks second among the world's exporters behind the US. In a world where Esperanto failed and German was not one of the main languages, German business was forced to address the language question early on. There is therefore a long history of German companies and businessmen being aware that language is an issue that is directly related to financial success. As one German businessman once said to me: "We buy in German but we sell in the language of the country concerned." This is a highly sophisticated approach to language in business, which companies in other parts of the world would do well to emulate. Such an attitude has, of course, ensured that the translation profession became well-established.

Corporate Identity

I write as a translator who worked in Germany for four years and has been active in the German market for over ten years. During that time it has become obvious that it is important to have a 'corporate identity' when dealing with German companies. A mature market expects to deal with mature partners and there are a number of 'badges' of identification. Items such as headed notepaper and business cards are basic requirements. A corporate brochure or leaflet (depending on size) may also be appropriate and helpful in establishing credentials with a client. This should not be too ostentatious and should give factual information about the products and services that a provider offers. Details of qualifications, experience and technical facilities should be at the forefront. In an increasingly European market a VAT registration number (or *USt-IdNr.)* indicates stability and continuity. A request for a quotation should be rendered speedily and accurately.

Your German partner will expect you to insist on an order confirmation, and translation providers should make this clear when a quotation is submitted. It is also essential not to assume that a project is going ahead until you have received the all-important confirmation. The establishment of a system whereby costs are immediately identified once an assignment is completed is much appreciated in a big company with a large number of cost centres. German companies view translation as a personal relationship and like to deal with the professional translator carrying out the translation. This allows many professional translators in a mature market to deal directly with clients simply as professional translators rather than through an agency. German companies appreciate prompt invoicing and prefer money to be transferred directly to a German bank or giro account as this allows them to use their standard procedures. The operational language used with your business partner must also be clear from the outset. Although the person you deal with may speak reasonable English they will almost certainly wish to conduct important business in German. It is therefore imperative not to assume that 'English is OK' but to conduct both written and spoken business in German from the outset and to move over to dealing exclusively in English only at the explicit request of your client. This of course means faultless written correspondence in German, which will involve having a native speaker of German to provide this expertise. Anything less than perfect German will reduce the translator's status in the eyes of the client.

Training

The culture of German industry is geared towards training and translators operating in this market will generally be highly trained. Make the most of your qualifications ensuring that they are prominently displayed, and be prepared to discuss your background, training and qualifications with an interested client. If you are phoning a client who has a doctorate, remember to address him or her as 'Herr/Frau Doktor X' – it's a small detail that counts.

Timing

This is a country where it is a status symbol to have a watch that is linked up by radio signal to the Braunschweig centre setting Central European time. Delivery on time is essential to doing any form of business in Germany. Work starts early and German business expects to be able to speak to its partners straight away – be ready to receive phone calls at 7.05 in the morning – and you'd better be bright and breezy! If you specify delivery by fax at a certain time, make sure the fax rolls not a minute later.

Public holidays are more frequent than in the UK, and it is important to check that a critical deadline has not been scheduled for a festival or public holiday. It is usual to wish a client a pleasant day if you happen to be faxing the day before a public holiday or at the start of a weekend.

Localization

Localizing client documentation means ensuring that there is a feedback loop through the company and its foreign subsidiaries to the translator. This ensures that documentation is specifically tailored to the market for which it is being produced and that there is also feedback from this market to the translator so that subsequent suggestions and corrections can be incorporated into documentation. A mature market will recognize the importance of this concept and its likely benefits in terms of sales in the target market. During the past ten years German companies have been increasingly willing to address these matters and make provision for the successful localization of their documentation. Translators in a mature market will view it as part of their function to point out the importance of localization and to make efforts to ensure that localization procedures are instituted in the companies for whom they produce work. A library of catalogues from different companies operating in a particular field will also go towards ensuring that documentation is localized in accordance with the conventions of a particular country.

Continuity

Continuity is terribly important in German business. If a company does business with you they want to know that you will be there in ten years time. For example, a company I had not had any contact with for four years faxed one morning out of the blue requiring a piece of work by the end of that week. There was no question of ringing up. The assumption was that because they had decided to do business in the past, they had made the right decision then and this included the assumption that I would always be at the end of the fax.

Things do not move fast in the German market. Companies may take many months to come to a decision about a series of catalogues, for example. Many factors will be taken into account such as budgeting, timing, etc. But once a decision has been made, things move fast and assume delivery on time.

Technology

Technology does not always take off immediately in Germany and new concepts can take time to become assimilated. This is a country of procedures that sets great store by the concept of 'tried and tested'. If something has worked successfully in the past there has to be a very good reason for making costly changes. This approach is epitomized by the continued reluctance of many businesses to accept credit cards. Modems to the outside world are still very much in their infancy even in big German companies, as a result of the monolithic structure of the German telecommunications market and lack of competition. More often than not it will be a businessman's private CompuServe or other E-Mailbox that will be used if delivery by modem is requested. However, times are undoubtedly changing, with the 'Handy' (mobile phone) developing into a status symbol and runaway success, so electronic transfer of text will inevitably become more widespread in the coming years.

Commitment

German companies value commitment in the 'partners' they work with. This is particularly true in the translation world where companies – especially small and medium-sized companies – rely on translators to promote their products and image abroad, very often without backup from an advertising agency. The drive to cut costs during the eighties saw many in-house translation bureaus closed down or drastically shorn of staff with more work being parcelled out to external operators resulting in the development of a growing agency market. Companies pay well but they expect absolute commitment from the translation provider. Tight deadlines have to be adhered to and if that involves weekend work – tough. A premium rate (30-50% surcharge) can, however, be negotiated for this kind of pressure without too much agonizing.

Commitment is also demonstrated by the translator simply showing initiative. Closeness to the customer is an especially important concept when the translator is based outside Germany. Visiting a trade fair at which you know a client is going to be present or arranging to meet a client at a trade fair is a fruitful way of maintaining personal contacts. Visiting the client periodically – particularly if operating from a different country – ensures that channels of communication are kept open and that any procedures and problems can be discussed and ironed out at regular intervals. Requesting and going on a tour of the production facilities enables you to understand the products better. German companies are proud of their products, and showing interest in the process of production is viewed as a mark of respect and contributes to elevating the status of the translator. Visiting the factory and seeing processes in action also increases translators' self-confidence and provides an invaluable source of information on terminology.

Standardization of Terminogy

Commitment may also involve making recommendations that can help a company to improve its efficiency and industrial documentation. This may take many forms ranging from pointing out flaws in a source text (generally written by an engineer rather than a copywriter) to making recommendations on house style, standardization of terminology, compilation of company-specific glossaries, etc. In some cases the technical documentation department may rely on the translator for feedback on the original text.

Company-specific terminology and lack of standardized company terminology are probably two of the greatest problems in any translation market – even a mature translation market. Gathering terminology in the field is an extremely effective method of mastering this difficulty and enhancing the translator's ability to produce high-quality work. Generally the client will assume that terminology is the translator's affair. However, if serious terminological problems arise that necessitate contacting the client it is important to make sure that any questions are pitched at the right level and that they are questions which the interviewee can answer. The translator's skills lie in fitting information obtained at source to the foreign-language text.

Reliability

The concept of reliability is central to the German way of doing business: deadlines are cast in stone and clients expect reliability to be absolute. It is also important to get the balance right and not to pursue a policy of enquiring whether 'everything is alright'. Last summer I thought I would take to heart ISO 2001's exhortation to obtain some feedback on the product and services I provided when visiting a customer in Germany. The answer was clear and definitive: 'You would soon hear from us if everything was not alright.' This concept is crucial to the way this mature translation market operates. The client pays for a quality product and expects an exemplary product every time.

Communication

Communication and dialogue are important and German clients appreciate knowing exactly where they are. If a deadline is requested the client expects to receive a quick confirmation that the deadline is in order. Likewise, a fax giving information about precisely when and how a document will arrive on the client's desk is a formality that is easy to perform. If a client comes through with a query it is important to deal with it quickly, efficiently, and undefensively, taking account of the client's point of view. However, if the client is simply wrong (for example, expecting 50 pages overnight), arguing the case rationally and with the support of expertise and evidence will normally mean that the translator rises in the esteem of the client.

Cooperation

The concept of the '*Partner*' is central to translating for the German market and in general for doing business in Germany. German clients generally expect to pay for quality, but then expect translation providers to have confidence in their ability to produce a quality job and take pride in producing that quality. A mature market demands a profession that has the skills and qualifications for cooperation without a go-between that effectively blocks the flow of information. Companies in Germany like a long-term relationship with a professional translator rather than working through an agency without direct contact with the translator.

Hierarchy

Hierarchies in German companies are much more rigid than in the UK. Tasks and functions are clearly assigned and it is important to accept that a certain person deals with arranging for documentation in English from a particular department even though the boss may ring or fax through occasionally with a document for translation. It is important to deal directly with whoever has commissioned the translation – to do otherwise would be regarded as inappropriate or ignorant of German business culture. Likewise, any queries or problems should be addressed to the initial commissioner before anyone else in the company is contacted, unless a contact has been specifically set up for dealing with queries. Working for a larger company may entail many different people and departments commissioning translations from different parts of the company. These people will have different styles, different budgets and different billing requirements, and the translator is simply expected to comply with the requirements.

Presents

Gifts and presents are not looked upon favourably in the German market and may be construed as bribes. Even a festive card at Christmas may be a little out of place unless the translator has been working for a client for some time. If at some point a gift seems suitable, it ought to be small and if possible specifically

British (or American, etc.), such as tea or marmalade; British wine has novelty value! Sometimes it may be appropriate to ask a client out for a business meeting over lunch or dinner, but this kind of activity is much less widespread in Germany than the UK and may well create embarrassment for both sides in some German companies.

Meetings

Meetings must be to the point and have a purpose. An appointment and a statement about the reason why a meeting is necessary are essential prerequisites for successful cooperation between client and translator. I also bear in mind two salient comments from a German industrialist when I once said that I thought a meeting might be helpful. His response was: "Firstly, is it necessary? Secondly, what will it achieve?" Time is of the essence when attending a meeting, and it is important to be sensitive to the client. Some German managers like to get down to business right away, others will take their time and have a cup of coffee with a little general chit chat before talking about business. Whatever mode of operation is adopted it is important to take up the cues and to have the facts, arguments and topics at your fingertips. Likewise, it is important not to try and prolong a meeting or bring up new topics once your partner has indicated that the meeting should now be brought to a close. Business cards for technicians and lower management are not as common in Germany as in the US and the UK but it should not be forgotten that a flourish of business cards is an integral component of any business meeting between professionals and middle and upper management.

Core product + service = End product

In a mature market such as that in Germany, translation can be viewed increasingly in terms of a product with added value. Regarded schematically, the **core product** consists of the basic translation carried out either by the human translator or a machine translation system. The translation is then provided with added value using as tools a wide range of services. Their complexity will de-

Product resources

- Human translator (translator skills: language of habitual use, office skills, expert skills, qualifications)
- Project manager
- Machine translation system
- Translation memory/manager/assistant
- Voice recognition system
- Hardware/software

Services

Resource services

- Dictionary library, catalogue library, standards library, CD-ROM library
- Access to specialist library facilities
- Online databases
- Client familiarisation (visiting the factory, consulting client documentation, etc.)
- Term banks
- Expert knowledge

Special services

- Delivery to tight deadlines
- Localisation (company terminology/style, Americanisation)
- Contextualisation
- Cultural adaptation (advertising)
- Glossary compilation/term banks/term archiving

Target text services

- Background research
- Editing
- Collocations conforming to natural language
- Terminology checking
- Specialist checking
- Industrial usage
- Incorporation of company-specific terminology
- Checking against the source language
- Proof-reading for spelling, typographical errors, technical accuracy, style
- Checking with existing documentation

Related services

- Submission of text as hardcopy/on diskette
- Overwriting source text files
- Providing dictated translations on cassette
- Special formatting
- Document conversion
- Desk-top publishing
- Proof-reading printers' proofs
- Administration (billing, quotations, contracts)
- Quality management
- Project management, translation processing
- Public relations (marketing, client consultation)
- Photocopying
- Client meetings, advice and consultation
- Telephone consultation
- Delivery by courier, electronic mail, fax, express delivery
- Archiving/storage facilities (keeping back-ups – hardcopy/ electronic, etc.)
- Client training/liaison/awareness
- Allied services (technical writing, advertising, journalism)

(See: T .Carrington-Windo, 'Translation: product or service?' in *Keeping the Customer Satisfied. Proceedings of the Eighth International Annual Conference of the Institute of Translation and Interpreting*, ed. by P. Mayorcas and G. Dunnett, London, 1995, pp.16-21) pend on the requirements of the client and the sophistication of the translation provider. Some of the services (e.g. dictionary library) will probably be reflected in the price of the **core product** (i.e. the line rate) whereas other services such as desk-top publishing will be charged in addition to the line rate and will constitute an added-value service. Alternatively an hourly rate may be charged (typically DM 90 to DM 120) for complex tasks such as overwriting source texts requiring the preservation of special characters.

The table opposite indicates the product resources that may be used to produce the core product and the services that are added by the translation provider.

Conclusion

Such a table is neither exhaustive nor does it cover the whole range of translation provision and practice. It is intended to highlight the diversity of services that a translation provider is able to offer in a mature market. The key to penetrating a mature market successfully is understanding the business culture and adapting to the needs and requirements of that market. The seven key features of the mature market in Germany are punctuality, continuity, commitment, reliability, cooperation, communication and service.

Part V – Machine Translation and Translation Tools

10. Basic tools of the trade

SIÁN MARLOW AND SEAN MARLOW

This section will concern itself with the basic tools of the trade of a (newly) qualified translator, and the usage of these tools. Whilst some experienced translators find that the best way to maximise their earning potential is through dictation, with someone else being employed to word-process their output, the vast majority of translators at present seem to end up doing the writing down themselves. This being the case, the translator's single most important tool is the word processor, i.e. the piece of software that transfers the translator's knowledge into editable hard (paper) or soft (electronic) copy, plus the hardware to run it on. At least, this will be the case until reliable direct input dictation software comes along, which may be only a matter of months now. If this software does establish itself and proves reliable, it will undoubtedly revolutionise the way in which most translators work at present, be they freelance or office-based. An equivalent step was the distribution of OCR (Optical Character Recognition) software in documentation departments in the mid 1980s: suddenly copy which would in the past be laboriously retyped became relatively easy to distribute in an electronic format.

Software

Word-processing software

Because of the overall importance in terms of usage, the first choice to be made is which word-processing software to use. I suggest the opinion of others be sought before deciding on the specific package and its release version; fashions tend to change and salesmen will only too eagerly sell you something perfectly adequate, but not what everybody else is buying... It is also a good idea not to consider the cost of the software in isolation but instead to make sure that a 'slush fund' is set up so that you can keep up with the inevitable future releases, which are bound to come along when you least need them. As the format to be provided is specified by the client, the 'best' word-processing software is not necessarily the one to buy, compatibility being a much more important issue. There is little point in giving specific recommendations in a book such as this, as the 'in' word-processing package can change within a matter of months. However, as more and more corporate users switch to using Windows rather than DOS as their user interface, and Windows NT and Windows 95 steadily gain ground, a product like Microsoft Word 7.0 would be a safe choice, especially as it gives tremendous compatibility with other leading packages, being able to save in their native format and thus preserve quite complex layouts accurately, including tables, headers, etc. Like most other systems, it can provide ASCII output, but it can also offer RTF (Rich Text Format) which is regaining popularity as a cross-platform text transfer standard, and it can also save in Word for Macintosh format, offering flexibility if your clients use Apples as well as PCs.

Operating systems

PC

Having decided on the primary tool, the word processor, the next decision has to be which operating system to run it on. There are four mainstream choices: the Power Mac, DOS, OS/2 or any flavour of Windows. The latter is almost certainly the safest choice, as something like 70 per cent of all Personal Computers in Europe are using one of Microsoft's Graphic User Interfaces, the most popular at present being Windows 3.11 for Workgroups. This has the advantage of being relatively easy to learn and set up, is well tried and has the advantage over the earlier Windows 3.1 in incorporating its own peer-to-peer network (meaning the sort of network where there is no computer whose sole task is to act as a server for data storage), which is useful if your translation business consists of more than one person, now or in the future. The recently introduced Windows 95 is at the time of writing still too young to be recommendable, but will undoubtedly take over from earlier Windows versions in the future. It would be prudent to let others experience the adventure of trying the latest technology, whilst continuing yourself to work with a stable, proven product instead. At present, Windows 95 has no advantages for a translator, and has the disadvantages of being slower on old hardware, as well as requiring more RAM (Random Access Memory) to run at all. As computers are being sold with Windows 3.11 for Workgroups and Windows 95 pre-installed, it may be advisable to put the price difference between the two towards either more hard disk space or more RAM, as these are considerably cheaper to buy with a new machine rather than as a later upgrade. Windows NT, the third member of the Windows group currently available, is undoubtedly a fine product, being the most stable (i.e. least prone to crashing just after you have worked on a translation for a while, and just before you remembered to save), and, if using Word 7.0, the fastest, but the set-up is not quite as straightforward as the previously mentioned user interfaces. A small point, but most of the popular games cannot be played on a system thus equipped – which may be a disadvantage if you have a family, or are that way inclined yourself – as it does not support 'sound cards', printed circuit boards that allow speakers and joysticks to be plugged into the PC.

The most popular operating system of the last 10 years, DOS (which stands for Disk Operating System), is no longer being developed by Microsoft, which implies it has no real future; and thus machines which can run this alone should not be considered unless you are on a seriously tight budget. It will do as a temporary solution, but certain clients will be loath to give work to translators using older DOS versions of word-processing software, as document formatting may need to be reworked by the client himself once the final translation has been submitted. Realistically, translators working in the rarer/more exotic languages, e.g. Japanese, Hungarian, Icelandic, etc. will have their work accepted regardless but companies will prove more choosy if you provide English, French or German, and as a new translator, the latest word-processing software and operating system can be used to gain a competitive edge against older, more experienced translators, who are generally not as willing to re-learn and re-invest as often as their clients would like them to.

The last product on Intel-based computers, OS/2, is, I am reliably informed, an excellent operating system; but is not advisable for translators unless they are already relatively familiar with Personal Computers and secretly enjoy surfing the Internet for the right software driver, if they are unlucky enough also to have slightly non-standard Video cards... Because of the fewer units of this operating system (which is produced by IBM) installed, as compared to the Microsoft DOS/Windows products, it does have the disadvantage that if you need unbiased advice, it will be more difficult to find.

Macintosh

The Macintosh operating system is an excellent choice for the lateral thinker. It can teach even the latest Windows clone a thing or two about user-friendliness; it is fast, well thought out and elegant. Whilst the established user base is not as good as that of the DOS/Windows/OS/2 PC, there are enough people out there using it for it not to go suddenly out of fashion, and if you intend concentrating on providing translations for the graphics, packaging or advertising industries, then it will be a bonus for you to add to your CV. Compatibility is not an issue, for if you buy a new Macintosh word processor, it will be 100 per cent compatible with its Windows equivalent (though check first that there is one!), although sometimes problems do arise when transmitting files via modem from a Macintosh to a PC or *vice versa*, especially if you use Russian, Greek or other non-Latin character sets. The advantage is that with a Macintosh operating system, you can get on with using a computer as a tool without constantly being forced to 'think' like it does. For confirmed Luddites trying to survive in the information age, there can be no finer computer tool.

Hardware

Whilst it may seem strange to consider hardware last, I believe it is more sensible to pick a software tool and operating system and then buy something to run them on, rather than buying hardware and subsequently using whatever it can. The following will concentrate on the technical side of hardware, with the ergonomic aspects of the set-up in general, and of computers in particular, being considered elsewhere in this piece.

Where to buy and what to look for

With hardware, where you buy will often make a greater difference to the final price than what you buy, and I would recommend costing the whole package before you make your final choice. By 'the whole package', I mean the services you are buying as well as the ugly plastic lump you will be staring at for most of your working life. Thus a warranty which includes on-site maintenance is essential, unless you want to become one of those so-called professionals who are forever explaining to their clients that the translation is late not because of any fault of theirs, but because the hard disk died, or the monitor shows only blue characters, or the prize-winning pet Siamese ate the mouse... Obviously, the more quickly a company is able to respond to a call-out, the better. The minimum would be on a 24-hour basis, with most good support sites being able to offer an eight-hour response time – unless, that is, you translate from a rocky crag on the Isle of Skye.

Similarly, if you do not feel 100 per cent confident with the technology, a support package such as that offered by Dell is invaluable, as it gives you the confidence of knowing there is an expert to talk you through any problem which may occur, often going out of their way to satisfy the customer by trying to fix problems not really of their own making. Computer magazines such as *PC Magazine* will regularly feature reliability and service surveys, and there are no better recommendations than those. Do not be afraid to buy your equipment from mail-order companies, as the person on the other end of the telephone is likely to know far more about computers than the average 16-year-old employed by one of the High Street chains and who is also responsible for toasters and spin dryers. The lower overheads of mail-order mean you also tend to get much more for your money. Again, read the reliability surveys in *Which?* and the like.

With hardware, depreciation is tremendously high, so do not be surprised if the value of the system you bought recently seems to fall daily. Specifications are constantly improving, and new upgrades are being offered on a monthly basis. Pick a reliable system with good support, and buy as advanced a system as you can afford, for it will last the longest. These days, this means a Pentium PC or one with an equivalent chip running at 75 MHz (the higher the MHz, the faster the computer) for Windows, or a Power Mac for the Apple OS, with 16 Mb RAM. This will last a good couple of years before it becomes obsolete. The law of diminishing returns means that to get the very latest and best, you will pay far more than the benefits it brings would seem to justify. Thus a 'leading edge' system would, at the time of writing, be a Pentium Pro, which, while three times as fast as the recommended system, might cost four times as much, because all its components will be 'up-specced' to cope with the speed of the processor.

Why buy a computer at all?

Having taken the word processor to be the primary tool, many will wonder whether the latest technology is worth it, since all they need is a glorified typewriter. Therefore, why not buy a 486SX, which will run all the software that a Pentium can, whilst often saving you the price of the software to run on it; or in the Macintosh world, why not look for a machine equipped with a Motorola 68040 rather than a Power Mac? The answer is future-proofing. All computers become obsolete hideously quickly, but hardware deemed obsolete the day you bought it is obviously at a disadvantage, so don't be surprised if you get blank looks in a couple of years' time when you try to upgrade the graphics capabilities or fit a bigger memory store. If 'dictation' software, i.e. systems capable of interpreting the dictated word, takes off – and at present it is on the verge of doing so – then you will need all the computing power you can get. Similarly, if Windows 95 generally replaces Windows 3.1 and 3.11 for Workgroups, and if Apple releases a version of the operating system incompatible with the pre-RISC (reduced instruction set) processors, then the few hundred pounds you saved by buying a 486SX or an LC475 will cost you dear.

Communications

As well as the main software and hardware, a part of your allocated budget will have to go on communications and support programs. Computer-Aided Translation tools and glossaries will be dealt with elsewhere in this book, being more suitable for the advanced computer user. But communications are a different story: whilst it is still possible to send disks to clients, it is a tremendous competitive advantage – due to the saving in terms of time – to be able to modem translations as soon as you have checked them. This can be done either directly or via service providers like CompuServe or an Internet gateway, assuming your clients have access to these. The service is not only efficient, but also cheap: for a relatively affordable £10 a month or so, it lets you transfer files at local telephone rates, even internationally. Anyone with more than a couple of clients abroad should consider this option very seriously indeed, or at least hedge their bets and buy shares in BT.

Current high-speed modems cost around £100, and are incomparably more pleasant to use those of even two years ago. While you will find a slow PC with old word-processing software annoying in the long term, a slow modem with old communications software will drive you – and worse, your client – absolutely hopping mad. Aim for something with BT approval and V.34 on the box, and that has had a good review in the computer press as your hardware of choice, and something with the Z-Modem protocol and a reasonably well-written and understandable manual (you may just find yourself reading this repeatedly) on the software front. Combined internal fax/modems are a mixed blessing: whilst they may increase your kudos with clients if you have a fax, and they are much cheaper than buying a separate fax machine, it is annoying to have to stop work every time your clients need to send you a fax, or *vice versa*. Technically it should be possible for modern computers to handle this sort of task in the background without stemming your creative flow, but sometimes theory and practice just do not coincide.

So it seems with combined fax/modems. Sometimes even experienced computer users find themselves at a loss to explain the somewhat strange quirks with which these systems seem to be afflicted. The advantages of subscribing to CompuServe or an Internet provider using your new modem include not only faster communication with clients which takes place when convenient for you, but these are quite good places to advertise your services (assuming you will have gathered a bit of skill in the meantime) and also provide you with the fastest means of contacting experts in various fields. Thus a technical translation question, worded in such a way as not to transgress client confidentiality (of course), posted in one of the fora, will usually get a response quickly. As the networks are truly global, it is as likely to come from Italy, if it is on, say, English into Italian automotive technology, as from next door, and all at the cost of a local call.

Secondary support programs

Accounts

One secondary support program you may need is a basic accounting package – lest the taxman come – of which there are many (accounting packages that is, but also, regrettably, taxmen). As with the modem software, pick a package that has a well-written manual, as most translators tend not to be experts in double entry book-keeping. And whatever you do, do not use the calculator that comes with Windows 3.11 for Workgroups for your accounting. If you suffer from the delusion that computers are good at counting, just try subtracting 2.01 from 2 on it...

Typing tutor

One quite good investment, if you are still hitting the keyboard like a demented woodpecker, would be a typing tutor. These can be quite enjoyable (rather more so than formal secretarial training, I find), and a tremendous boon when you have got yourself into the situation of having taken on too much work, and dawn is moving inexorably closer as you hammer away at the keyboard with aching index fingers.

So much then as to the basic computer tools you will need to start off with; using your word-processor will soon become second nature as long as you do not pick up any bad habits (translators who still use the space bar to align text in columns please note!): you may also find it handy to book in on a two-day training course. Being able to set up stylesheets, change fonts, save in various formats and use and know how to adapt the spell-checker should be regarded as the minimum you need to learn from any course. Take the opportunity to ask the course instructors for their hardware and software recommendations – they generally not only know their subject, but will be able to give you advice on equipment that will meet your specific requirements.

Office Ergonomics

Equally as important to the translator as the equipment he has to use in his day-to-day work is the way in which this equipment is put to use. Ergonomics can be summed up as being as comfortable as is possible whilst trying to do the work required. With this in mind, the following section aims to look at how to ensure your own comfort and safety while working at your computer, while at the same time ensuring that you suffer no long-term injury as a result of poor working practice or positioning of the body.

Your computer environment

It is fair to assume that most (if not all) translators use a computer for their work. The location and position of your desk, computer, monitor and keyboard (and mouse if you have one) are of fundamental importance if you are to stay healthy. If such considerations are not observed, there is a chance that you could end up a victim of Repetitive Strain Injury (RSI), a condition caused by repeating the same movement over and over again (such as when typing), or by adopting an incorrect position when working. The objective of the section which follows is to give you a brief insight into how your equipment should be arranged to minimise strain on your body.

Your desk

Ideally, you should position your computer on a desk which is of the optimum height to suit your requirements and has plenty of space for all your bits and pieces. Obviously, your computer will be the most important (and most used) piece of equipment on this desk, and it should therefore be positioned centrally so that you do not have to strain to reach it. A document holder which keeps the documents from which you are working almost vertical can be an asset, especially since this will save you from having to move your head up and down in order to look first at the document, then at the screen. If your desk is large enough for you to place dictionaries and other reference works on it, so much the better. Never be tempted to keep your reference books on your lap, though – the sitting position you would have to adopt to stop them sliding off would not be the safest or the most comfortable for you.

Your chair

You should never use a standard kitchen chair for working at a desk, particularly if your work involves using a computer. A height-adjustable office chair with adjustable backrest (for your lower back) is the best investment you can make in this respect. When trying out chairs, though, do ensure that your feet are able to rest flat on the ground – if you can do this, you are in the best working position. Make sure also that you find the chair comfortable when sitting squarely on it: remember that you will be occupying it for at least a few hours a day for many weeks to come!

Your computer

It is vital that your computer be positioned correctly as outlined below.

Keyboard

Place the keyboard on the desk with the 'legs' at the rear folded out; this tilts the keyboard forward slightly and makes it easier to use. You can use a wrist mat placed in front of the keyboard to support your wrists when typing, although these seem to be falling out of favour at the time of writing (if for no other reason than the fact that they take up a considerable amount of valuable desk space).

Mouse

Place the mouse on its mat within easy reach of the keyboard so that you do not have to stretch or move your body (except your arm!) to reach it.

Base unit

If you have a 'tower' base unit, stand this to one side of your desk. If, however, you use one of the horizontal types, you will probably have to give up some of that valuable desk space in order to accommodate it. Some people like to place their monitors on top of the base unit, but this is not recommended as it results in too high a monitor position with most full-size base units. If you do prefer to keep your monitor on top of your base unit, remember to take this into consideration when you buy a desk.

Monitor

The monitor, which ideally should be of the low-radiation type and fitted with an anti-glare screen, should be placed on the desk and tilted slightly upwards so that you can look at it without having to move your head. Your neck should be comfortably straight when looking at the screen. If it is not, the angle of the monitor can be adjusted slightly up or down. Also, it is more comfortable, particularly when working with a text in a document holder which is positioned to one side of your monitor, to keep the monitor directly in front of you. The recommended distance between you and your monitor is 60-66 cm, although this can vary from individual to individual.

Document holder

There are a number of types of document holder on the market which can be used to hold your translation texts steady and in a position which enables you to translate without having to turn your head repeatedly or to look up to your screen and then down at a text. The most effective document holder a translator can use is the type fitted with a clip at the top (to hold documents steady – this is particularly useful when working with jobs on thermal fax paper, which have a tendency to slip) and with an electrically-operated bar across. This bar is dual-purpose: it acts as a secondary paper holder, whilst at the same time allowing the translator to see which part of the document he is working with. The advantage of acquiring a holder with an electrically-operated bar is that you do not have to keep moving your arms backwards and forwards to shift the bar down as you translate; all you do is use the foot pedal provided, which gives the bar smooth downward movement. And not only does a document holder of this type mean that you continue to work in the most comfortable and ergonomically sound position possible; it also saves the hours of frustration which would otherwise be spent every time you lost your place in a translation because of the telephone.

Positioning the body when working at a computer workstation

If you work for long periods at a time without taking a break, you will find that your muscles become tired this is due to the tenseness of the muscles, which prevents proper circulation of the blood.

Therefore, when sitting at your desk working on a translation, you should adopt a position recommended by physiotherapists: that is to say, try to remain as relaxed as possible, particularly in the neck and shoulders. Keep your upper arms level with your body, and your lower arms at right angles to your upper arms. Your wrists should be kept straight (as if you were playing the piano). Sit up straight, allowing the backrest of your chair to rest comfortably against your lower back. Sit squarely on your chair, and rest your feet on your footstool if you have one (this is in fact recommended); otherwise, keep your feet flat on the floor.

If you are sitting correctly, you will find that as long as you take the frequent breaks recommended for computer operators (two to three minutes every 40 minutes, and a full 15 minutes after every two hours), you will not feel stiff or sore after a few hours at the keyboard. If you do feel some discomfort, however, try adjusting your sitting position slightly until you feel more comfortable when working.

In addition, you may find it helpful to leave your computer for short breaks every now and then, particularly if you are starting to feel uncomfortable or stiff. Walk around or do a few simple stretching exercises. Remember, no matter how urgent a translation is, you must take regular breaks away from your computer if you are to function as well as you can. Short breaks not only make you feel better physically; you will also feel refreshed and work more efficiently if you take the time to leave what you are doing, even if you can spare only a few minutes.

If, however, you feel that the position of your body when working leaves something to be desired, consult a physiotherapist. He will be able to review your working position and suggest improvements. If you feel that you are starting to show signs of RSI, it is vital that you consult a physiotherapist without delay: left untreated, RSI is a potentially disabling condition and could cut short your working life by a number of years.

Finally, if the telephone rings when you are working on a particularly urgent translation, never be tempted to cradle the telephone under your chin and carry on working while having a conversation! This is a very easy mistake to make, particularly when you are busy, but if you do this you will soon find that neck and back pain can result.

Looking after your eyes

When working with a computer, your eyes are the most vulnerable part of your body. When working for any length of time on your computer, you should observe a few rules to ensure that your sight is not damaged. Opticians used to recommend that you spend no more than four hours a day on computer-based work, but it is now recognised that most people will spend longer than this regardless of the official recommendations, so certain measures which can help protect your eyes from serious damage during prolonged work with a computer are essential.

- Try to work with dark text on a light background – this is less tiring for the eyes.
- As mentioned above, ensure that you are sitting around 60 - 66 cm from your screen (although this distance may be varied, depending on personal preference).
- Try to take two to three-minute breaks for every 40 minutes you spend working on the computer.
- If you are working with the computer for a more prolonged period, it is recommended that you take a 15-minute break after every two-hour session.
- Try to ensure that there are no windows directly behind or in front of your computer monitor. Any window in a room should be to the either side of your computer to prevent glare on the screen. Windows should be equipped with blinds which can be pulled over the window in strong sunlight.
- Also in respect of lighting: ensure that there is adequate lighting in the room in which you are working, but try to avoid positioning your computer screen where the light reflects off the screen. It is possible to purchase anti-glare screens – this may be the best solution, if you can afford one. You should at all costs avoid working in a room where a faulty fluorescent tube is flickering.
- If you can, work in a room in which you are isolated and which people do not use as a means of getting from one room to another. Such movement can cause distraction (reflections on your screen, as well as the noise involved) and fluctuations in the level of light on your screen.

- If you wear spectacles, try to purchase a pair which have a special anti-glare coating: this can greatly facilitate working on a computer.
- If you wear contact lenses and experience discomfort (such as dry, gritty eyes) while working with the computer, have a word with your optician. He will be able to prescribe high water-content lenses for you, and you may find that purchasing lenses on a frequent replacement scheme (where new lenses are provided once every three months, once a month or every day) helps alleviate the problem. Also, you may find that switching to an all-in-one care solution (as opposed to separate solutions for each stage of the cleaning process) helps.

If you do experience problems with your eyesight, consult your optician immediately. If you are employed by a company instead of working freelance, your employer is required to provide and pay for eye examinations for all employees who work regularly with computer screens this piece of EC legislation came into force on 1 January 1993.

Should this eye examination prove that spectacles should be prescribed specifically for use with computer monitors, then your employer is also legally required to contribute to the price of these. However, do note that if you wear spectacles to correct some other sight problem such as myopia as well, you have to fund these yourself.

All that remains to say in this respect is that if you take good care to ensure that your working environment is as safe and as well arranged as possible so that you do not suffer from RSI, eye strain or any one of a number of other afflictions caused by working for long periods of time while sitting or typing in an incorrect position, you will make sure that you enjoy a long and (hopefully) profitable working life.

Reference Material

It is unlikely that translators will ever experience the 'paperless office'. Computers create more paperwork than ever before: most translators will print out a preliminary version of a translation for reading through before submitting a final copy as it is easier to proofread your own work – and find your own mistakes – on paper than to scan through it on screen. Moreover, translators would have a hard time surviving without paper dictionaries, no matter how good their computers are. Admittedly, it is possible to purchase copies of works of reference on CD-ROM, but as far as translators are concerned, the more works of reference they have to consult, and the more easily accessible these are, the better.

In the following section I would like to describe just a few of the sources of reference open to translators.

Dictionaries

There are many different types of dictionary available to the translator. As well as the standard bilingual and monolingual dictionaries, it is possible to purchase dictionaries which target specific subject fields. These dictionaries are particularly useful if you can find any relevant to your own specialist subjects.

Bilingual dictionaries

The standard bilingual dictionaries such as the Collins Robert *French-English-French* or the Norstedts *Swedish-English-Swedish* are designed to be used by anyone, from GCSE students to translators with many years of experience. The main difference between these two categories lies in how these books are used: while a student may use a bilingual dictionary to look up a word previously unknown to him, a translator will almost always use it to jog his memory or to suggest alternative translations for words.

As mentioned above, specialist dictionaries are a good source of reference. All translators should have their preferred subject fields, so a good investment to make when starting out as a freelance translator, for example, would be some of the dictionaries more relevant to your subject. These are sometimes difficult to find, but some of the larger city bookshops (who also operate mail-order services) may be able to help. That said, translators should be aware that in many cases such dictionaries are compiled by one person rather than by a board, and as a result they may know all there is to know about the subject, but their grasp of the target language may not be as good as they think! Therefore, when buying such specialised dictionaries, it may be as well to contact someone who is familiar with the dictionary (such as another translator) and to ask him for his opinions before parting with your hard-earned cash, especially since such dictionaries can be rather expensive. Alternatively, you could turn to your national association of translators for guidance – they might also be able to advise you on where a copy of the dictionary you need can be found. If the dictionary has already been reviewed in their publication, asking for a reprint of the relevant article may result in you finding an expert opinion on the dictionary in question.

Monolingual dictionaries

Monolingual dictionaries in the source language are a less used, but no less invaluable, source of reference. The standard dictionaries often contain many words which the compilers of bilingual dictionaries considered irrelevant, such as colloquialisms, but which do appear in texts for translation from time to time. Monolingual dictionaries can also provide the translator with a deeper understanding of the unfamiliar word or suggest alternative translations for words already known.

Monolingual specialist dictionaries can be particularly helpful to the translator. These will describe precisely what is meant by a term, thereby allowing the translator (who presumably is *au fait* with the subject matter of the translation) to determine what is meant by the unfamiliar word. A particular example is American English, where something like the SAE glossary of automotive terms reveals how wide the gulf between British and American usage of the language has become.

Co-operation with clients and other translators

When all your works of reference have been explored and a translation of the term you are looking for has still not been revealed, you may have to consult your client. If you are able to describe to your client what the word you are looking for actually means (don't take it for granted that they will speak the source language of your translation) – you could perhaps quote a section of the text which describes the term in question – then your client may be able to proffer a suitable translation.

It may be that the term causing you problems is an example of inhouse terminology for which a company-approved translation exists. In such cases, it is always valuable to ask your client whether a glossary of inhouse terms has been compiled. If so, suggest that this be sent to you for use now and with future translations. If not, there is nothing to stop you compiling your own and, if you wish, submitting it to your client with a request for comments and corrections. Of course, this procedure works the other way around, too: if you disagree with some of the terms suggested in a client's glossary, do not be afraid to let them know. They may refuse to change the contentious term, but you will at least have made them aware that there may be problems with their glossary.

It is likely that from time to time you will be faced with a term which is completely unfamiliar to you, which goes unmentioned in any of your reference works and on which your client is unable to offer any assistance. This is a good time to ask other translators whether they have ever encountered this term before. This is a particularly useful exercise as it not only encourages co-operation (and therefore a certain degree of consistency) between translators, but it also prevents the feeling of isolation often experienced by freelance translators. However, do in all circumstances beware of breaching client confidentiality when consulting third parties: the client's right to complete confidentiality is of paramount importance, and when consulting other translators you must be careful not to divulge any information (such as details of a prototype product or the contents of a vital contract) which may compromise the position of your client. Where at all possible, you should endeavour to avoid even naming your client.

Glossaries – compiling your own

While we are on the subject, compiling glossaries is a good way of retaining a record of all the research you have done. If you compile a glossary when doing a translation for a particular client or on a particular subject, it will save you from having to look up all those terms again.

Glossaries can be compiled whenever you like when doing a translation: before you start, while you work, or when you have finished. You can use standard word-processing software for this, and the advantage of the Windows multi-tasking environment is that you can compile your glossary using one application while you translate using another, or you can even use more than one window in the same application to create several documents at once. I personally find that compiling the glossary as you go along prevents inconsistency to a large extent and also allows you to revise ideas you may have had along the way. Of course, any glossary you compile can be arranged into alphabetical order if you so desire, and keeping a copy of your glossary on disk means that you can call it up on your computer whenever necessary and add to it or revise it as required.

Glossaries supplied by a client

It is inevitable that one of your clients will supply you with a glossary at some stage and request that you use it for your translation. If the glossary is exhaustive and consistently well researched, you may find that it is an excellent aid to you in your work.

But what happens when the glossary has been compiled by someone (or worse, a number of someones) at an overseas office with a less than fluent grasp of your native language? You may find, at best, numerous spelling mistakes and, at worst, some of the terms you are being asked to use may be nonsensical to the average native speaker. The way around this is to consult your client. Tell him that you are less than happy with the glossary, and ask whether you may amend the glossary as you see fit (you are the translator, after all!). This will generate one of two responses:

- The client may tell you that the glossary is 'final' and that you must adhere to it. If this is the case, do as you are asked, but feel free to put a disclaimer on your translation to the effect that you were asked to use the client's terminology, which may not coincide with your preferred terms as a translator.

- If, however, your client is a little more willing to accept that some of his terms may leave something to be desired, the easiest way to proceed is to go through the glossary first, picking out the terms which you know or can find out about, entering them in the glossary as you go. Any terms you are not sure about can then be researched later when you encounter them in context as you translate. Do bear in mind, however, that if a client has allowed you to amend his glossary, it is only polite to let him know what changes you have made to it.

Other glossaries

You will come across glossaries in a number of places – at the end of technical reference works, in computer manuals, magazines or product catalogues to name but a few sources. It is quite often very handy to keep a record of where you found these glossaries, what information they contained, etc. and to keep the relevant books or magazines with your other reference literature. The information will then be at your fingertips when you need it.

Past translations

Again, you may find these to be an invaluable source of reference material. You may think that you would remember your past translations well enough to recall what you used for translations of certain terms, but experience will prove that this is most definitely not always the case! Past translations are best stored on computer disks (which use less space), with client comments on your translations kept in files in chronological order nearby. If you choose to store your past translations in this way, however, do remember that you will need to keep a record of precisely what can be found on each disk. This will facilitate rapid retrieval of information as and when you need it.

Standards

Standards (reference documents produced by associations such as BSI in the United Kingdom or DIN in Germany) can be very useful to translators. Such documents are usually of a technical nature and often include glossaries of terms and abbreviations, frequently in just one language, but occasionally in two or even more languages, thereby forming an excellent reference source for the translator. If you work for large companies, you may find that they produce their own in-house standards which you can use as reference literature and are particularly useful for terminology – you only have to ask for a copy. If such standards are not available, international or national standards can be purchased from BSI in the United Kingdom.

Less obvious sources of reference material

Reference material can be found in the unlikeliest of places. In theory, anything which is written down can be used by the translator as reference material.

Reference material from shops

When out shopping, you can pick up a number of useful reference items such as those listed below:

- in-store catalogues
- product information leaflets
- company information leaflets

These may seem unlikely sources of any useful information for the translator, but if you have the space to store them, they may come in handy just when you least expect it. Imagine being asked to translate, for instance, a text on video cameras. Do you have to call them 'video cameras', or can the term 'camcorders' be used regardless of make? The reference material you collect while shopping will certainly be able to help you in such matters, or at least give you the telephone number of someone who might know the answer.

Reference material in the post

If you are one of the people regularly singled out by companies as the kind of person who would probably like to know all about their new product via 'junk mail', you may find it interesting to note that not all junk mail is junk! That is to say, some of the leaflets, special offers, free samples, etc. that litter your doormat with monotonous regularity may actually be of use to you in your work. Suffice it to say, discard such material only when you know for certain that you will never do a translation on life assurance/bank loans/hearing aids...

Storage of reference material

When you have collected together all this material, you must find a way of storing it so that you can actually locate it when you need it. If office space is at a premium, you may find yourself having to be selective as to what stays on your shelves and what ends up in the bin; but whatever the situation, make sure you use a logical filing system for all your material. Store it by subject, client or product name, but do ensure that you are uniform in your methods so that any elusive but extremely helpful one-page leaflets do not go astray.

Using the telephone as a source of reference

Finally, if all your painstaking research using your reference material has proved fruitless and your client cannot answer your questions, do not be afraid to use the telephone to contact an expert in the field. Admittedly, you do feel a bit of an idiot the first few times you telephone your local garage and ask pertinent questions such as what the holes in wheel rims are 'officially' called (this question received the response, 'Well, we call 'em holes'), but you do get results! You can contact your local garden centre, dentist, doctor, or anyone who knows something about the subject in hand. You may occasionally find that the person on the other end of the telephone is singularly unhelpful, but more often than not people will feel flattered that you bothered to contact them as a potential expert on the subject (particularly if you start off by saying something like 'I'm doing a translation on X and I've heard that you know quite a lot about this, so I decided to call you and ask...').

One interesting point in this respect is that you should always make sure that when thanking your contact for his help, you leave your name and telephone number (and address where applicable) just in case the company concerned ever has any translations it needs doing. After all, you will have made it clear during your conversation that the subject area the company deals in is one of your specialist areas. Remember, translators are often selected at random from the Yellow Pages or similar, and by telephoning them for help you are bringing yourself to their attention as a potential supplier of translations. However, remember that the golden rule once again is, respect the confidentiality of your client.

If a request for information by this means is turned down, thank your contact politely for his time, then try another source of information – perhaps another company in the same field. Do not be disheartened if your contact refuses to help – just keep trying.

On the other hand, many people are more than helpful and will go out of their way to answer your questions or, if this is not possible, to get you the telephone number of someone who can. Remember that you are taking up their time (which is at least as valuable to them as yours is to you), so always be polite, and thank them for their time and assistance.

To conclude, remember that when searching for an adequate translation for words or phrases previously unknown, the translator should always be prepared to search everywhere for the term he requires: some of the most appropriate translations of unfamiliar foreign terms can be found in the most peculiar of places!

11. Terminology Management Systems

KLAUS-DIRK SCHMITZ

1. Introduction

The present age is characterised by an increase in knowledge in almost all technological, economic, political and cultural fields. Modern communication and publication methods and media allow a swift and wide transfer of this knowledge. But the spread of knowledge is not limited to a closed group of specialists or one language community. Translators and interpreters play an important role in this multilingual communication process across language boundaries.

Since a high percentage of specialised knowledge is documented and published by means of language, correct terminology is a prerequisite for efficient knowledge transfer, so that translators are faced with the problem of collecting, storing and retrieving terminology when they produce a professional translation of a specialised document.

In the past, translators used glossary lists and file cards to manage their terminology. Today there is a wide range of software tools available to support the process of translation, documentation and technical writing. These programs include computer-aided translation systems, electronic dictionaries, terminological data banks on CD-ROM and, of course, terminology management systems.

2. Historical Background

The first approaches in the use of computer technology in managing terminological data started in the early 1960s. There was an urgent need for national and international institutions and for multinational companies with large translating and interpreting services since a great number of translators frequently had to co-operate on large translation projects under great time pressure in order to meet a given deadline. Due to the restrictions resulting from the hardware and software components available at that time and due to the organisational infrastructure needed for operating mainframe computers, only the wealthier organisations and institutions could afford to implement and run their own terminological data banks. It is therefore not surprising that the first terminological data banks were set up in large language services belonging to governmental organisations and major enterprises, in standards organisations and in language planning organisations, for example:

- LEXIS (Federal Office of Languages, Germany)
- TERMIUM (Language service of the Canadian government)
- EURODICAUTOM (Commission of the European Community)
- TEAM (Siemens AG, Germany)
- AFNOR (French Association for Standardisation)
- BTQ (Office de la langue française, Canada)

Although the individual terminological databanks mentioned differ in content (languages, subject fields), size, structure and function, they usually have the following data fields in common:

- main term / main phrase
- subject field / classification
- definition
- context / example
- synonyms
- source
- comment / note
- administrative information (date, author, quality, ...)

Most of these large terminological databanks have been maintained and used within the corresponding institution down to the present day, so that they contain hundreds of thousands of entries. The terminological data of some of the large data banks is also accessible for external users on microfiche (LEXIS), on CD-ROM (TERMIUM, AFNOR, TERMDOK2 with parts of EURODICAUTOM and TERMIUM) and via network (EURODICAUTOM on ECHO-HOST and on the World Wide Web).

```
 File   Edit   Window   Print   Configure

                        EURODICAUTOM  1 (2)
  Next      Previous    Extended Search

enTE:  1)central processing unit;2)central processor;main frame;CPU
enDE:  unit which generally incorporates the main storage,the
       arithmetical and logical elements and the control elements
enNO:  main frame=terme not recommended
daTE:  centralenhed
daDE:  enhed som almindeligvis indeholder hovedlageret,
       regneelementerne, de logiske elementer og kontrolanordningerne
deTE:  Zentralheinheit
deDE:  eine Zentraleinheit enthaelt in der Regel den Hauptspeicher,die
       arithmetischen und logischen Elemente und die Steuer-und
       Kontrollelemente
frTE:  1)unité centrale de traitement;2)unité centrale
frDE:  une unité centrale de traitement comprend généralement la
       mémoire principale,les éléments arithmétiques et logiques et les
       organes de commande et de contrôle
esTE:  unidad central de procesamiento
esDE:  una unidad central de procesamiento comprende generalmente la

       Index                     Exit
```

Figure 1: EURODICAUTOM on TERMDOK2

The first generation of term banks with their pragmatic and often institution-specific design was followed by research-oriented developments which, on the one hand, helped reveal the conceptual weakness of the individual data banks and, on the other hand, created new concepts, which again led to the development of corresponding software. Examples of this are the DANTERM database, developed at the University of Copenhagen, and the Ericsson CAT system, used in the language departments of some German companies and governmental organisations. Both systems are based on a concept-oriented approach of terminology management and run on medium-sized computers. But with the breakthrough of microelectronics and the population of (networking) personal computers in language departments and at the translator's workplace, the Ericsson CAT system lost the support it had enjoyed and disappeared from the market.

At the same time, the development of PC-based terminology management systems began. These operated in a standardised hardware and software environment (MS-DOS) and could be used together with other programs such as word processing systems. The first of these systems were launched in the mid-1980s and were designed for the single translator's workstation. Most of them allowed only simple management of bilingual terminology with considerable restrictions on the number of data fields and maximum length of storable data. Today, the modern terminology management systems available on the market follow the concept-oriented approach of terminology management with a very elaborate data structure and sophisticated look-up features. These systems can be used by freelance translators as well as language departments with a local area network of personal computers.

3. Concepts, Types and Features of Termnology Management Systems

3.1 Basic elements of terminology management

Terminology science can be characterised as the study of concepts and terms in special language communication. Terminology work is based on the principles of terminology science and includes all activities concerned with the preparation, acquisition, processing and presentation of terminological data. The more administrative side of terminology work can be described as terminology management and is supported by computerised tools.

The terminological entry is the basic unit in terminology management. It is composed of systematically arranged and well-defined terminological data categories and includes all terminological information belonging to *one* concept and its related terms.

A terminological data category is the smallest unit used in handling terminology. It is crucial to the systematics of work with terminology that each data category contains only *one* type of information and only that type of data for which the data category is provided, e.g. in a data category 'definition' only the definition of a concept should be stored and not the source of the definition as well.

Terminological data categories can be grouped under various headings, depending on whether they are concept-related, term-related or contain administrative data.

Concept-related terminological data categories contain those data elements that refer to the concept underlying this entry or describing the relationship between this concept and other concepts. Typically concept-related data categories are:

- definition
- subject field / domain
- illustration / symbol / formula
- classification / notation
- superordinate concept
- subordinate concept
- co-ordinate concept

Term-related terminological data categories contain those data elements that refer to one particular term attributed to the concept underlying this entry. The set of term-related data categories must be repeated for each term assigned to the concept both within one language (e.g. for synonyms) or for several languages. Possible term-related data categories are:

- term (including synonyms and phraseological units)
- context / example
- grammatical information
- geographical restriction
- linguistic restrictions
- register
- project code / company code
- status of the term

Administrative data categories refer to the entry as a whole or to individual concept-related or term-related data categories within this entry. Administrative data categories are:

- identification number (entry number)
- date (creation / last update)
- author (creator / checker / editor)
- source
- reliability
- note / annotation / comment

The above terminological data categories are defined and explained with examples in ISO 12620 together with many other possible data categories. Some authors of introductions to terminology work distinguish between obligatory and optional data categories, but the choice of data categories for the terminological entry depends very much on the user groups involved, the planned application and the purpose of the terminology management. For translators, a minimal terminological entry is defined as consisting of the following data categories:

- term / synonym
- definition or explanation
- context
- source
- subject field / domain
- date
- author
- note

3.2 Types of terminology management systems

Translators often start by replacing a file card system with a computerised approach using some existing software tool with which they are familiar. Usually the terms are recorded in a word processing file as a simple word list or a table with the source language term on the one side and the target language term on the other. Although this approach allows the user to look up a term, find a translation, paste the term into a target language text and print out a term list in alphabetic order, a word processing system is not an adequate tool for managing terminology in an efficient way with a minimal entry structure of necessary data categories. Also, a word processor's search facility is very slow where several thousand terminological entries have to be managed.

A more systematic approach involves the use of database systems like MS-Access or spreadsheet programs like MS-Excel in managing terminology. These programs allow the user to define the terminological data categories, build up a structure for terminological entries and search for a term in a very efficient way. Unfortunately, most of these systems have problems with the management of linguistic data having a variable length, for example, a definition may be composed of only a few words, but may also be longer than one page. In addition, some programming effort is necessary to give a general-purpose software tool a specific and efficient user interface for a translator or terminologist.

The best computerised replacement for the old file card approach is a terminology management system. Terminology management systems can be defined as software tools specifically designed to manage terminological data for use by translators and terminologists. They are not unlike database management systems, though without the full functionality of such systems, are customised for efficient handling of linguistic and terminological data.

Surveys of computerised tools for translators list some 50 different terminology management systems. Most of these were developed in Central European countries, and some are very experimental and not (yet) or no longer available. About 20 systems based on different approaches are available on the market and are useful tools for translators and terminologists; the choice of system depends very much on aspects discussed in section four and on the type and design of the terminology management system.

Bilingual or language-pair-based terminology management systems are more likely to meet the requirements of term-oriented or lexicographic terminology work, but these programs usually offer only a limited number of terminological data categories and a very simple entry structure. Problems arise if, for example, a German-English terminological database has to be used for an English-German translation. It is sometimes possible to cope with more than two languages by using some tricks, but these tools are not adapt at managing multilingual terminology.

Figure 2: MTX-Reference for Windows

Multilingual terminology management systems come closer to a concept-oriented approach, so that they fit much better into multi-user environments. Some of the systems on the market are confined to a fixed number of languages, and some give the user bilingual access to an entry, depending on the languages needed for a specific translation. We also find systems with a very poor entry structure (only the terms themselves in several languages along with two or three additional data categories) and systems with a highly sophisticated entry structure. Some of these more complex systems support synonym autonomy, where synonymous terms can be fully documented with data categories such as grammatical information, context example or project code.

The third class of terminology management systems in terms of system philosophy includes all systems with a free entry structure. These systems allow users to define their own data categories and their own entry structure, so that the software can be adapted to suit a user's specific terminological needs and can grow as future requirements change.

105290 | NT40: Übertragungstechnik

Deutsch Restdämpfung

Note:

Grainfo: nf

Def.: Vereinbarter Begriff zur Darstellung der Betriebsdämpfung, der
Spannungsdämpfung und der Einfügungsdämpfung eines
Land: Stromkreises für den Spezialfall, daß beide Abschlußwiderstände

English circuit equivalent

Note:

Grainfo:

Def.: Conventional term used to represent composite attenuation,
transductile attenuation, and insertion loss of a circuit in the
Land: particular case where the impedances between which the circuit

Français équivalent d'un circuit

Note:

Grainfo: nm

Def.: Terme conventionnel adopté pour représenter l'affaiblissement
composite, l'affaiblissement transductique et l'affaiblissement
Land: d'insertion d'un circuit dans le cas particulier où les impédances

Figure 3: RailLexic

MultiTerm '95 - TEST1.MTW

File   Edit   View   Search   Help

Index **Englisch**   Target **Deutsch**

accumulator   battery storage

Entry Number   1
Subject   Windenergie
Notation   N-5.2.1.
Anlagedatum   11.02.94
Autor   nutz
battery storage *Sub*
accumulator   *Sub*
        Quelle Crabble S.191
        Definition Storage of energy in the form of potential chemical reactions, with their energy
        being recovered in the form of electricity.
        Quelle AWEA 1991
        Kontext The storage of electricity in accumulators is expensive and the battery charge is
        comparatively short-lived.
Batterie   *f.*
elektro-chemischer Speicher *m.*
Akkumulator   *m.*
        Quelle Molly S.227
        Definition Elektro-chemische Speicher sind Vorrichtungen, welche die elektrische Energie
        in Form von chemischer Energie speichern und bei Bedarf diese wieder in elektrische
        Energie umwandeln und abgeben.
        Quelle Rummich S.201
        Kontext Elektrische Energie kann direkt in Batterien gespeichert werden, wenn sie als
        Gleichstrom vorliegt.

Synonym -> Grammar

Figure 4: MultiTerm 95

3.3 Users and working environments

Besides the traditional user groups of terminology management systems, such as technical translators, interpreters, terminologists, standardisation specialists and language planners, we now find other user groups such as technical editors, experts in individual subjects, documentation specialists, information mediators and knowledge engineers at work with these systems.

The various users in these groups use terminology management systems in different organisational environments: some work on their own (e.g. as freelance translators); others are employed in an autonomous company (e.g. in a translation bureau or language service); still others may work in a department or division of a large enterprise or organisation with homogeneous information processing facilities.

A typical freelance translator offers his service in two or three languages to different customers. Very often we find a specialisation in one language direction (with the mother tongue as target language) and in only a few subject fields.

Faced with computerised terminology management, a freelance translator will try to replace his old file card system with terminology management software that runs on his personal computer and is compatible with his word processing system. Since his terminology work is often done under time pressure when he is completing a translation, only a simple terminological entry with a few data categories is filled with information. Of course, entries consisting of nothing but source and target language terms will be of little use in the future. A date to indicate the topicality of the entry, a subject field and a project or customer code are very important and can easily be added automatically. Context examples and grammatical information are useful if the target language is not the translator's mother tongue, and definitions or explanations will help him understand the concept some years on. Sources for the terms, context examples and definitions give information on the value of the data and pointers for further investigation.

The terminology management system use by a freelance translator should be able to record all the data categories in the minimal terminological entry mentioned under 3.1, although time pressure means that not all data categories in each entry will be filled with information.

A terminology management system used in a translation bureau or language service should meet all the requirements listed for freelance translators. However, since more languages, more subject fields and more people are involved, additional data categories and system features are necessary.

Since the user of the terminological information is not (always) the creator of the terminological entry, the existence of correct definitions and context examples with the corresponding sources is very important. A data category 'quality status' should indicate the value and the correctness of the information in the entry. Proper use of the terms may be indicated by data categories containing information on linguistic or geographical restrictions. The subject field classification has to be much more elaborate, since more domains are covered by a language service than by a freelance translator.

If several users are to work with the terminology management system, the software should be able to run in a multi-user environment. Besides the technical requirements for holding the terminological database on the server and the simultaneous access of different users from client computers, access rights for different user groups should be implemented. Features for importing and exporting data, and for selecting terminological entries under different criteria are necessary, particularly if external translators are involved in translation projects.

Terminology management systems used in the (language) departments of large enterprises or organisations have to meet the same requirements as systems used in language bureaus. Minor differences may be found in the subject field classification (more sophisticated for the domains of the company) and in the customer code (replaced by a project or department code). The terminology management system sometimes has to interact or to interchange data with other application programs or databases in the organisation, i.e. with a documentation system. If only for this reason, the terminology management system must run in a hardware and software environment that is compatible with the company's data processing equipment.

4. Evaluating and Selecting Terminology Management Systems

This section describes the important criteria used to evaluate terminology management systems, although this account cannot claim to be exhaustive. For certain programs and in specific application environments, other aspects may have to be considered in addition to those outlined.

The following discussion of benchmarks for evaluating terminology management systems can be used for a market analysis or a survey of existing terminology management systems, for example, as a basis for selecting and purchasing a specific program that suits a user's specific needs and work environment.

4.1 Technical aspects

The technical aspects of program evaluation for terminology management systems refer to the hardware and software environment required by a particular program. To what extent these technical features are crucial in selecting a terminology management system depends very much on the existing or planned computer equipment in any given work environment.

Most terminology management systems offered on the market run on IBM-compatible personal computers; only a few require an Apple Macintosh computer or a UNIX-based minicomputer.

From the software point of view, the type and version of the operating system under which a terminology management system runs are important when evaluating the system. This aspect is closely linked with the processor type family and, hence, with computer type (see below).

In most practical applications, the terminology management system will be used together with word processing software. Since the personal computer is designed as a single-task machine that cannot run more than one program at a time, mechanisms for quasi-multitasking are needed.

Most older terminology management systems are designed as terminate-and-stay-resident programs (TSR programs). After loading a TSR program into the main memory, the word processor is started. If the user needs to look up a term in the terminology file while working with the word processor, a hot key activates the TSR program. In TSR terminology management systems, mechanisms are programmed to transfer terms from the word processor to the terminology software and vice-versa. TSR programs can be used together with most familiar word processors that run in non-graphic mode.

Modern terminology management systems run under the graphic user interface MS-Windows, which allows different application programs to be run quasi-simultaneously in different windows. Mechanisms (DDE interface) for transferring information from one window to another window help the user cut and paste the search term from the word processor to the terminology management system, or cut and paste the target language term from the terminological entry into the translation in the word processor window.

If the terminology management system is to be used in a multi-user environment, the software should allow both the program and a common terminology database to be stored and accessed by all users on a network file server.

In addition to the software aspects to be taken into account when evaluating terminology management systems, consideration should also be given to some of the hardware features of the computer system.

The microprocessor's clock frequency, expressed in MHz, is usually an indicator of an application program's processing speed. Since programs for the management of terminology contain more commands for accessing data on the hard disk than time-consuming commands for making calculations, the access time value of the external storage device is much more important than the processor's clock frequency. Only in terminology management systems running under a graphic user interface like MS-Windows does a fast microprocessor cut the time needed to set up the screen and the time for man-machine interaction.

The capacity of the main memory, expressed in kilobytes (KB) or megabytes (MB), should be sufficient to operate the terminology management system. If the terminology management system is used in memory-resident mode, additional programs (e.g. the word processor) should also be able to fit into the main memory. For TSR terminology software, main memory capacity of 1 MB is adequate, whereas programs running under MS-Windows prefer a main memory capacity of 4 MB or more.

Hard disk capacity is needed for storing the application programs and the data files. In terminology management, data file size depends on the system-specific entry structure and the data categories involved, the expected number of entries, and the data storage architecture of the terminology management system. To evaluate a specific program, it is necessary to build up some typical terminological entries as they occur in practice and to multiply the reserved bytes of the data files by the number of entries expected in the next few years.

4.2 Terminological aspects

The most important criterion when evaluating terminology management systems is the suitability of the software for the terminology work to be undertaken. Since there are different types of terminology work, the software products available vary greatly, which may be a result of different system philosophies.

To evaluate the utility of a particular terminology management system in a specific environment, it is necessary to examine in detail whether all the required terminological and administrative data categories are supported by the system, whether the system's entry structure meets the user's (or users') requirements, and whether the system philosophy is in line with the philosophy of the user's own terminology work.

It is also important to ensure that the maximum length of the data occurring in practical terminology work can be stored in the system's data categories and that multiple data of the same type (e.g. more than one context example for one term) can be handled by the system (repeatability of data categories).

For terminology management systems with a defined set of data categories, the user-friendliness of the system can be supported by suppressing or ignoring any data categories not needed in specific applications or for specific users.

Some terminology management systems on the market include additional modules for building up and managing classification systems, concept systems or thesauri. In evaluating a program, the user has to decide whether he needs these features.

4.3 User interface aspects

The user interface of terminology management systems is assessed using the general criteria used in evaluating other kinds of user programs.

The operating manual, Help function and online tutorial will support the user in learning to operate the terminology management system or in troubleshooting and dealing with errors. Since terminology management systems are often used in a multilingual environment, the languages in which the manual, Help function and tutorial are available and the language of the user interface (commands and messages), as well as their quality, completeness and readability, should be included in the evaluation procedure.

The user can interact with the terminology management system via commands, function keys, traditional or pull-down/pop-up menus by using a keyboard or mouse. The type of interaction should be convenient for the user and should be in conformity with the form of interaction with the word processor or other programs.

The information displayed on screen (system operation and terminological entry) should be easy to read and clearly arranged. Frames, colours and screen display attributes can help here. Fixed templates for data categories and the terminological entry can support readability if the information does not have to be distributed between several screens. In addition to the terminological entry, the dictionaries selected or the subject fields, source and target language and other options (e.g. insert/overwrite mode) should be displayed on the screen. In showing a specific entry, some terminology management systems inform the user of the preceding or following alphabetical entry/entries.

One very important aspect of the user interface and the retrieval efficiency of a terminology management system is how a look-up term is input. Does the user have to type in the complete term or only the first letters? Is there the option of using wildcards for truncation or a character pattern if the term is not completely known? Can the user look up parts of a multi-word term or of a string compound? Does the software support a 'free-text search' in data categories other than in the term category (e.g. in the definition or context field)? Is it possible to restrict the look-up procedure by using filters (e.g. for subject fields)?

Closely connected with the search facility is the question of how the system responds to a term not found or to a wildcard search. Some terminology management systems merely display a message 'term not found' on screen, others automatically show the alphabetical term that matches best. After a wildcard search, a hitlist of matching terms should be presented from which the user can select the desired term.

Since in practice most terminology management systems are used along with a word processor, the various ways of selecting and transferring information must be taken into consideration. In selecting information, the data element sought can be chosen by naming the corresponding data category, by moving the cursor or marking bar to the element or by marking with the mouse. As for the type and quantity of transferable information, some terminology management systems allow only one of the target language terms to be selected, while others permit other data elements or the whole entry to be selected.

Besides the transfer of information from terminology management system to word processor, it might be useful to reverse the process, i.e. to transfer the look-up term from the word processor to the terminology management system. This feature should be included only in the evaluation procedure if the text to be translated is available in practice in a machine-readable form.

4.4 Organisational aspects

From an organisational point of view, the user must assess whether a certain terminology management system fits into his own work environment. As a general precondition all hardware and software requirements should be compatible with the existing or planned hardware and software infrastructure.

The maximum number of languages and the maximum number of dictionaries or glossaries that can be handled by a terminology management system should be greater than or at least equal to the actual number of languages and dictionaries that are to be used in practical terminology work. The maximum number of entries that can be stored in a dictionary is not as important a criterion for the evaluation. Modern terminology management systems are limited in the number of entries they can handle only by the capacity of the hard disk, or the maximum number is so high that there are no restrictions for practical work.

All the working languages to be used by the terminology management system have to be supported by the standardised alphabetical sorting function and by the correct character set. Since program developers cannot be expected to foresee all the languages that might be employed, some terminology management systems allow the user to define his own alphabetical sorting arrangements. For non-Latin character sets such as Greek or Cyrillic, additional program modules or predefined character sets are available. Modified operating systems should be used to cope with languages like Arabic, Japanese or Chinese.

If the terminology management system is to be used in a multi-user environment, the software should support a network application. This includes correct handling of a competitive writing access to the same entry by different users. From an organisational point of view, the program should allow the system administrator to define different access rights, different subsets of data categories and different screen masks for different user groups such as foreign correspondence clerks, translators or terminologists.

If an interchange of terminological data is planned with other departments or colleagues (using the same terminology management system or other data processing systems), the terminology management systems will have to allow for an import and export of data. This interchange facility should permit the user or the system administrator to define the extent, structure and layout of the data or should import or export data corresponding to an inter-change standard such as MATER (ISO 6156) or MARTIF (ISO 12200).

The interchange mechanism of a terminology management system can also be used for exporting terminological data to a word processing or a desktop publishing program (with the necessary layout tags) or for printing a dictionary or glossary. If a user decides to replace his (old) terminology management system with a new system, the interchange mechanism saves him from having to key in all the data again by hand.

Complete terminology files or dictionaries are available for some terminology management systems. These files can be accessed only by the appropriate program. The availability of such diction-aries may be a very important criterion for choosing a particular program, but it must not be forgotten that bought-in terminology is, in most cases, only a first step in a user's terminology work and does not relieve him of the effort of making his own entries.

4.5 Commercial aspects

The commercial aspects of program evaluation refer mainly to the purchase and operating costs terminology management systems. When a customer decides to buy a certain terminology manage-ment system he has to consider whether he can continue to use his present hardware (microprocessor type and hard disk capacity) and application programs (e.g. the word processor).

When the prices of different terminology management systems are compared, it is necessary to assess whether important auxil-iary tools such as import-export routines, character sets or classi-fication modules are included in the software package – and in the price – or whether they must be bought separately.

For multi-user and network environments, a multiple software li-cence for a given number of users may be cheaper and more effi-cient than buying several single copies of the program. In some cases, auxiliary programs or additional dictionaries need be bought only once. It is also possible in specific organisational environ-ments for some users to be given (only) a cheaper read-only ver-sion of the terminology management system, whereas other users need to work with the full version.

Apart from the acquisition costs, additional expenditure may be necessary for installation, service, the hot line and training courses.

The good name and the reliability of the software developer or local dealer are important evaluation criteria, but are not usually easy to assess. The number of terminology management systems already installed and the experience of other users may help indicate the quality of the software and the future support likely to be given by the developer.

Bibliography

Ahmad, Khurshid; Rogers, Margaret (1992): Terminology management: a corpus-based approach. In: Turner, R. (ed.) *Translating and the Computer 14: Quality, Standards and the Implementation of Technology*. London: ASLIB.

Ahmad, Khurshid; Rogers, Margaret; Thomas, Patricia (1987): Term Banks: A case study in knowledge representation and deployment. In: Czap, Hans; Galinski, Christian (eds.) *Terminology and Knowledge Engineering. Indeks Verlag: Franfurt/M. Selected papers from the First International Congress on Terminology and Knowledge Engineering*, Trier, FRG, 19 September -1 October 1987.

Ahmad, Khurshid; Heyer, Gerd (1995):*Final Report of the Translator's Workbench Project, April 1992 - September 1994*. ESPRIT 6005.

Arntz, Reiner; Picht, Heribert (1989): *Einführung in die Terminologiearbeit*. Hildesheim, Zürich, New York: Olms.

Auger, Pierre (1991): Terminographie et lexicographie assistées par ordinateur : état de la situation et prospectives, Actes du colloque *'Les industries de la langue, perspectives des années 1990'*, Montréal 21-24 novembre 1990, OLF-STQ, Québec.

Auger, Pierre (1994): Les outils de la terminotique: Typologie des logiciels d'aide à la terminologie et/ou d'automatisation de la chaîne de travail en terminographie. In: *Terminologies nouvelles*, 11/94, 46-52.

Blanchon, Elisabeth (1992): Choisir un logiciel de terminologie. In: *La Banque des Mots*, Numéro spécial CTN 1991, CILF, Paris.

Blanchon, Elisabeth (1994a): Logiciels de terminologie. In: *Terminometro*, No. 16, Oktobre 1994, 1-67.

Blanchon, Elisabeth (1994b): Terminological databases software: the changing market. In: *Mitteilungen für Terminologie und Wissenstransfer*, 1-2/94, 3-9.

Blatt, Achim; Freigang, Karl-Heinz; Schmitz, Klaus-Dirk; Thome, Gisela. (1985): *Computer und Übersetzen. Eine Einführung*. Hildesheim, Zürich, New York: Olms.

Budin, Gerhard; Wright, Sue Ellen (1994): Data elements in terminological entries: An empirical study. In: *Terminology*, Vol. 1(1), 1994, 41-59.

Budin, Gerhard; Wright, Sue Ellen (1996): *The Handbook of Terminology Management*. Amsterdam, Philadelphia: Benjamins.

Cabré, M. Teresa (1994): Terminologie et dictionnaires. In: *Meta*, XXXIX, 4/1994, 589-597.

Cotsowes (1990): [Conference of Translation Services of West European States. Working Party on Terminology and Documentation] *Recommendations for Terminology Work*. Bern: Swiss Federal Chancellery. (also available in German, French, Italian and Spanish).

Day, Joan M. (1990): CD-ROM. What can it offer the translator? In: Picken, Catriona (ed.) (1990): *Translating and the Computer 11*. London: Aslib, 75-78.

De Besse, Bruno; Pulitano, Donatella (1990): Les logiciels de gestion de la terminologie. In: *Terminologie et Traduction*, n°3, 1990.

Deschaetzen, Caroline (1990): Bilan des dictionnaires électroniques et gestionnaires de dictionnaires. In: *Terminologie et Traduction*, n°3, 83-94.

Deschaetzen, Caroline (1990): Outils de bureautique et de télématique pour la traduction. In: *Lebende Sprachen* 3/90.

Felber, Helmut (1984): *Terminology Manual*. Paris: UNESCO General Information Programme and UNISIST.

Fischer, Ingeborg; Freigang, Karl.-Heinz; Mayer, Felix; Reinke, Uwe (1994): *Sprachdatenverarbeitung für Übersetzer und Dolmetscher. Akten des Symposiums zum Abschluß des Saarbrücker Modellversuchs*. Universität des Saarlandes, 28.-29. September 1992. Hildesheim: Olms.

Freugang, Karl-Heinz; Mayer Felix; Schmitz Klaus-Dirk (1991): *Micro- and Minicomputer-based terminology databases in Europe. TermNet Report 1*. Wien: TermNet.

GTW (1994): [Gesellschaft für Terminologie und Wissenstransfer e.V.] *Empfehlungen für Planung und Aufbau von Terminologie-datenbanken*. GTW-Report. Saarbrücken: Fachrichtung 8.6, Universität des Saarlandes.

Henning, Jean-Michel (1985): L'évolution des logiciels de gestion terminologique. Actes du colloque '*Terminologie et technologies nouvelles*'. OLF-CGLF, Paris 9-11 décembre 1985, OLF, Québec.

Heyn, Matthias (1994): Impacts of Neural Network Technology on Computer Aided Translation. To appear in: *TAMA '94: Proceedings. Proceedings of the 3rd TermNet Symposium. Terminology in Advanced Microcomputer Applications.* Vienna, November 1994.

Hohnhold, Ingo. (1988): Der terminologische Eintrag und seine Terminologie. In: *MDÜ - Mitteilungsblatt für Übersetzer und Dolmetscher* 5/34,4-17.

Hohnhold, Ingo (1990): *Übersetzungsorientierte Terminologiearbeit*. Stuttgart: InTra.

Hvalkov, Sonja (1985): *Etude comparative des données terminologiques des banques de terminologie DANTERM, B.T.Q., EURODICAUTOM, Q.F.L. et SIEMENS*, Århus: Handels-høj-skolen i Århus.

ISO DIS 1087-2 (1994): *Terminology Work - Vocabulary, Part 2: Computational aids in terminology.*

ISO 6156 (1987): *Magnetic tape exchange format for terminological/lexicographical records (MATER).*

ISO 12200 (1996): *Terminology-Computer applications - Machine-Readable Terminology Interchange Format (MARTIF) - An SGML application.*

ISO DTR 12618 (1993): *Computational aids in terminology - Creation and use of terminological databases and text corpora.*

ISO DIS 12616 (1995): *Translation-oriented terminography.*

ISO 12620 (1996): *Terminology-Computer applications - Data categories.*

Kageura, Kyo (1994): Differences in linguistic representations of concepts in Japanese and English complex noun terms. in: *Terminology*, Vol. 1(1), 1994, 103-119.

Kugler, Marianne; Ahmad, Khurshid; Thurmair, Gregor (1995) (Eds.): *Translator's Workbench: Tools and Terminology for*

Translation and Text Processing. Research Reports ESPRIT. Berlin, Heidelberg, New York: Springer.

Mayer Felix (1990): Terminologieverwaltungssysteme für Übersetzer. In: *Lebende Sprachen* 3/90, 106-114.

Mayer, Felix (1993): Entry Models in Translation-Oriented Computer-Assisted Terminography. In: Schmitz, Klaus-Dirk (ed.)(1993): *TKE '93. Terminology and Knowledge Engineering. Proceedings of the Third International Congress on Terminology and Knowledge Engineering*, 25-27 August 1993, Cologne. Frankfurt: Indeks.

Melby, Alan (1984): Creating an environment for the translator. In: King, Margaret (Hrsg.) (1987): *Machine Translation Today: The State of the Art. Proceedings of the Third Lugano Tutorial, Lugano Switzerland*, April 2-6 1984. Edinburgh: Edinburgh University Press, 124-132.

Melby, Alan (1989): New tools for terminology management on microcomputers, Terminologie diachronique. In: *Actes du colloque organisé à Bruxelles les 25 et 26 mars 1988*, Centre de terminologie de Bruxelles, Institut libre Marie Haps, CILF, 1989.

Melby, Alan (1992): New Aspects of Terminology Management. In: *Actes de TAMA '92, Applications terminologiques et microordinateurs*, organisé par TermNet les 5 et 6 juin 1992 à Avignon, Paris, 1992.

Melby, Alan; Budin, Gerhard; Wright, Sue Ellen (1993): Terminology Interchange Format (TIF): A Tutorial. In: *TermNet News* (40), 1993, 5-64.

Mossmann, Yvan (1994): Terminologistik: Eine neue Dimension der Terminologiearbeit. In: Fischer, Ingeborg; Freigang, Karl-Heinz; Mayer, Felix; Reinke, Uwe (Hrsg.)(1994): *Akten des Symposiums zum Abschluß des Saarbrücker Modellversuchs, Universität des Saarlandes*, 28./29. September 1992. Hildesheim: Olms. 21 - 30.

Picht, Heribert; Draskau, Jennifer (1985): *Terminology: An Introduction*, Guildford (UK): University of Surrey.

Reinke, Uwe (1993a): Der Austausch terminographischer Daten. Wien: *TermNet*.

Reinke, Uwe (1993b): Towards a Standard Interchange Format for Terminographic Data. In: Schmitz, Klaus-Dirk (ed.)(1993): *TKE '93. Terminology and Knowledge Engineering. Proceedings of the Third International Congress on Terminology and Knowledge Engineering*, 25-27 August 1993, Cologne. Frankfurt: Indeks.

Reinke, Uwe (1994): Zur Leistungsfähigkeit integrierter Übersetzungssysteme. In: *Lebende Sprachen* 3/94, 97-104.

Rondeau, Guy (1979): Les banques de terminologie bilingues et multilingues: état de la question. In: *META* XXIV, 2, 253-263.

Sager, Juan C. (1990): *A practical course in terminology processing*. Amsterdam, Philadelphia: Benjamins.

Sager; Juan C. (1994): *Language Engineering and Translation: Consequences of automation*. Amsterdam, Philadelphia: Benjamins.

Schmitz, Peter A. (1994): Translationsorientierte Terminographie auf dem PC - Ein neuer Weg von der Terminologiedatenbank zum Fachwörterbuch. In: Fischer, Ingeborg; Freigang, Karl-Heinz; Mayer, Felix; Reinke, Uwe (Hrsg.)(1994): *Akten des Symposiums zum Abschluß des Saarbrücker Modellversuchs, Universität des Saarlandes*, 28./29. September 1992. Hildesheim: Olms. 31-62.

Schmitz, Klaus-Dirk (1990): Rechnergestützte Terminologieverwaltung am Übersetzerarbeitplatz, *Terminologie et Traduction*, n°3, 1990, 7-23.

Schmitz, Klaus-Dirk (1992): Guidelines for the Design and Implementation of Terminological Data Banks. In: *Actes de TAMA '92, Applications terminologiques et microordinateurs*, organisé par TermNet les 5 et 6 juin 1992 à Avignon, Paris, 1992.

Schmitz, Klaus-Dirk (1993): Rechnergestützte Terminologieverwaltung in der Praxis. In: Bundesverband der Übersetzer und Dolmetscher (Hrsg.) (1994): *Das berufliche Umfeld des Dolmetschers und Übersetzers - aus der Praxis für die Praxis*. Tagungsakte des Kongresses vom 23. - 25. April 1993. Bonn: BDÜ.

Schmitz, Klaus-Dirk (1994a): Interaktionsarten bei
  Terminologieverwaltungssystemen. In: Fischer, Ingeborg;
  Freigang, Karl-Heinz; Mayer, Felix; Reinke, Uwe
  (Hrsg.)(1994): *Akten des Symposiums zum Abschluß des
  Saarbrücker Modellversuchs, Universität des Saarlandes,*
  28./29. September 1992. Hildesheim: Olms. 109-132.

Schmitz, Klaus-Dirk (1994b): Verarbeitung fachsprachlichen
  Wissens in Termino-logie verwaltungssystemen. In: Spillner,
  Bernd (Hg.) (1994): *Fachkommunikation. Kongreßbeiträge
  zur 24. Jahrestagung der Gesellschaft für Angewandte
  Linguistik GAL* e. V. Frankfurt/Main: Lang.

Schmitz, Klaus-Dirk (1994c): Überlegungen zum Einsatz und zur
  Evaluierung von Terminologieveraltungssystemen. In:
  Lebende Sprachen. 4/94, 145-149.

Schmitz, Klaus-Dirk (1994d): Sprachliche Einheiten und deren
  Behandlung in Terminologieverwaltungssystemen. In:
  Grinstad, Annelise; Bodil Nistrup Madsen (Hg.)(1994):
  *Festskrift til Gert Engel i anledning af hans 70 års
  fødselsdag.* Handelshøjskole Syd.

Schmitz, Klaus-Dirk (1995): *Computational aids in terminology -
  Creation and use of terminological databases and text
  corpora* (Draft), ISO/TR 12618, DIN-NAT 5, Nr. 5-95.

Schütz, Jörg (1994): *Terminological Knowledge in Multilingual
  Language Processing.* Luxembourg: Office for Official
  Publications of the European Communities.

Stoll, Cay-Holger (1989): A concept-oriented approach to terminology work on PC. In: *META* 34, 3/89, 615-628.

Termnet (1993): *Proceedings of the 2nd TermNet Symposium
  'Terminology in Advanced Microcomputer Applications -
  TAMA'92',* Avignon, 5 - 6 June 1992. Vienna: TermNet.

Verhaest, Frank (1990): Evaluation de cinq gestionnaires de
  glossaires, *Actes du colloque 'Les industries de la langue.
  Perspective des années 1990,* Montréal 21-24 novembre
  1990, OLF-STQ, Québec, 1991.

Wright, Sue Ellen (1993): Special Problems in the Exchange of
  Terminological Data. In: Schmitz, Klaus-Dirk (ed.)(1993):
  TKE '93. Terminology and Knowledge Engineering. Pro-

ceedings of the Third International Congress on Terminology and Knowledge Engineering, 25-27 August 1993, Cologne. Frankfurt: Indeks.

Wright, Sue Ellen (1994): Das Terminologie-Austausch-Format (TIF). In: Arntz, Reiner; Mayer, Felix; Reisen, Ursula (Hrsg.)(1994): *Terminologie als Produktivitätsfaktor in volkswirtschaftlicher und betriebswirtschaftlicher Sicht. Akten des Symposions*, Köln, 15.-16. April 1994.

12. Machine Translation

HAROLD SOMERS AND CLARE RUTZLER

Introduction

For many years now, computers that can interact perfectly with humans, and which are in many ways superior to humans, have had a leading role in science fiction. They can speak in any languages human or alien and have encyclopaedic knowledge of any topic one cares to name. The important point is, however, that this *is* science fiction. The reality, especially concerning translation and interpreting, is quite different.

This article concerns the use of computers in translation, and will cover not only systems aiming to produce translations essentially without help from a human – Machine Translation proper, henceforth MT – but also systems for use by a translator, so-called Computer-Aided Translation (CAT). Although for the most part we will be concerned with the translation of written text, we will also mention briefly current progress towards MT systems dealing with speech translation.

When computers were first invented, it was assumed that these 'electronic brains' would eventually be able to simulate perfectly human behaviour, and even outperform humans at certain tasks, including translation. In the eyes of non-linguists particularly, it was assumed that language translation would be one of the first non-numeric applications of computers to be perfected. Thus, the promise of Fully Automatic High Quality Translation 'FAHQT' came into being. The exciting possibilities brought about by the advent of the computer conjured up dreams of machines which would churn out pages and pages of perfect translation per day. It soon became obvious that this was not to be.

Early History

Like the invention of television, numerous names have been associated with the idea of using computers to perform translations including Georges Artsrouni and Petr Smirnov-Troyanski, who both independently took out patents in 1933, and Alan Turing, among war-time computer scientists, but the founding father is generally agreed to be Warren Weaver whose discussions with colleagues in the immediate post-war period led to him sending a memorandum in 1949, reprinted in Locke & Booth 1955, to some 200 of his colleagues. This is acknowledged as the launch of MT research in the United States (see Hutchins 1986:pp.24-30). Although Weaver's original idea to use some of the techniques of code-breaking proved unproductive, the general idea was seen as a worthwhile goal, and soon attracted government funding, at least in the USA. In 1951, Yehoshua Bar-Hillel became the first full-time MT researcher. A year later MIT hosted an international conference. A Russian – English system developed jointly by IBM and Georgetown University was demonstrated in 1954. A dedicated journal appeared, and work began in other countries, notably the UK, USSR and Japan. The next ten years saw worldwide activity, led by the USA, which invested $20 million in MT research.

There were numerous groups conducting research in MT from the mid-1950s onwards and two basic approaches were adopted. Some groups took a 'brute force' approach and based their work on the assumption that it was desirable, and indeed necessary, to come up with a working system as soon as possible, in order to take advantage of the enthusiasm which reigned at that time. They saw word-for-word translation systems as an adequate starting point which could be improved upon using feedback from the output. The basic need was for larger computer storage and it was not felt necessary to solve all the foreseeable problems before trying to develop a system. Unfortunately, it was on the basis of this enthusiasm that hopes of a fully automatic system in the short term grew rapidly. Other research groups preferred to take a slower, deeper, 'perfectionist' approach, basing their research on linguistic issues, trying to take the human thought processes into account. They could be thought of as the early pioneers of Artificial Intelligence. But their approach was equally hampered by the limitations of the computer technology of the time.

Despite all this enthusiasm, however, major problems began to appear. The trouble was that computing technology was at that time so underdeveloped that the subject was essentially theoretical and no one had envisaged the practical difficulties that solving these problems would entail: after all, MT brings together the complexities of natural language and the simplicity of computational power which sees language as little more than apparently meaningless strings of characters.

The major problem for early MT research was the lack of co-operation between experts in the two domains involved, namely linguistics and computer science. Translators and linguists have traditionally had a fear of all things computational and they considered it impossible to define language in a manner rigid enough to produce good translation. The computer scientists, on the other hand, had no linguistic training, and lacked an understanding of the intricacies of language: they believed that MT was primarily a mathematical problem. This gap between the two camps, and to some extent the mistrust that existed between them, lay at the heart of MT's shaky and in many ways disastrous entry into the world.

Overawed by the new computing technology and unaware of the difficulties of natural language processing, the early fathers of MT extravagantly proclaimed the advent of 'automatic translation'. These claims soon became known even outside the field of MT research and the pressure to produce a fully automatic system grew rapidly. A lot of money had been invested in MT and the Cold War brought with it the need for a large amount of translation from Russian to English. This was the language pair most often experimented with in the early stages. As time went on, it became apparent that original assumptions were simplistic and the early promises unrealistic. Gradually a deeper understanding of the global problems began to emerge and with it the prospect of producing the desired system declined. Disquiet among the investors began to grow and a report on the state of play was commissioned by the main funders, the US Government.

The now infamous 1966 ALPAC report was hugely critical of MT as a whole, concluding that MT was more expensive, slower and less accurate than human translation, and that there was no long-term or eventual prospect of usable MT. The conclusions of the

ALPAC report were seen by many to be unduly critical, and the report's authors were accused of ignoring favourable results and being biased towards out-of-date results which showed MT in a bad light, e.g. Pankowicz, quoted in Josselson 1971. Nevertheless, it is significant that of the two MT researchers on the committee, neither believed that research should continue as it was, and that the emphasis should be rather shifted to Computational Linguistics CL. Neither of the MT specialists believed in the continuation of MT research as such; at RAND Corporation for example, the emphasis had shifted since the early 1960s towards basic research in (CL). The two linguists on the committee did not believe in trying to formalise language. It is evident, then, that even before the tests began, MT had a huge mountain to climb in trying to prove its worth. The ALPAC report may have convinced most people outside the field that MT had no hope of success but many on the inside saw the report as short-sighted and narrow-minded. They had already realised many of the problems of automating the translation process, (e.g. Bar-Hillel 1951, Locke & Booth 1955, Yngve 1957) and did not accept that MT was doomed to failure forever. However, funds were no longer available and many MT research projects came to a halt.

Even if early approaches had been naive, it had certainly been recognized long before the ALPAC committee began their work that translation was a complex task. Researchers had already come to the conclusion that MT was always going to be dogged by what Yngve called 'the semantic problem', and which Bar-Hillel 1960 characterised with the following famous example: consider the word *pen* in:

1. Johnny was looking for his toy box. Finally he found it. The box was in the pen. Johnny was very happy.

We have to understand that this must be the 'playpen' meaning of *pen* since the 'writing implement' meaning does not make sense in the 'real world'. Bar-Hillel believed that this need for real-world knowledge would arise time and time again in translation: a computer would effectively need to be able to 'understand' the text it was translating. He quickly realised that the kind of knowledge brought to bear by humans when performing translation tasks of this nature was simply beyond any imaginable computer. He therefore concluded that FAHQT was simply impossible and he had already said so fifteen years before the ALPAC report came to the same conclusion – (Bar-Hillel) 1951. Unlike the ALPAC report, however, he did see a future for MT, as long as humans were somehow involved collaboratively in the process.

The Semantic Barrier

In fact, the 'semantic barrier' is in reality a linguistic barrier, since the kinds of problems that would apparently require the machine to understand the input result from a variety of linguistic situations. One word sums up the problem in general: 'ambiguity'. Broadly, ambiguity problems can be divided between lexical and structural in one 'dimension', and between monolingual and translational in another.

Lexical ambiguity

Lexical ambiguity arises from the fact that a single word can have more than one interpretation, and hence more than one translation. This is true from a monolingual perspective because morphology can be ambiguous (e.g. does *drier* mean 'more dry' or 'machine which dries'?) or because words can represent different parts of speech *(round* can be a noun, or a verb, or an adjective, or an adverb, or a preposition), or because words can have multiple meanings (e.g. *bank* 'financial institution' or 'side of a river'). All of the above have an impact on translation, but in addition languages differ hugely in the way in which words correspond to concepts in the real world: for example, the English word *leg* corresponds to French *jambe*, *patte* or *pied*, depending on whose leg it is. German has two words for 'eat', distinguishing human eating, *essen,* from animals performing the same activity, *fressen.* Spanish has only one word, *paloma,* for the birds distinguished in English as *doves* and *pigeons*. Examples like this are extremely widespread, and not difficult to find. These are problems which are not entirely unfamiliar to human translators, but they represent a particular difficulty for MT since computers often lack the necessary global understanding of the context to make the correct decision regarding their translation. Sometimes the solution is relatively easy: depending on the subject matter of the text, for example, one or other reading of an ambiguous word may be more likely e.g. *rail* as a type of bird or metal track that trains run on. Alternatively, neighbouring words may give a clue. Consider the word *ball* which can indicate a spherical object or a dancing event. The correct interpretation is easy to get in sentences like 2 and 3, since the verb *roll* requires a spherical object as its grammatical subject, and *last* requires a durative event as its subject.

2. The ball rolled down the hill.

3. The ball lasted until midnight.

But consider the verb *hold* which means 'grasp' when its grammatical object is a physical object, but means 'organize' when its object indicates an event. So the two words *hold* and *ball* are both ambiguous in the sentence fragment 4.

4. When you hold a ball ....

Structural ambiguity

Structural ambiguity is perhaps a slightly more subtle problem. This arises when the combined lexical ambiguity of the words making up a sentence mean that it has several interpretations. It is rather rare to find such examples in real life, as the context will usually determine whether, in a sentence like 5, we are talking about permission to partake of a hobby or work in a canning factory.

5. They can fish.

However, for the computer, such problems can be quite common. More common are so-called 'attachment ambiguities' such as 6, where some knowledge of the scientific domain is needed to know whether *thermal emission* is used for analysis or for investigation, a distinction that may have to be made explicit in the translation.

6. Investigation of techniques of stress analysis by thermal emission.

Often-quoted further examples include 7, the potentially three-way ambiguous 8, and the perennial 9.

7. Visiting relatives can be boring.

8. Time flies like an arrow.

9. The man saw the girl with a telescope.

While these are truly ambiguous for a computer without access to contextual knowledge, consider the very similar sentences 10-12, which are unambiguous to a human, but could present the same sort of ambiguity problem to a computer lacking the relevant linguistic knowledge.

10. Visiting hospitals can be boring.
11. Blow flies like a banana.
12. The man saw the girl with a hat.

Different levels of ambiguity

Structural ambiguities such as those illustrated above can be further classified according to the 'range' of the ambiguity they represent. 'Local ambiguities' are the most superficial and, accordingly, often the easiest to deal with in translation, for example because they persist in the target language. The attachment ambiguities already illustrated in 6, 9 and 12 are examples of this, where the ambiguity lies not in the words themselves but in their juxtaposition. Further examples 13 and 14 show this more clearly.

13a. Did you read the story about the aircrash in the jungle?
  b. Did you read the story about the aircrash in the paper?
14. John mentioned the book I sent to Susan.

This can be contrasted with 'global' ambiguity caused by combinations of part-of-speech ambiguities: different analyses involve different part-of-speech choices and hence radically different translations, as in 15 and 16.

15. He noticed her shaking hands, i.e. 'her hands were shaking' or 'she was shaking hands with people'
16. I like swimming, i.e. to do or to watch.

A further categorization of ambiguity reflects the 'depth' at which the ambiguity arises. For example, the two sentences in 17 have a similar 'surface structure', but at a deeper level differ in that John is the implied subject of *please* in 17a, but its object in 17b. Compare 18 which is truly ambiguous in this respect.

17 a. John is eager to please.
  b. John is easy to please.
18. The chicken is ready to eat.

Example 19 provides us with another subtle ambiguity of this type: to see that it is ambiguous, compare the sentences in 20, and consider a language which distinguishes the different interpretations in case-marking, as in Finnish, or in the choice of the verb, as in German.

19. John painted the house.

20 a. John painted the window frame.

   b. John painted the panorama.

   c. John painted the canvas.

   d. Da Vinci painted the Mona Lisa.

As a final example, consider the examples in 21-22, which illustrate the problem of 'anaphora resolution', that is, identification of antecedents of pronouns. In translating into a language where pronouns reflect grammatical differences, this is an important, but difficult, task for the computer. Consider what background information you, as a human, use to make the correct interpretation.

21 a. The monkey ate the banana because it was hungry.

   b. The monkey ate the banana because it was ripe.

   c. The monkey ate the banana because it was tea-time.

22 a. The soldiers shot at the women, and some of them fell.

   b. The soldiers shot at the women, and some of them missed.

Solutions to the Problem of Ambiguity

Many of the problems described in the previous section were recognised very early on by the MT pioneers. Of the possible solutions suggested, some remain popular to this day, while others have been superseded.

The earliest approach, inspired by work on 'Information Theory' by Shannon & Weaver 1949 involved using statistical methods to take account of the context. Lexical ambiguities would be interpreted one way or another depending on the surrounding words. This was typically implemented in a fairly crude way. For example, faced with a word which could either be a noun or a verb (of which there are many such words in English), one technique would be to look to see if the preceding word was an article *a* or the *A* similar technique might be evolved for translational ambiguities. For structural ambiguities, the program would look at longer sequences of parts of speech, and identify which was the more probable. While such techniques are often effective, in the sense that they deliver the right answer, they do not contribute to the notion of having the computer simulate understanding of the text in any sense.

Recognising these limitations, researchers soon hit on the idea of involving a human user to help prepare the input for translation (pre-editing) or tidy up the output after the system has done its best (post-editing). It was also recognised that limiting the scope and domain of the texts to be given to the system could result in better translations. All these ideas, which we shall look at in more detail below, and which are now commonly referred to by vendors of commercial MT software, were proposed way back in the early days of MT research.

Perhaps a more significant solution to these problems, however, was the incorporation of more sophisticated techniques of analysing the text to be translated, using methods proposed by linguists, and making use of linguistic theory coupled with more elaborate computer programs. Inasmuch as this approach distinguishes the early research in MT from much of the work done in the 1970s and 1980s, systems developed with these techniques are known as 'second generation systems'. We shall look in more detail below at the important features of these systems. It is interesting to note, however, that the vast majority of commercial MT systems now available owe much more in basic design to the techniques first suggested almost 50 years ago, even if in computational and software terms the similarities are almost invisible.

MT: The User's Perspective

As just mentioned, there has been a shift in emphasis from fully automatic translation towards the reduced aim of computer-assisted or-aided translation (CAT). We can distinguish broadly between two types of CAT: in one, we have the use of partially automated computer tools by the human translator, which we can call 'machine-aided human translation' (MAHT). The word processor is the most obvious tool now essential to almost all translators (assuming that the target language uses an alphabet for which word-processing tools have been developed). Texts can be received and delivered over a computer network or in machine-readable form on diskettes, and translations can be stored for future reference without filling endless filing cabinets with paper. On-line dictionaries, grammar and spelling checkers, an increasing number of terminological databanks and other automated specialised information sources have dramatically increased the speed and efficiency with which human translators can work.

The second type of CAT is where it is essentially the computer which performs the translation, though still under the control of the human user, who may or may not be a translator. This involves stages of contribution by the human to the process of translation, either before or after the machine has done what it can, or interactively during the translation process.

As soon as we start thinking about the relationship between a system and its users, we must consider the different profiles of possible users of a CAT system. The obvious one is perhaps the translator looking for a way to speed up the translation process. But equally valid is the scenario where the user may be the person who actually wants to make use of the translated document, for example a scientist who has been sent a technical article in Russian or Japanese, and wants to know roughly what it is about, to see whether and which parts of it need translating 'properly'. Alternatively, the user might be the original author of a document, who wants to send a translation of it to someone in another country. Under certain circumstances, the document may be of a sufficiently stereo typed nature (for example, certain types of business letter, or a price list) that this work could be done by a system without the need for a human who knows the target language to check the output, as long as the recipient is warned that he or she is receiving 'unrevised machine translation output'.

In this latter case, we would want to be sure the text that the system got to translate 'unsupervised' was so straightforward that the system would not make any serious mistakes. There are two ways to do this: one involves 'restricted input', the other 'sublanguage'. Both may involve the user in 'pre-editing'.

Restricted input

Restricted input systems, as the name suggests, operate on the understanding that the texts they are asked to translate will be constrained in some way, notably avoiding words or constructions that the system will not be able to translate. Computationally, it is relatively easy to check whether a text contains any 'unknown' words, and not much more difficult to ascertain whether the sentences can be 'parsed' by the system, that is to say, that the structure can be recognized. If unknown words or 'illegal' structures are detected, the user can then be asked to correct them, perhaps with reference to a style manual. Although at first sight there might be a negative reaction to this idea of a computer dictating what a writer can or cannot write, it should be pointed out that technical writers are quite used to the idea of pre- and proscribed vocabulary and style. The notion of 'artificial languages' may be familiar to some readers cf. Sager 1993, p.32ff – though the term can be confusing since it is also sometimes used to describe formal codes such as programming 'languages'. Many users of current, and earlier commercial MT systems have reported tremendous success with the idea of restricted input (Elliston 1979, Pym 1990, Newton 1992, and others). Notably, it has been reported that having texts written according to a style-sheet that permitted them to be machine translated actually led to an improvement in readability and style of the original text from the point of view of end-users (Lawson 1979, p.81f). Certainly, the idea of a restricted subset of Basic English for consumption by non-native readers predates Machine Translation (see Arnold et al. 1994, p.156ff for further discussion).

Closely related to the notion of restricted input is the so-called sublanguage approach. 'Sublanguage' is a term which was introduced by researchers working in Canada, notably on the Météo system which translates weather bulletins (Kittredge & Lehrberger 1982). The notion will be familiar to readers under different names such as 'register', 'LSP' and so on. The idea is that for certain text-types and subject domains, the language used is naturally restricted in vocabulary and structures. It is fairly clear that the words used in a particular text will reflect the subject matter of the text: the term 'jargon' is often used disparagingly though it is also a useful technical term for linguists. If an MT system can recognise the subject matter of a text, then many possible lexical ambiguities may be resolved. Put another way, the lexicon for a sublanguage system can be greatly reduced in size, since many words, or alternative meanings and translations of words, can simply be omitted.

What is perhaps less obvious is that the same applies to the syntactic constructions found. For example, instruction manuals will typically contain many imperatives and simple declarative sentences. A legal contract may contain many conditional and hypothetical verb tenses. The often recurring and – of more interest – absent constructions for a given sublanguage mean that the grammars used by the system can be simplified, and again potential ambiguities can be reduced or eliminated. So sublanguages are usually defined in terms of their specialised vocabulary and the range of constructions used. This may or may not be done with reference to some notion of a 'general' grammar of the language, since it is to be noted that many sublanguages permit constructions that in another context would actually be regarded as ungrammatical. For example, in medical reports, the verb *present* is used intransitively to describe symptoms as in 23: a construction that would sound odd under other circumstances. Similarly, sentences in weather bulletins often lack a tensed main verb, as in 24.

23. The patient presented with a sore throat.

24. Clear now, becoming cloudy later.

The sublanguage approach recognizes that certain sublanguages, for example that 'sublanguage of weather bulletins', 'stock market reports' and 'instruction manuals' have the natural lexical and syntactic restrictions that will make MT easier, and more reliable. It is also recognized that some sublanguages actually make MT harder. For example, some legal texts, such as patents, contain syntactic constructions that are in fact much more complex than everyday language, because helpful punctuation is generally omitted, which makes them less amenable to translation by machine. Telexes, similarly, with their ellipses and generally 'telegraphic' style introduce more ambiguities as compared to the 'standard' language. A further point of interest, especially to researchers, is the extent to which corresponding sublanguages across languages share syntactic features or not. It has been claimed by Kittredge 1982, that the grammars of corresponding sublanguages have more in common across language pairs than with other sublanguages of the 'parent' language; that is to say, notwithstanding the obvious lexical differences, the sublanguages of English and French instruction manuals are more similar than the English sublanguages of, say, stock market reports and holiday travel brochures. This point is of course somewhat debatable, and certainly some parallel sublanguages are quite strikingly different, cooking recipes, knitting instructions and some kinds of job ad, for example.

The sublanguage and restricted input approaches are very similar then, in that they rely on the fact that the potential complexity of the source texts is controlled. Perhaps the key difference between the two and one which makes, for some observers, one approach acceptable where the other is not is the *source* of the restrictions. In sublanguage systems, the restrictions occur naturally, since a sublanguage is defined by Sager et al. 1980 as "semi-autonomous, complex semiotic systems based on and derived from general language [whose] use presupposes special education and is restricted to communication among specialists in the same or closely related fields," , and it "reflects the usage of some 'community' of speakers, who are normally linked by some common knowledge about the domain which goes beyond the common knowledge of speakers of the standard language" according to Kittredge 1985. Sublanguage MT systems are designed to handle the special structures found in the already existing sublanguages. We can contrast this with restricted input systems, where the restrictions often arise from the perceived shortcomings of some existing MT system. The fact that the resulting controlled language may turn out to be more appropriate to the community of end-users is a happy accident which should not hide the fact that it is the MT system which defines the 'sublanguage' and not vice versa.

Pre-editing

Whatever the source of the restrictions on the system, it is usually necessary for there to be some check that the source text actually adheres to the restrictions. In the case of a sublanguage system, it may be hoped that this will happen naturally, though most sublanguage texts are 'noisy' to some degree or other, for example, when the weather report includes friendly comment such as 25:

25. ... so you'd better take your umbrellas, folks.

Certainly in the case of artificially imposed restrictions, a phase of preprocessing is normally needed, during which the source text is made to conform to the expected input norms of the system.

This preprocessing is called 'pre-editing', and it may be carried out essentially manually (in much the same way that an editor prepares an article or book before publication), or the system itself may be able to assist, by pointing out possible deviations from the agreed restrictions, as mentioned above. This may be in a kind of 'submit-and-return' system where the text is given to the system and comes back with inappropriate vocabulary and constructions highlighted. Or the system may have an interactive pre-editing facility where the user, or rather the pre-editor, and the system work through the text together. The system may even be able to suggest corrections itself, on the basis of its 'self-knowledge' about the vocabulary and grammar it 'knows' how to handle.

Post-editing

The other side of the human-assisted MT coin is post-editing, where a human user takes the results of the MT process and corrects or generally tidies them up ready for the end-user. Several points need to be made about this process. The first is one that is often ignored by critics of MT who fail to point out that most human translation is subject to revision, so the need to revise MT output should not necessarily be seen as an added cost. Indeed there is even evidence that revising MT output is in some senses easier than revising human translations, notably from the point of view of 'peer sensitivity'. Many observers report increased productivity e.g. Magnusson-Murray 1985, though there have been some dissenting voices e.g. Wagner 1985, though these come mostly from translators who have been diverted from the task of translating to the, for them, more limiting task of post-editing.

This brings us to the second point, which is the question of what the profile of the post-editor should be. As just mentioned, involving translators in the task of post-editing is not necessarily the most effective way to use MT, since in many cases – for example where the 'raw' MT output is really quite poor quality – the translators may really become resentful of the fact that they could have produced a better translation from scratch. Furthermore, the skills

needed for post-editing MT output are different from those of translators and even of revisors of human translations (cf. Vasconcellos
1986): the types of errors that need to be corrected are quite different from those made by a human translator, which will, one
hopes, primarily be questions of style. An MT system may well
make quite banal errors, of grammatical agreement, for example,
or choice of tense, which a native speaker simply would not produce, unless because of a typographic or cut-and-paste error. Depending on the exact scenario, one can envisage post-editing as a
separate task in its own right, requiring different training and skills,
not least of which would be some understanding of how the MT
system itself works and thus what the possible cause of some error
might be. Certainly, under some circumstances, one could leave
the task of post-editing to the end-user, which brings us neatly to
the third point.

The amount of correction that needs to be done to the output from
an MT system will crucially depend on the end use to which that
text is to be put. One of the major advantages claimed for MT is
that it can provide a rough and ready translation, a 'gist', of a text
which would otherwise have been completely inaccessible to the
end-users (for example, because it is written in a foreign script)
and from which they can identify whether the text needs to be
translated 'properly', and if so, which parts of it in particular. End
users, as domain experts, may be able to understand a low quality
translation despite perhaps quite damaging translation errors (for
example, a misplaced negative), simply because they know the
field well enough to 'second guess' what the original author was
probably trying to say. It has been reported (Martin Kay, personal
communication) that early users of the Systran MT system which
was used by the US Air Force to translate documents from Russian into English got used to the kind of slavicised English that the
system produced, claiming that it was 'more accurate' than the
results of post-editing by translators who were not domain experts, a finding backed up by other evaluations of (Systran van
Slype 1979, Bostad 1986), Habermann 1986 and other systems,
(e.g. Sinaiko & Clare 1972) who found that mechanics' quality
ratings of technical translations were consistently higher than translators'.

Interactive systems

While pre- and post-editing involve a human working on the translation either before or after the MT system has done its work, another possibility is that the user collaborates with the system at run-time in what is generally called 'interactive mode'. Interactive systems pause to ask the user to help them make linguistic decisions while the program is running. This might be the case where the source text has an unknown word (the user is asked to check its spelling and provide some grammatical information both about the source word and its translation), a lexical or syntactic ambiguity (the system cannot find sufficient criteria to make a choice, so consults the user), or a choice of target translation, again either lexical or syntactic.

Some modern commercial systems have a choice of interactive or default translation. In the latter case, the system will make all the choices for itself, perhaps arbitrarily, or based on some 'best guess'. For example, in the case of attachment ambiguity, as illustrated above, a good guess, in the absence of any other indications, based on general frequency in English, is to attach to the nearest noun, e.g. 26, though of course sometimes this will give a false interpretation as in 27:

26 a. percentage of children educated privately

　　b. decoration of rooms with no windows

27. total number of delegates broken down by sex.

One obvious problem with interactive systems is that the interactions slow down the translation process. In particular, there is evidence that users quickly tire of continued interactions requesting the most banal information or repeatedly asking the same question (e.g. Seal 1992): 'over-interaction' can lead to user alienation.

Another problem is the profile of the user that is implied by an interactive system: the program seeks help in understanding the source text, so it cannot be used by someone who knows only the target language, i.e. the end-user who wants to read the text; similarly, it asks questions about the style or syntax of the target text, so it cannot be used by someone who doesn't know the target language, for example someone writing a business letter to an overseas client; in fact, it also asks for decisions about the relation between the source and target language, how to translate an unknown word and so on, so the ideal user is probably a translator. And typically translators feel that they could probably do a better job more quickly without the intermediary of the system at all.

Two solutions to this problem offer themselves. The first is to give more control to the translator-as-user, inviting them to decide on a case-by-case basis whether to translate portions of the text manually, interactively, or automatically with post-editing (cf. Somers et al. 1990). Certainly the latter two options will save the user a certain amount of typing at the very least, and the idea is that as the user gets to know the system, they will learn how well it is likely to translate a given portion of text, which might be a whole paragraph, a sentence, or even a smaller stretch of text, and be able to decide on the quickest way to deal with it.

The second solution is to allow the system to 'learn' from its experience, and 'remember' the corrections that the user suggested. Some systems have even been designed (e.g. Nishida & Takamatsu 1990) so that they can 'learn' new translation rules and patterns from user's interactions or from a record of post-editing changes.

Translator's workbench

It has been suggested that all of the functions described above could be combined into a flexible package for translators, often called a 'Translator's Workbench'. This idea seems to have been first suggested by Martin Kay in his now much-cited 1980 research manuscript; Melby 1982 describes a similar idea. Running on a personal computer, possibly linked by a network to a more powerful mainframe computer, the idea is that the translator can have access on-line to terminological resources, dictionaries and other reference materials, as well as full or human-aided translation software. For output, spelling and grammar checkers as well as desk-top publishing packages for re-formatting the finished work would all be available at the click of a button. For texts not already in machine-readable form, a scanner should be attached to the system. One function that should be mentioned particularly is to access previously translated texts on similar topics in what has come to be called a 'Translation Memory'. The origin of this very simple idea is somewhat obscure – the 'bilingual concordance' mentioned by Kjærsgaard 1987 is an early relevant proposal, as is Harris's 1988 notion of 'bi-texts'. The idea, in relation to MT, is that when translating a new piece of text (a sentence, for example) it is useful to have at one's fingertips examples of similar sentences and their translations. This allows the translator to ensure consistency of terminology and phraseology, and also, in the case of an exact match, to turn translation into a simple cut-and-paste editing job! A somewhat inflexible version of this tool was included in the ALPSystems MT software in the mid-1980s (see Weaver 1988), though more recent work on flexible pattern-matching, as well as highly efficient storage and retrieval techniques have made this kind of tool potentially much more useful (cf. van Hoof et al. 1995).

Use of Linguistic Techniques

Although some users found the output from early, essentially word-for-word, systems satisfactory, it clearly was not ideal. The rather crude reordering techniques of early systems, often a simple inversion of words, were obviously inadequate. From around 1960, syntax was the main thrust of MT research, to be incorporated into a predominantly direct translation system. Much research was carried out to formalize the rules which lay behind inherent human knowledge of sentence structure, identifying the grammatical categories (noun, verb, etc.) of strings and grouping them together (noun phrase, verb phrase, etc.). The result of syntactic analysis in MT is often represented by a linguistic parse tree, or phrase-structure tree. Besides coding morphological information, these representations will generally include identification of subjects, objects, complements and heads, resulting from syntactic analysis.

The transformational grammar of Noam Chomsky was particularly influential in early research in this field, though it was not developed with MT specifically in mind. It argued that many of the syntactic differences between languages are in fact superficial, and that there is an underlying deep structure which is the same for all languages. If this is so, analysing a source language string will produce a representation which is language-independent, the so-called 'interlingua', from which the target language string could be directly generated. Alternatively, and more realistically, the source-text analysis could be expected to go just so far in eliminating trivial source-language idiosyncrasies, resulting in an intermediate representation that encoded the basic syntactic relationships underlying the string, though still reflecting the nature of the source language: so for example, subject and object relationships would be maintained. There would then need to be some kind of 'transfer' stage which would convert the source-language dependent representation into the corresponding target-language deep structure, preserving the meaning, but changing, if necessary, the syntactic relations. For example, to translate 28a into German requires a structure where the English subject *he* becomes the German indirect object, while the object *the film* becomes the subject of the German sentence 28b. The pros and cons of these two approaches are discussed below.

28 a. He liked the film.

    b. Der Film gefiel ihm.

It quickly becomes apparent that syntactic analysis alone is also not sufficient to translate all text types successfully. The question of ambiguity poses a difficult problem, some aspects of which still have not been solved. As mentioned above, ambiguity can occur at the lexical level, or a whole sentence can be ambiguous. Some types of ambiguity can be resolved by syntactic analysis, but often more subtle techniques are required. Humans have the ability to refer to the context and even to their own abstract general knowledge and common sense to find the correct interpretation. A computer does not implicitly have this capability and this knowledge must be made explicit in order for it to be exploited. The field of semantics is important for correct interpretation and much research continues into how best to encode this knowledge. Semantic restrictions are often used to limit the possibilities of word combination. For example, a verb such as *eat* normally takes an animate subject and an edible object, but of course this information, about animacy and edibility, must be encoded somewhere in the system.

Nevertheless the problem of accessing contextual, pragmatic and real-world knowledge remains a big one. This knowledge undoubt edly contributes to human understanding of language strings, but in an MT system it is not obvious how to go about extracting the appropriate knowledge from the context, or representing in a convenient accessible and efficient manner all the possible knowledge about the real world that a human translator might use to resolve an ambiguity, problem. It should be noted that a huge percentage of potential ambiguities are simply not noticed by humans because of the ease with which they can access this knowledge.

Basic design features

The incorporation of more sophisticated linguistic, and computational, techniques led in the 1970s and 1980s to the development of the so-called 'second generation' of MT design, characterised in particular by the 'indirect' approach to translation, in which the source text is transformed into the corresponding target text via an intermediate representation. This may purport to be a representation of the meaning of the text, or else, rather less ambitiously, a representation of the syntactic structure of the text. A further distinction is the transfer-interlingua issue already mentioned. The difference between the two approaches is illustrated by the well-known 'pyramid' diagram Figure 1, probably first used by Vauquois 1968: the deeper the analysis, the less transfer is needed, the ideal case being the interlingua approach where there is no transfer at all.

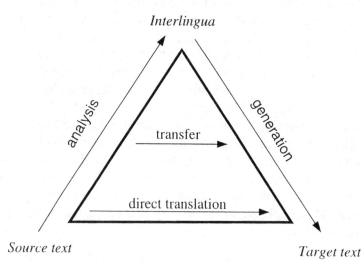

Figure 1. The 'pyramid' diagram

The interlingua approach

Historically prior, the interlingua approach represents a theoretically purer approach. The interlingual representation is an abstract representation of the meaning of the source text, capturing all and only the linguistic information necessary to generate an appropriate target text showing no undue influence from the original text. This turns out to be very difficult to achieve in practice, however. Even the very deepest of representations that linguists have come up with are still representations of text, not of meaning, and it seems inevitable that a translation system must be based on a mechanism which transforms the linguistic structures of one language into those of the other. This is unfortunate in a way, as there are many advantages to an interlingual approach, especially when one thinks of multilingual systems translating between many language pairs (consider that a system to translate between all eleven current official languages of the European Union would need to deal with 110 different language pairs), but the best attempts to implement this idea so far have had to be on a very small scale, and have generally turned out translingual paraphrases rather than translations.

Transfer

The more practical solution has been the 'transfer' approach, which views translation as a three-stage process:

- analysis of the input into a source-language syntactic structure representation,
- transfer of that representation into the corresponding target-language structure,
- synthesis of the output from that structure.

Although this approach has the disadvantage of requiring an additional stage of processing, there is a corresponding advantage in that the approach focusses on the contrastive element of translation, since it is precisely in the transfer stage that the differences between the languages can be brought out. Current systems working within this framework adopt an approach where transfer is reduced as much as possible, ideally to the translation of the lexical items only, by the adoption of a 'deep' intermediate representation which neutralises as much as possible the idiosyncrasies of the surface forms of the language, such as gender agreement, word order, tense, mood and aspect in verbs and so on.

The issue of transfer vs. interlingua has been widely discussed in the literature: see particularly Arnold et al. 1994: p80ff, Hutchins & Somers 1992: p71ff, and further references cited there.

Computational formalisms

Another theoretical issue in the design of an MT system is the computational one of how to compute and manipulate the representations described above. Since there are broadly two problems here – what to do and how to do it – the former linguistic, the latter computational, attempts are often made to separate the two by providing computational formalisms or programming languages which a linguist can easily learn and work with. This usually means formalisms which are very similar to the grammar formalisms found in theoretical linguistics. But there is a further theoretical distinction between 'declarative' and 'procedural' formalisms. In a declarative formalism, the linguists have to think in terms of static relationships and facts, and leave it to the computer to figure out how to combine them, whereas with a procedural formalism they have to be more explicit about what to do and when. We can exemplify this quite easily: consider the fact that *mice* is the plural of *mouse*. We might use this information in a number of different procedures, for example in confirming that the subject of a sentence agrees with the verb, in determining how to translate *mice*, which is not in the bilingual dictionary, or when translating into English. So there is an obvious advantage in stating this piece of 'declarative' information independently of the procedures which use it.

Latest Research Directions

The linguistic and computational techniques described above have been used with a certain amount of success in a number of systems, some of which have been developed into commercially available software, while others have remained clearly no more than research systems. Meanwhile, as we will see in the final section below, increases in the processing power of personal computers, and more attention paid to 'peripheral' aspects such as user-friendliness, have meant that MT systems based more on the original 'first generation' approach, though with a slightly less naive linguistic background, are finding their way onto the commercial scene, and enjoying some success.

These two facts put together have meant that in the last three or four years, some researchers have been looking out for a completely new approach to MT, feeling perhaps that the second generation approach is a little 'burnt out'. The new approach is inspired by the factors, mentioned above, which have enabled 'translation memory' to become a working reality, namely the possibility of extensive storage of and fast access to previous translations.

Non-symbolic approaches to MT

The new paradigms for MT research eschew to a certain extent the linguistically motivated 'analysis and intermediate representation' approach of the second generation systems, and try to take advantage of sophisticated pattern-matching and search techniques, coupled with statistical analysis, and the relatively new computational approach known as 'connectionism'.

The purely statistical approach of the IBM group (Brown et al 1990) is based on a bilingual corpus, the Canadian parliamentary proceedings. This research system attempts to translate from English into French purely on the basis of probabilities calculated by considering millions of words of parallel text. The statistical probabilities determine choice of lexical equivalents (taking into account 'fertility', that is the chance that one English word corresponds to more than one French word, e.g. *implemented – mise en application)* and the target-language word order (taking into account 'distortion', that is the fact that English and French word order is not identical).

Another approach, called 'example-based MT', has been proposed by several research groups, cf. Somers 1992/3. Here, translation is produced by comparing segments of the input text (usually sentence by sentence) with a bilingual corpus of typical examples, extracting the closest matches and using them as a model for the target text. There are thus two stages: 'matching' the input with the examples, and 'recombining' the target-language fragments thus extracted. This approach is claimed to be more like the way some humans go about translating, and is also said to result in more stylish, less literal translations, since it is not essentially based on structural analysis of the input. The approach will work best when the text to be translated and the corpus of examples to be consulted are sufficiently restricted in style and content, and are closely related. Obvious cases from the commercial world are where a manual for a piece of equipment is revised, or the documentation when a new product is marketed, which can be broadly based on texts produced for similar or related products. The similarity of this to the 'translation memory' approach described above is obvious: the main difference is that whereas translation memory is seen as a tool to help the translator, example-based MT is seen as a methodology for essentially automatic translation in its own right. Nevertheless, much of the technology is shared by both.

Implementations of example-based MT vary in a number of aspects. For instance, in a 'hybrid' system, the technique may be used only for cases which are particularly problematic for traditional methods, e.g. Sumita & Iida 1991; in these and other systems, the bilingual examples may be hand-picked so as to be representative of the particular problems addressed, while other systems (e.g. Somers et al. 1994) are based on a naturally occurring corpus.

The results produced by both these efforts at 'non-symbolic' MT (i.e. techniques which do not rely on linguistic theory or rule formalisms) are still fairly tentative at the moment, and, while not suggesting that the long-awaited revolution is upon us, are sufficiently interesting to merit further investigation.

Speech translation

Mention should also be made here of speech translation, i.e. the possibility of automatic recognition and translation of spoken language. The enormity of this particular problem has long been recognised. Getting computers to 'understand' speech and turn it into text, for example in an automatic dictation machine, is already a difficult task. The main problems relate to differences in the human voice from speaker to speaker, or for the same speaker over time, for example, due to excitement, or having a cold, and so on. While the human brain is able to ignore these differences in the acoustic speech signal, it is quite another matter to program a computer to do so. Humans have all sorts of means at their disposal for making quite fine-grained distinctions in decoding speech, notably, their understanding of context, their expectation that what they are hearing will make sense (e.g. in 29 *necks drain* should obviously be *next train*), and their ability to guess on the basis of past experience.

29. What time is the necks drain to town?

All these are skills which are extremely difficult to program into a computer. Some success has been achieved in decoding speech under controlled conditions, e.g. using a good microphone in a quiet room, speaking slowly and clearly. But it is obvious that decoding speech as it naturally occurs, with background noise, or down a telephone line, is another matter. But even if the words themselves can be decoded, that is not the end of it: natural speech is often marred by hesitation noises *(ummm, er, ah)*, coughs and sighs, false starts and unfinished sentences. Speech is rarely perfectly grammatical in a, nor even, if we are honest, does it always make sense. All these make recognition and particularly translation particularly difficult, especially using traditional MT techniques (cf. Miike et al. 1988). As any interpreter knows, speech is not 'spoken text', and to try to translate it using the same techniques is doomed to failure.

For all these reasons, there has been very little serious work on speech translation. One or two programs, for demonstration purposes, have offered 'translation' of limited vocabularies 200 words or so, commands such as *Stop, Start*, numbers, letters of the alphabet. Another approach, using crude pattern-matching techniques, can generate target-language text on the basis of key segments recognised in the input stream, in the manner of a holiday-maker's phrasebook: this gives good translations if the phrase you want is in there, but no flexibility. But these are not significant developments. A few recent projects are making more serious efforts to tackle the problem (see Kurematsu 1993, Kay et al. 1994, Kitano 1994), attempting to put together all the latest techniques in both speech processing and translation. In most cases, the domain tackled is highly restricted, e.g. an imaginary conference office dealing with enquiries about registration, the programme of speeches and so on. The MT world awaits its results with interest.

MT Today

Perhaps the most striking recent development in MT is the availability, at last, of relatively inexpensive, relatively useful commercial MT software. Reviews of MT in the past have been forced to conclude that while all the research has been of great interest to computational linguists, the end-result has not been especially appreciated by potential users. In the mid-1970s, two or three MT systems were launched commercially in what was arguably a considerable marketing disaster. The systems, ran only on large, expensive mainframes, often not the computer that a potential customer would already have bought for other purposes. More important, the quality of translation was usually dire; and to add insult to injury, the shortcomings of the systems were well hidden from the prospective customers by unsupportable boasts concerning efficiency gains. The users of such systems, typically translators who had to be retrained against their will, were rightly sceptical, and, perhaps unfortunately, remain so to this day, despite huge changes in the performance of commercial MT systems, and indeed in the way they are marketed.

Second time around, the situation is in all respects much better. While it would be inappropriate here to mention any commercial systems by name, there are several which are instantly affordable, even if only for a cautious look and a trial run with some unsensitive material. They nearly all run on the kind of hardware PCs that many translators – freelance or staff – already have, and are familiar with. Attention has been paid to the user interface, and to the activities around the periphery of translation, such as text capture, de- and re-formatting, and publishable-quality printing. Most important of all, false claims about translation quality and the need for revision by the user are no longer made. Companies marketing MT today make it clear that users must be trained, must invest a certain amount of time in customizing the system and accustoming themselves to using it. And of course not all translation tasks are suited to MT in the first place.

The important improvements which resulted in the revival of MT were of course largely linguistic and computational, many developed subsequent to the criticisms of the ALPAC report. Nevertheless, attitudes towards the concept are in many ways equally important. Translators were originally very hostile to the prospect of MT because on the one hand they were largely computer-illiterate and on the other they felt that their skills and jobs were being undermined by these developments. Since the improvement in machine aids for translation and the increasing computer literacy of translators, they have come to realise the benefits they stand to gain from MT systems. It is conceivable that translating as a profession will evolve in line with these advances and that the post-editing and resource management skills, such as developing on-line word-lists, associated with use of an MT system will become as much a part of the translator's everyday job as the word-processing skills that they have had to acquire in recent years.

Following the demise of the earliest commercial systems, the exaggerated claims that had been made have been reduced or eliminated and the stated aims revised. It has become obvious that not all text-types can be treated in the same way. Computers fall far short of being able to translate stylistically rich or extremely ambiguous texts. On the other hand, technical texts do not pose the same problems and are much more suited to the new technology.

From the very first experiments, MT output clearly did not match up to the quality of human translation. However, some experts were surprised at how much of the output text they could understand. It is now accepted that different levels of output quality are required for different purposes. Documents intended for distribution to customers or ones where accuracy is of paramount importance clearly need to be of higher quality than those which were intended to be internal 'for information only' documents, or to decide whether a text needs to be translated fully. In these cases, especially where the receiver has no knowledge of the source language, it is often true that any translation is better than none at all. Willingness to accept output which may need post-editing is an important step towards accepting MT.

Since it is no longer expected to produce FAHQT, MT now rates quite highly for the quality of output. Of course the issue of assessing quality is still a thorny one and there is no consensus as to the best method. The primary objective has to be the adequate fulfilment of users' needs and if the user is satisfied with even low quality output, then the given system should pass the test. But simply allowing potential customers to try the system out for themselves before agreeing to purchase may not be the best way to 'sell' MT: commitment also has to be there. Output often improves after the system, particularly its dictionaries, has been configured to the users' needs and this takes time. It is also true to say that once translators become accustomed to looking at raw MT output, the job of post-editing becomes significantly quicker and easier, but the translator has to learn to edit without completely rewriting. The cooperation of translators in their role as post-editors will provide the developers with the essential feedback needed to improve the system. People who have a good understanding of the system and can quickly put right errors or update entries will certainly be an asset and, in general, people with a positive view of MT are essential for any kind of useful development. Companies regularly using MT will begin to recruit people who have a positive attitude to it (cf. Vasconcellos 1993, p.180).

References

ALPAC 1966. *Languages and machines: computers in translation and linguistics*. A report by the Automatic Language Processing Advisory Committee, Division of Behavioral Sciences, National Research Council, National Academy of Sciences, Washington DC.

Arnold D., L. Balkan, R.L. Humphreys, S. Meijer & L. Sadler 1994 *Machine translation: an introductory guide*, Manchester: NEC Blackwell.

Bar-Hillel, Y. 1951 The state of machine translation in 1951. *American Documentation* **2**, 229-237; reprinted in Y. Bar-Hillel, (1964): Language and information. Reading, Mass. Addison-Wesley.

Bar-Hillel, Y. 1960 The present status of automatic translation of languages. *Advances in Computers*, **1**, 91-163.

Bostad, D.A. 1986 Machine translation in the USAF. *Terminologie et Traduction*, 1986/1, 68-72.

Brown, P.F. et al, 1990 A statistical approach to machine translation. *Computational Linguistics*, **16**, 79-85.

Elliston, J.S.G. 1979 Computer aided translation: a business viewpoint. In: B.M. Snell ed. *Translating and the computer*. Amsterdam: North-Holland, 149-158.

Habermann, F.W.A. 1986 Provision and use of raw machine translation. *Terminologie et Traduction*, **1**, 29-42.

Harris, B. 1988 Bi-text, a new concept in translation theory. *Language Monthly*, **54**, 8-10.

Hutchins, W.J. 1986 *Machine translation: past, present, future.* Chichester: Ellis Horwood.

Hutchins, W.J. & H.L. Somers 1992 *An introduction to machine translation*. London: Academic Press.

Josselson, H.H. 1971 Automatic translation of languages since 1960: a linguist's view. *Advances in Computers*, **11**, 1-58.

Kay, M. 1980 *The proper place of men and machines in language translation*. Research Report CSL-80-11. Xerox Palo Alto Research Center, Palo Alto, California. October 1980.

Kay, M., J.M. Gawron & P. Norvig 1994 *Verbmobil: a translation system for face-to-Face dialog*, Stanford: Center for the Study of Language and Information.

Kitano, H. 1994 *Speech-to-speech translation: a massively parallel memory-based approach*. Boston: Kluwer Academic Publishers.

Kittredge, R.I. 1982 Variation and homogeneity of sublanguages. In: *Kittredge & Lehrberger* 1982, 107-137.

Kittredge, R.I. 1985 The significance of sublanguage for automatic translation. In: S. Nirenburg ed. *Machine translation: theoretical and methodological issues*, Cambridge: Cambridge University Press, 59-67.

Kittredge, R.I. & J. Lehrberger eds 1982 *Sublanguage: studies of language in restricted semantic domains*. Berlin: de Gruyter.

Kjærsgaard, P.S. 1987 REFTEX - a context-based translation aid. In: *Proceedings of the Third Conference of the European Chapter of the Association for Computational Linguistics* Copenhagen, 109-112.

Kurematsu, A. 1993 Overview of speech translation at ATR. In: S. Nirenburg ed. *Progress in machine translation*, Amsterdam: IOS Press, 33-41.

Lawson, V. 1979 Tigers and polar bears, or: translating and the computer. *The Incorporated Linguist*, **18**, 81-85.

Lawson, V. ed. 1985 *Tools for the trade: computers and translation 5*, Amsterdam: North-Holland.

Locke, W.N. & A.D. Booth eds 1955 *Machine translation of Languages*. Cambridge, Mass.: MIT Press.

Magnusson-Murray, U. 1985 Operational experience of a machine translation service. In: *Lawson* 1985, 171-180.

Melby, A.K. 1982 Multi-level translation aids in a distributed system. In: J. Horecký ed. *COLING 82: Proceedings of the Ninth International Conference on Computational Linguistics*. Amsterdam: North-Holland, 215-220.

Miike, S., et al 1988 Experiences with an online translating dialogue system. In: *Proceedings of the 26th Annual Meeting of the Association for Computational Linguistics* Buffalo NY, 155-162.

Newton, J. 1992 The Perkins experience. In: J. Newton ed. *Computers in translation: a practical appraisal*. London: Routledge, 46-57.

Nishida, F. & S. Takamatsu 1990 Automated procedures for the improvement of a machine translation system by feedback from postediting. *Machine Translation*, **5**, 223-246.

Pym, P.J. 1990 Pre-editing and the use of simplified writing for MT: an engineer's experience of operating an MT system. In: P. Mayorcas ed. *Translating and the computer 10: the translation environment 10 years on*. London: Aslib, 80-96.

Sager, J.C. 1993 *Language engineering and translation: consequences of automation*. Amsterdam: John Benjamins.

Sager, J.C., D. Dungworth & P.F. McDonald 1980 *English special languages: principles and practice in science and technology*. Wiesbaden: Brandstetter.

Seal, T. 1992 ALPNET and TSS: the commercial realities of using a computer-aided translation system. In: *Translating and the Computer 13: the theory and practice of machine translation - a marriage of convenience?* London: Aslib, 119-125.

Shannon, C. & W. Weaver 1949 *The mathematical theory of communication*. Urbana: University of Illinois Press.

Sinaiko, H.W. & G.R. Klare 1972 Further experiments in language translation: readability of computer translations, *ITL*, **15**, 1-29.

Somers, H.L. 1992/3 Example-based and corpus-based approaches to machine translation. In: *Proceedings of International Symposium on Natural Language Understanding and AI* Iizuka, Fukuoka, July 1992, 87-101; La traduction automatique basée sur l'exemple ou sur les corpus. In: P. Bouillon and A. Clas eds La traductique: etudes et recherches de traduction par ordinateur. Montréal 1993: Les Presses de l'Université de Montréal, 149-166.

Somers, H.L., I. McLean & D. Jones 1994 Experiments in multilingual example-based generation. In: *Proceedings of CSNLP 1994: 3rd Conference on the Cognitive Science of Natural Language Processing* Dublin.

Somers, H.L., J. McNaught & Y. Zaharin 1990 A user-driven interactive machine translation system. In: *Proceedings of SICONLP '90: Seoul International Conference on Natural Language Processing* Seoul, 140-143.

Sumita, E. & H. Iida 1991 Experiments and prospects of example-based machine translation. In: *Proceedings of the 29th Annual Meeting of the Association for Computational Linguistics* Berkeley, 185-192.

Van Hoof, A., et al 1995 Translation memory. In M. Kugler, K. Ahmad & G. Thurmair eds *Translator's workbench: tools and terminology for translation and text processing*. Berlin: Springer, 83-99.

Van Slype, G. 1979 Evaluation of the 1978 version of the SYSTRAN English-French automatic system of the Commission of the European Communities. *The Incorporated Linguist*, **18.3**, 86-89.

Vasconcellos, M. 1986 Functional considerations in the postediting of machine-translated output. *Computers and Translation*, **1**, 21-38.

Vasconcellos, M. 1993 Is MT right for you? *Byte*, January 1993.

Vauquois, B. 1968 A survey of formal grammars and algorithms for recognition and transformation in machine translation. In: *IFIP Congress-68* Edinburgh, 254-260; reprinted in Ch. Boitet ed. Bernard Vauquois et la TAO: *Vingt-cinq ans de traduction automatique - analectes*. Grenoble 1988: Association Champollion, 201-213.

Wagner, E. 1985 Rapid post-editing of Systran. In: *Lawson 1985*, 199-213.

Weaver, A. 1988 Two aspects of interactive machine translation. In M:. Vasconcellos ed. *Technology as translation strategy*. Binghamton, NY: State University of New York at Binghamton SUNY, 116-123.

Yngve, V.H. 1957 A framework for syntactic translation. *Mechanical Translation*, 4.3, 59-65.

13. New Technology for Translators

GEOFFREY SAMUELSSON-BROWN

This chapter is a personal view and was compiled in less time than I would have liked – the age-old problem of the translator. I must acknowledge the assistance and support given to me, often at very short notice, by developers and suppliers of the technologies referred to in this chapter. My thanks to them for their patience and time in answering what were probably very naive questions, for reviewing the draft version of this chapter, and introducing logic and coherence to a motley collection of assembled facts and figures. My particular thanks go to Françoise Moreau-Johnson, Speech Recognition Specialist, IBM United Kingdom Limited; Ian Gordon, Managing Director of Trados UK Ltd.; David Kitchen, Technical Support Manager, Speech Processing, Philips Dictation Systems; and Peter Angell, Managing Director, Endeavour Technologies Ltd.

Introduction

When I first started translation as a freelance in the mid '70s, about the time when early speech recognition systems were being researched, I wrote my translations out by hand. At best I could achieve a translation rate of around 300 words per hour after which the translation was copy-typed and then sent back to me for checking (if the delivery time allowed!). I leave it to your imagination to consider the level of quality and presentation this permitted.

It was suggested to me by the agency for whom I worked at the time that I ought to try dictating my translations and submit them on tapes. These translations were subsequently typed by an audio typist. My translation output grew enormously and I could, at a push, dictate around 2500 words an hour. If I spoke articulately, and gave punctuation and formatting instructions while dictating, the audio typist was able to produce a very good draft. In any event, it was necessary to make corrections and possibly changes to the draft and, since I was mindful of the work of retyping, I was reluctant to make any major changes. These were the days of dry transfer lettering for different fonts and true 'cut and paste operations' on a drawing board or light table. Any work to be produced as camera-ready copy needed to go through expensive and time-consuming typesetting and artwork stages.

A few years later I bought my first dedicated word processor and worked together with an audio typist who, again, worked from my dictation. Even though this equipment was archaic by today's standard, it did allow me a lot more editorial freedom. What I dreamed of at the time was something that would combine the dictaphone and the computer so that, as if by some magic, my spoken words would appear on screen. Now, fifteen years later, that dream has become reality – I can talk to the computer and the spoken word appears. Furthermore I can produce camera-ready pages on screen and e-mail them without even moving from my desk.

When working with repetitive text, word processing systems can be used to do automatic search and replace. It is quite easy to set up a number of search and replace macros to deal with repetitive text and most translators are fairly adept at this. You could regard this as a very primitive form of computer-aided translation (CAT). In fact, this is the basic philosophy of some CAT packages – the software searches for text that it recognises and replaces it with the target text.

Technology is developing at a frightening pace and the demands made on the translator do not show any signs of abating. In fact, the translator is becoming more and more dependent on information technology and, if the translator does not adapt to change, he or she may become uncompetitive.

What I hope to do in this chapter is to give a broad overview of technological development in just two of the sectors that affect the translator – speech recognition and computer-aided-translation. This overview is a purely personal reflection and I am unashamed in admitting that my view may be woefully ignorant in some respects. But if I can raise your awareness of the information technology changes that you will face then my efforts will not have been in vain.

Speech recognition systems

I first encountered speech recognition systems in the early '90s. These systems had been developed primarily for the legal profession and others whose practitioners dictated a significant proportion of their work. Readers who wish to find out more about the development of this technology should read R.A.Sharman's excellent article (1994). In the early '90s you needed a very powerful computer by contemporary standards and the software was expensive (8MB of RAM and 60MB of hard disk!). I could see the value of the application but the translation company for which I work was not in the position for this to be a viable proposition. The software alone cost over £2,000 at 1993 prices. The system would work only with a small number of word processing packages. Today, a typical system costs in the region of £850 and will run on what is now a standard configuration PC.

There are few of the, dare I say, more mature translators who are efficient keyboard operators. Efficiency can be hampered by the amount of reference material that may need to be consulted while translating. Keyboarding is very much a hands-on operation whereas talking into a head-set microphone leaves your hands free to leaf through whatever you might have on your desk. You don't even need to be in front of your screen to dictate. There is also the threat, after years of keyboarding, of repetitive strain injury if you have not been diligent in arranging an ergonomic workplace. Being free from the keyboard means that you can assume a working position that is the most comfortable.

Principle of speech recognition

The principle of a speech recognition system (Philips 1993) is that it records the speech signal, digitises it, formats in a certain way, compares it with a collection of possible words, decides which of these words is most likely to have been articulated, generates the text, and allows for corrections of misunderstandings via some form of correction editor. This principle is outlined in Figure 1.

The speech input is analysed acoustically and is compared with a collection of words represented in the same way. Information from three sources is used to recognise a word: the phoneme inventory, the pronunciation lexicon, and the language model. The output, in the form of a sequence of words which has scored the highest probability rating in the comparative process, is the word sequence that is recognised.

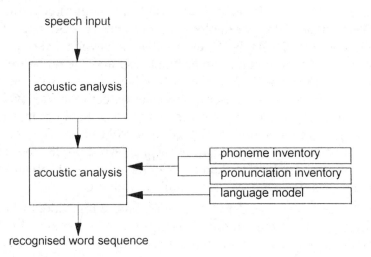

Figure 1. The principle of speech recognition

Speech sampling

Written words consist of characters while spoken words consist of phonemes, the smallest distinctive speech sounds in a language that are used to distinguish words. You could use the analogy that these are the 'atoms' of speech. Speech signals of spoken words comprise a succession of phonemes which must be related to a succession of characters. This relationship should be unambiguous. The speech signal needs to be recorded for this to be possible.

An oral signal can be recorded in analogue format by a microphone but the signal needs to be digitised before it can be processed. This is performed by registering the amplitude and frequency of the speaker's utterances at certain time intervals. It is then necessary to decide how many samples are to be taken per unit of time. Sampling algorithms based on the quality of the speech required, and the memory available to store the signals are the criteria on which the decision is based. Any redundancy in the signal is reduced as a result.

Pronunciation lexicon and training

The number of phonemes is limited as is the number of characters in the alphabet and is language-dependent. To give an example, between 40 and 50 phonemes are required in German and English. A decision must be made where a phone, or word, starts and where it ends. In the case of continuous speech (as developed by Philips), there are no anchor points in the signal from which the beginning or the end of the word can be deduced. It is necessary in the case of continuous speech to identify beginnings and ends of words by comparing a large number of signals of known words to extract the separate phonemes. To this end, text (both spoken and written) is used in which all the necessary phonemes are included in a large number of combinations with others.

In any system, whether discrete utterances or continuous speech, it is necessary for the system to learn the user's voice. The degree to which this is done depends on the system to be used. But more of this later when considering individual systems. The exact form of a phoneme signal depends on the speaker. Every speaker has his or her own characteristic signal form. The uniqueness of each voice means that the system needs to learn the characteristic phoneme signal of new users. Recordings of the intended user are needed to provide the system with all the essential characteristics of the user's voice to build up a phoneme inventory for that user. Once these are available, an arbitrary succession of phonemes can be drawn up to decide what the speech signal of an arbitrary (written) word looks like. This collection, called the speaker's reference, together with the lexicon, results in a set of speech signals for the 'library' of words that can be recognised.

Let's look at the principal players in the UK. These are IBM, Endeavour Technologies Limited (ETL) and Philips. The common denominator is that speech recognition systems identify speech patterns, interpret them as words or command macros, and either reproduce words on screen or implement macro instructions.

Common to IBM and ETL is that

each..word..must..be..spoken..as..a..distinct..
utterance..with..a..brief..pause..between..each..word

if the software is to interpret each word correctly. Macros such as *enterIBMaddress* can be dictated as a continuous utterance since the software recognises this as a distinct sound pattern and carries out the command macro accordingly. Naturally, the macro will need to be programmed into the system. The following screen shot shows IBM's VoiceWriter with its command window and the text which appears on screen as it is recognised.

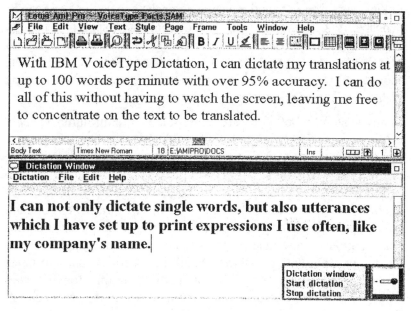

With IBM VoiceType Dictation, I can dictate my translations at up to 100 words per minute with over 95% accuracy. I can do all of this without having to watch the screen, leaving me free to concentrate on the text to be translated.

I can not only dictate single words, but also utterances which I have set up to print expressions I use often, like my company's name.

Figure 2. IBM's VoiceWriter

Statistics offered by IBM and ETL indicate that the software can accept around 80 words per minute. I know that I would be hard pushed to match this speed when dictating to achieve more than 2500 words an hour and usually reckon on about 1700 words an hour. Translating in this way is extremely demanding in terms of mental stamina. If you can achieve and sustain four hours of effective translation time a day then you will be doing extremely well. Dictating your translations will allow you to complete your draft in a much shorter time thereby leaving more time for editing and quality control. What is more important, it will allow you more time for other activities such as hobbies and leisure or, if you're a glutton for punishment, more translation assignments.

Since the Philips system deals with continuous text, it requires considerably more computing power. In addition to providing speech recognition, the system also provides document management. Dictation is of course performed in real time but, because of the amount of processing required and the lag in processing (typically 1.5 times the rate of speech) speech flow is analysed in a server and the result made available for post-recognition editing. Since the system is designed primarily for firms that have their own secretarial services, it is expected that the system will be run on a network. This is illustrated in Figure 3.

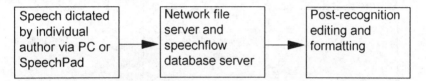

Figure 3. Philip's system for continuous speech recognition

The person dictating is not confined to sitting in front of a PC since a hand-held dictation machine that uses a speech card is available. This hand-held system is known as the SpeechPad and it allows speech to be recorded onto a SpeechCard (PC-card S-RAM) as PC-DOS files according to IVA's worldwide digital dictation standard. The contents of the card can be downloaded to a PC when required. Figure 3 shows the dictation screen in which the user has identified the dictionary (radiology) to facilitate recognition. Since speech recognition and post-recognition editing are performed off-line, the person dictating identifies the person who will carry out the editing.

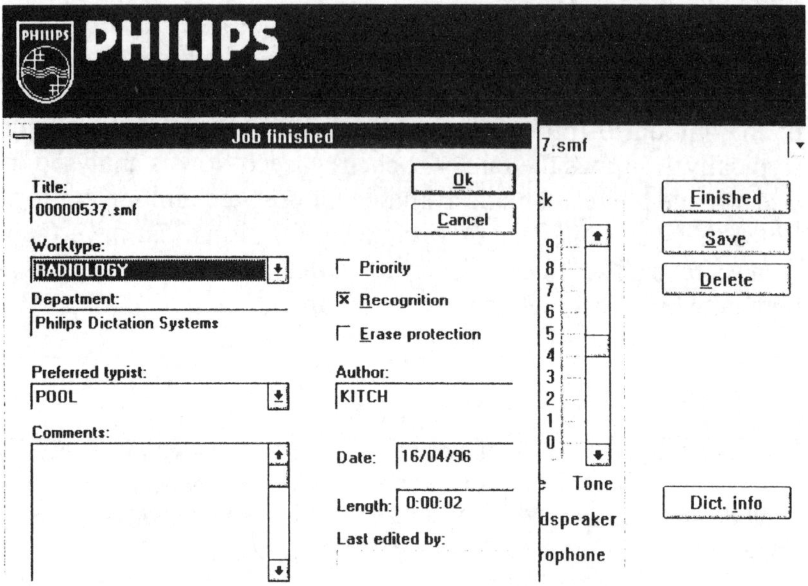

Figure 4. Philips dictation screen

Computer-aided translation systems

Since I work for a translation company, I have a vested interest in improving efficiency and profitability. There is a limit to what the human translator can achieve in a given time and the profession is still very labour-intensive. A lot of translation work can be intensely boring particularly when you see a text that is fairly similar to something you translated some while ago. It is difficult to convince a client that you need to make a complete re-translation of a text when there are perhaps only various sentences or paragraphs that are the same. You as the translator need to identify what needs to be translated and I know from experience that it is often better to make a completely new translation rather than assuming that some sections are identical and finding out later that there were slight differences.

There are ways of getting round the problem. These include getting the word processing software to make a comparison and highlight the differences or getting the client to mark the differences. I have not found the former an easy application to master nor have I encountered too many clients willing to perform the latter task.

This is where computer-aided translation comes into its own. Again, the major players include IBM, ETL as well as Trados. Put very simplistically, a CAT system will search through previous translations to find a match and then perform the necessary substitution. If there is a close but not exact match, it will offer what is known as a fuzzy match which can the be edited to produce an exact match. The following screen shot from IBM Translation Manager shows a screen shot that displays a number of windows which you may choose to have up on screen at any time.

The translation window at the top displays the translated text, segment by segment. In brackets you will see the specific markups for the word processing package you are using – (Word for Windows) in this case. You can choose to have these protected or unprotected. The segment you are working on will be highlighted in a distinctive colour to facilitate your work. Regrettably this cannot be reproduced here.

The second window displays the original text and will not be changed as you translate. A segment of text will be scanned by the software to see if there is a direct match or a fuzzy match. This will be offered for substitution or modification. These matches, if found, will be displayed in the Translation Memory window.

The translation memory is something that you will gradually build up as the number of translated segments is added. Translation memory compilation is an iterative process and, to facilitate searching, you will need to create a range of memories to suit particular clients. Obviously, the fewer the matches the system needs to scan, the quicker the substitution process. You can ask the software to make automatic substitution but this process will stop as soon as an unrecognisable segment is detected.

TranslationManager - Translation Environment FLEITCH.DOC[DLS]

File   Edit   Options   Cursor   Translate   Spellcheck   Style   Window   Help

Original

Bei der Qualitätssicherung in der fleischverarbeitenden Industrie fallen eine Vielzahl von Daten an, die ohne moderne EDV nicht effizient erfaßt und ausgewertet werden können. Dies beginnt bei der Bestimmung von Faktoren zur Aufzucht und Haltung der Tiere, die bereits maßgeblich die Fleischqualität beeinflussen, bis zur Kontrolle des verbraucherfertigen Produktes. So werden bei der Anlieferung der Tiere Herkunftsort, Zustand wie die Hautbeschaffenheit und das Lebendgewicht bestimmt. Ziel ist eine zuverlässige Indentitätskontrolle des Tieres auch während der Schlachtung. Darüber hinaus übernimmt das EDV-System auch die Steuerung der geschlachteten Tiere in den Kühlräumen. Bei Fleischlieferungen sollen neben der terminierten Ankunftszeit auch Beladungsdichte

Translation

of data is produced which cannot be recorded efficiently or analysed without modern EDP.
This begins with factors such as the rearing and keeping of the animals which significantly influence the quality of the meat and continue up until the control of the product in its final form.
The place of origin of the animals and their condition (e.g. skin condition and live weight) are determined in this manner when the animals are delivered.
The objective is to achieve reliable identity control of the animal, even during slaughtering.
In addition, the EDP system also takes over the controlling of the

Dictionary: GERM-ENGL GERMAN:

Bestimmung	Faktor	Haltung	Tier	Qualität
c) determination	d) factor	e) bearing	g) animal	h) quality
Kontrolle	fertig	Produkt		
k) control	m) finished	o) product		

beginnen
a) begin
b) start
beeinflussen
i) affect

f) carriage

Translation Memory: DLS

0 — Dies beginnt bei der Bestimmung von Faktoren zur Aufzucht und Haltung der Tiere, die bereits maßgeblich die Fleischqualität beeinflussen, bis zur Kontrolle des verbraucherfertigen Produktes.
1 — This begins with factors such as the rearing and keeping of the animals, which significantly influence the quality of the meat, and continue up until the control of the product in its final form.

Figure 5. Screen shot displaying IBM Translation Manager (Windows version)

In addition to setting up translation memories, you can compile a number of client-specific dictionaries. You can display up to ten dictionaries at any one time. The greatest benefit of this is that you can display client dictionaries in descending order of importance followed by general subject dictionaries and then general dictionaries. Thus the software will prompt you with client-specific terminology that can be substituted and included in the translation.

This procedure clears any doubt about what terminology you should use.

Dictionaries can be compiled and updated online. Entries should even include what might be considered common terms if only for the sake of consistency. Many translators find comfort in having hard copy dictionaries and it is a simple matter to export dictionaries to a word processing package for reformatting to suit personal taste and requirements. Interim updates can be made offline on the hard copy and the computer dictionary updated later.

During the brief time that I have been able to look at TRADOS® Translator's Workbench for Windows, I get the impression that the fundamental approach to CAT is similar to that of IBM Translation Manager. Workbench allows networking in projects where several translators work together and require a high level of coordination to ensure quality. Workbench automates this co-ordination by allowing common access to the same translation memory over a computer network. Translated segments are stored immediately in a translation memory and are available to every translator in the team, both for translation of additional segments and for concordance searches.

As long as the text is being worked on, the Workbench retains the source sentences as hidden text together with the corresponding target sentences. This means, for instance, that the translator or editor can use the word processor to make corrections or perform spell checking without the Workbench being active. The Update facility allows changes made this way to be automatically reflected in the translation memory.

The operations procedure implemented by the Workbench can best be illustrated by the looking at its various utilities:

Import Workbench loads a structured ANSI file into a translation memory.

Export Writes translation units from a translation memory to a structured ANSI text file according to predetermined filter criteria.

Analyse Determines repetition statistics for a group of texts. This facilitates accurate estimation of project duration and cost. Sentences that occur frequently can be extracted and pre-translated either manually or using a machine translation system.

Translate Translates a text without user interaction by comparing it with a translation memory. All sentences with a similarity level that exceeds a user-defined threshold are automatically translated.

Update This compares the translation units with sentences stored in the translation memory. The text must contain the hidden source sentences inserted by interactive or batch translation, but the target sentences may be modified directly in the word processor without the use of Workbench. New translations are added to the translation memory, and translations for existing sentences are updated.

'Quick and dirty' translations

On occasions we receive requests to carry out a rough translation so that the client has an idea what the source text contains. I would like to quote the scenario presented by ETL.

The client has received a foreign language document and has no idea what it is. The client can deal with this in any of four different ways:

1. Ignore it. After all, the chances are it is junk mail. If it is not, the client could be making a costly mistake and missing a valuable opportunity.

2. The client could ask a busy colleague who has some language skills to do the best he can do to make sense of it, bearing in mind that it is not his job and he probably can't spare the time anyway.

3. Get a complete translation made of it and incur cost that you may not be able to justify. This translation may take a number of days and may only confirm that the information is of no use. One solution is to fax a number of pages to the translator, the problem being which pages the client should send.

4. Get a 'quick and dirty' translation made by CAT software. This will show whether post-CAT editing will add any value to the information extracted in this manner.

Text scanning

One of the requirements for CAT is to have the source text in an acceptable electronic format. Even though very few clients are without word processing systems, very few respond positively when asked for the text in electronic format. Thus we considered the application of text scanning to circumvent this problem.

Just two years ago (1994), we envisaged the scenario whereby we would scan incoming documents, put them through a CAT system, and then carry out post-CAT editing and quality control. The level of accuracy that could be achieved at the time was not high enough to make the scanning part of the operation feasible. Even though the system stated a recognition level of say 97%, it may not have recognised characters correctly. At worst, a level of around 75% accuracy was achieved and this was unacceptable. Trying to scan fax-quality documents was out of the question. The upshot of this was that a considerable amount of pre-translation editing of the source language text was required before CAT could be applied and we put that idea on hold.

The scenario is now much improved and scanning produces a much more usable electronic version of hard copy. Technology has closed the circle and present-day capabilities can be illustrated in the following.

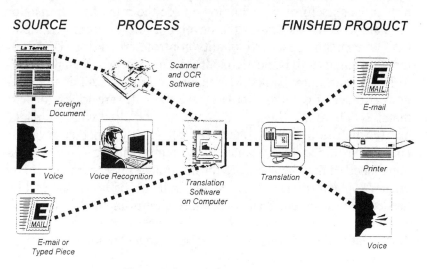

Figure 6. translation process
(Take in illustration of ETL's scenario)

291

Hardware requirements

The hardware requirements that are stated by software suppliers should be considered a minimum since the more powerful your machine, the faster the application will run. The cost of a faster processor and a generous amount of RAM will more than compensate for the frustration felt by watching an application grinding through slowly and less efficiently. Although a standard 14" SVGA colour screen will suffice, a 17" high resolution screen will add to your efficiency. Most software will run on a 486 PC with 8MB but the recommendation is for a Pentium PC with 16MB and a 17" monitor.

Adapting to new technology

Many professions have seen the demise of their traditional ways of working. Imminent technological change has often resulted in fruitless efforts to prevent that change and there are so many examples of this that the translator must be aware of, and adapt to, change. I have lived through the change from translations being produced on a typewriter to translations being produced in electronic format and whizzed around the globe in seconds.

It is estimated that the requirement for translations will increase by around 15% per annum. Naturally this will provide an opportunity and a spur for new technology. I see the role of the translator in years to come as that of the developer and of adding value to CAT in terms of post-CAT quality control and editing. Development resources will be needed in the development and quality control of terminology banks. My understanding of CAT is that of a powerful set of database tools where the software looks for text matches. There may be a rude dictionary supplied with the package but before it can operate really efficiently it needs to be refined and added to.A translation produced using CAT will be unpolished. It may be adequate for information purposes but, if any greater sophistication is required, the skills of the translator will be needed to provide editorial and quality control input. While it will take some while for this technology to have an impact on some spheres of translation, the translator will ignore such technological development at his peril.

Equipment suppliers

Endeavour Technologies
Surrey House
114 Tilt Road
Cobham
Surrey KT11 3JH
Tel: 01932 866500 Fax: 01932 860522

IBM United Kingdom Limited
PO Box 41
North Harbour
Portsmouth
Hampshire PO6 3AU
Tel: 01705 492249

Philips Dictation Systems
The Crescent, Colchester Business Park
Colchester
Essex CO4 4YQ
Tel: 01206 755 555 Fax: 755 666

Trados UK Ltd
Shepherd's Bank
Kettleshulme SK12 7QU
Tel: 01663 734515 Fax: 01663 734516

References

In addition to general publicity material from all companies referred to in the chapter, I am grateful for being given access to the following publications:

1. *Speech Recognition in the Office: How the Technology Supports Dictation*, Sharman R.A., 1994, IBM (UK) Laboratory
2. *Speech in – text out*, Philips Research Topics, No. 3, 1993, Philips Research Laboratories

Appendix I

FIT - Regular Members   1. 11. 1995

- Asociación Argentina de Traductores e Intérpretes, Santa Fe 883 - E.P.,1059 Buenos Aires, Argentina
- Colegio de Traductores Públicos de la Ciudad de Buenos Aires, Callao 289-4 Piso, 1022 Buenos Aires, Argentina
- Australian Institute of Interpreters and Translators (AUTIT), 13 Peacedale Grove, Nunawading, Victoria 3131, Australia
- Österreichischer Übersetzer- und Dolmetscherverband UNIVERSITAS, Gymnasiumstrasse 50, A-1190 Vienna, Austria
- Österreichischer Verband der Gerichtsdolmetscher, Postfach 14, A-1016 Vienna, Austria (Candidate)
- Übersetzergemeinschaft im Literaturhaus, Interessengemeinschaft von Übersetzern literarischer und wissenschaftlicher Werke, Seidengasse 13, -1070 Vienna, Austria
- Chambre belge des traducteurs, interprètes et philologues - Belgische Kamer van Vertalers, Tolken en Filologen, sec.gén.: Rue des Sapins 19, B-4100 Seraing, Belgium
- Sindicato Nacional dos Traductores (SINTRA), Rua da Quintanada 194, 10°, Sala 1206-1207, BR 20091 Rio de Janeiro, Brazil
- Union des Traducteurs en Bulgarie, ul. Gr. Ignatiev 16, BG-1000 Sofia, Bulgaria
- Conseil des traducteurs et interprètes du Canada (C.T.I.C.), 1, rue Nicholas, bureau 1402, Ottawa, Ontario K1N 7B7, Canada
- Association des traducteurs et traductrices littéraires du Canada, 3492, rue Laval, Montréal (Québec) H2X 3C8, Canada
- Santiago Translators' Professional Association, Las Urbinas No. 53, office 22, Santiago, Chile

- Croatian Association of Scientific and Technical Translators (HDZTP), Palmoticeva 22/1, 4100 Zagreb, Croatia
- Cyprus Association of Translators and Interpreters, 51A Riga Fereou Street, CY-3091 Limassol, Cyprus (Candidate)
- Obec Prekladatelú, Pod nuselskymi schody 3, 120 00 Praha 2, Czech Republic
- Union des Interprètes et Traducteurs (JTP), Senovázné nám. 23, 11282 Praha 1, Czech Republic
- ESF - Erhvervssprogligt Forbund, Skindergade 45-47, Postboks 2246, DK-1019 København, Denmark (Candidate)
- VDÜ- Verband deutscher Schriftsteller, Bundessparte Übersetzer, c.o. Fr. A. di Ciriaco-Sussdorf-WDR, Apellhofplatz 1, D-50667 Köln, Fed. Rep. of Germany
- Bundesverband der Dolmetscher und Übersetzer e.V. (BDÜ), Geschäftsstelle: Rüdigerstrasse 79a, D-53179 Bonn, Fed. Rep. of Germany
- Verband der Übersetzer und Dolmetscher Berlin e.V, Postfach 220, D-10182 Berlin, Federal Republic of Germany (Candidate)
- Suomen kääntäjien ja tulkkien liitto - Finlands översättar och tolkförbund r.y., Museokatu 9 B 23, FIN-00100 Helsinki, Finland
- Association des Traducteurs littéraires de France (A.T.L.F), 99, rue de Vaugirard, F-75006 Paris, France
- Société française des traducteurs (S.F.T.), 22, rue des Martyrs, F-75009 Paris, France
- Union Nationale des Experts Traducteurs-Interprètes près les Cours d'Appel (UNETICA) Secr. gén.: 9, rue Sylvabelle, F-13006 Marseille, France
- Société hellénique des traducteurs de littérature (EEML), 7, rue E. Tsakona, Paleo Psychiko, GR-15452 Athens, Greece
- Panhellenic Association of Translators, 8, Kominon Street, GR-54624 Thessaloniki, Greece

- Panhellenic Association of Professional Translators, P.O.Box 31892, Athens 10035, Greece
- Hellenic Association of Translators - Interpreters in the Public Sector, Kazanova 80, GR-185 39, Piraeus, Greece (Candidate)
- Asociación Guatemalteca de Intèrpretes y Traductores, (AGIT), 9a calle 7-30, Zona 9, Guatemala C.A., Guatemala
- Hong Kong Translation Society Ltd., P.O. Box 20186, Hennessy Road Post Office, Hong Kong
- A Magyar Irók Szövetségének Müfordítói Szakosztálya, Bajza utca 18, H-10061 Budapest VI, Hungary
- Indian Scientific Translators Association, INSDOC Building, 14 Satsang Vihar Marg, New Delhi-110067, India
- Association of Indonesian Translators (HPI), Jalan Semarang No.12, Jakarta 10310, Indonesia
- Iraqi Translators' Association, Ali Bldg., 3rd Floor, Sinak-Al-Khulafa Avenue, Bagdad, Iraq
- Irish Translators' Association, The Irish Writers Centre, 19 Parnell Square, Dublin 1, Ireland
- Israel Translators Association, c.o. Ms. Ophira Rahat, P.O.B. 9082, Jerusalem 91090, Israel
- Associazone Italiana Traduttori e Interpreti (A.I.T.I), Segr. Naz.: Vittoria Lo Faro, Via dei Prati Fiscali 158, 00141 Roma, Italy
- National Translation Institute of Science and Technology of Japan (N.A.T.I.S.T.), c/o Mr. T. Koretsune, 1-25-24 Sakura-Josui, Setagaya-Ku, Tokyo 156 / Japan
- Japan Society of Translators (JST), c/o Orion Press , 1 - 13, Kanda Jimbocho, Chiyoda-ku, Tokyo 101, Japan
- Union of Literary Translators of the Republic of Macedonia, P.P. 3, 91001 Skopje, Former Yugoslav Republic of Macedonia
- Organización Mexicana de Traductores, A.C., Matias Romero 99, Desp. 2, Col. del Valle, 03100 México, D.F., Mexico (Candidate)

- Asociación de traductores profesionales, Av. Revolución 1341-14, 01040 Mexico 20 D.F., Mexico
- Association marocaine des interprètes et des traducteurs de conférence (AMITRAC), c.o. ISESCO, 16 bis, Avenue Omar Ben Khattab, BP. 755 AGDAL Rabat, Morocco
- Namibian Association of Translators and Interpreters (NATI), P.O.Box 30331 Pioniers Park, Windhoek 9000, Namibia
- Nederlands Genootschap van Vertalers, Postbus 8138, NL-3503 Utrecht, Netherlands
- New Zealand Society of Translators and Interpreters (Inc.), c/o Dr. Sabine Fenton, Director, Center for Translation and Interpreting Studies, Auckland Institute of Technology, Private Bag 92006, Auckland, New Zealand
- Nigerian Association of Translators and Interpreters (NATI), P.O. Box 1861, Marina, Lagos, Nigeria
- Norsk Faglitteraer Forfatter-og Oversetterforening, Bygdøy allé 21, N-0262 Oslo, Norway
- Norsk Oversetterforening, Postboks 579, Sentrum Oslo 1, Norway
- Statsautoriserte Translatørers Forening, Kongensgate 15, 0157 Oslo 1, Norway
- Science and Technology Translators' Association of the Chinese Academy of Sciences, 52 SanLIHE Road, 100864 Beijing, People's Republic of China
- Translators' Association of China, Wai Wen Building, Baiwanzhuang Road 24, 100037Beijing, People's Republic of China
- Stowarzyszenie Tlumaczy Polskich, ul. Marszalkowska 2, PL-00581 Warsaw, Poland
- TEPIS - Polish Society of Economic, Legal and Court Translators, P.O. Box 33, 00-967 Warsaw 86, Poland
- Associacao Portuguesa de Tradutores, c.o. Mr. Fr. Magalhaes, Rua de Ceuta 6-5° E, 2795 Linda-a-Velha, Portugal

- Korean Society of Translators, Room 604, Midopa Kwangwhamoon B/D, 145 Tangjudong, Chonroku, Seoul, Republic of Korea
- Association des Interprètes et Traducteurs Littéraires du Congo, B.P. 825, Brazzaville, République Populaire du Congo
- Uniunea Scriitorilor din Romania, 115 Calea Victoria, R-71102 Bucharest 1, Romania
- Union of Translators of Russia, 125047 Moscow, P.O.Box 136, Russia
- Soviet po Khoudojestwennomu Perevodou Soyouza Pisateley, Powarskaja ul. 52, 121069 Moscow, Russia
- Association of Slovak Translators and Interpreters Organizations (APTOS), Laurinská 2, 81508 Bratislava, Slovak Republic
- Association of Scientific and Technical Translators of Slovenia (DZTPS), Petkovskovo nabrezje 57, 61000 Ljubljana, Slovenia
- Suid-Afrikaanse Instituut van Vertalers en Tolke, P.O. Box 27711, Sunnyside 0122, South Africa
- Asociación dos Traductores Galegos, Instituto da Lingua Galega, Praza da Universidade, Santiago de Compostela a Coruña, Galicia, Spain (Candidate)
- Agrupación de Interprètes de Conferencia de España-AICE, Apartado de Correos 50680 - 28080 Madrid, Spain, (Candidate)
- Asociación Profesional de Traductores, Correctores e Interprètes de Lengua Vasca, EIZIE, Etxague Jenerala 6 behea, E-20003 Donostia - San Sebastian, Spain
- Asociación Profesional Española de Traductores e Interprètes (A.P.E.T.I), Calle Recoletos 5, 3° izqda., E-28001 Madrid, Spain
- Translators' Committee of the People's Writers' Front, 57/10 Sirinivasa, Ratnavali Road, Kalubovila West, Dehiwala, Sri Lanka

- Swedish Association of Professional Translators - SFÖ, Marestorp, S-280 72 Killeberg, Sweden (Candidate)
- Federation of Authorized Translators in Sweden - FAT, Rimbogatan 19, 753 24 Uppsala, Sweden (Candidate)
- Association Suisse des Traducteurs, Terminologues et Interprètes (A.S.T.T.I.), Postgasse 17, CH-3011 Berne, Switzerland
- Association des Traducteurs dans l'Union des Ecrivains Arabes, c/o M. Ali Okla Orsan, Mazzé-Auto-Strad, BP-3230, Damascus, Syria
- Chama cha Wafasari wa Tanzania (CHAWATA), Tanzanian Translators' Association, P.O. Box 35180, University Hill, Dar es Salaam, Tanzania
- The Translators Association, 84 Drayton Gardens, London SW10 9SB, United Kingdom
- Institute of Translation and Interpreting, 377 City Road, London EC1V 1NA, United Kingdom
- Inter-Trans Committee of the Institute of Linguists, att.: Ms. E. Ostarhild, Director and Chief Executive, 24a Highbury Grove, London N5 2DQ, United Kingdom (Candidate)
- Colegio de Traductores Públicos del Uruguay, Ciudadela 1426, Piso 3 esc. 302, Montevideo, Uruguay
- American Translators' Association (A.T.A.), 1735 Jefferson Davis Highway, Suite 903, Arlington, VA 22202-3413, USA
- Colegio Nacional de Traductores e Intèrpretes, Apartado Postal 52108, Sabana Grande, Caracas 1050 A, Venezuela
- Savez drustava znanstvenih i technickih prevodilaca Jugoslavije, Kicevska br.9, YU-11000 Belgrade, Yugoslavia
- Savez drustava udruzenja knjizevnih prevodilaca Jugoslavije, Francuska 7, YU-11000 Belgrade, Yugoslavia
- Bureau zaïrois de traduction (BUZAT), B.P.: 4956, Kinshasa / Gombe, Zaire

Appendix II

FIT - Associate Members   1.11.1995

- Provinciale Hogeschool voor Vertalers en Tolken, Brusselsepoortstraat 93, B-9000 Gent, Belgium

- Ecole des Interprètes Internationaux, Université de l'Etat à Mons, Avenue du Champ de Mars, B-7000 Mons, Belgium

- Institut Supérieur de Traducteurs et Interprètes de la Communauté franÿaise, 34 rue J. Hazard, B-1180 Bruxelles, Belgium

- Institute of Translation Studies, Charles University, Hybernská 3, CZ-110 00 Praha 1, Czech Republic (Candidate)

- Euro-Schulen Organisation (ESO), Hauptstrasse 26, D-63811 Stockstadt, Fed. Rep. of Germany

- Ecole Supérieure d'Interprètes et de Traducteurs de l'Université de Paris (E.S.I.T), Centre Universitaire Dau phine, Place du Maréchal de Lattre de Tassigny, F- 75116 Paris, France

- Association des Anciens Elèves de l'ESIT, Centre Universitaire Dauphine, F-75116 Paris, France (Candidate)

- Japan Translation Association, NS Building, 2-2-3 Sarugaku-cho, Chiyoda-ku, Tokyo 101, Japan

- Japan Translation Federation, 8-10 Hachobori, 2-chome, Chuo-Ko, Tokyo 104, Japan

- Japan Association of Translators, 2-19-15-808 Shibuya-ku, Tokyo 150, Japan

- Yarmouk University, Department of English, Chairman,Irbid, Jordan

- Ecole de Traducteurs et d'Interprètes, Université SaintJoseph, P.O. Box 175-208, Beirut, Lebanon Bureau administratif, 42 rue de Grenelle, F-75343 Paris, Cedex 07, France

- Université de Balamand, Deir El-Balamand, B.P. 100, Tripoli, Lebanon (Candidate)

- Universidad Intercontinental, Ecole de Traduction, Insurgentes Sur no. 4135, Tlalpan, Mexico D.F., Mexico

- Instituto Superior de Intérpretes y Traductores, Rio Rhin no 40, Col. Cuauhtémoc, B.P. 06500, Mexico D.F.

- Ecole Supérieure ROI FAHD de Traduction, Université Abdelmalek Essaadi, Route du Charf, B.P. 410, Tanger, Morocco

- Ecole Supérieure de Traducteurs et Interprètes (ASTI) du Centre Universitaire de Buea, P.O. Box 63, Buea, République Unie du Cameroun

- Moscow Linguistic University, Ostozhenka 38, 119034 Moscow, G-34, Russia

- Moscow International School of Translation and Interpreting (MISTI), P.O. Box 51, Moscow 123103, Russia

- Faculdad de Traductores e Intérpretes de Granada, C/ Puentezuelas 55, 18002 Granada, Spain

- Ecole de Traduction et d'Interprétation, Université de Genève, 102 Bvl Carl-Vogt, CH-1211 Genève 4, Switzerland

- University of Salford, Department of Modern Languages, c.o. Dr. Myriam Carr, Salford M5 4WT, United Kingdom

- United Bible Societies, Service Center/New York, c.o. Mr. Philip C. Stine, Translation Research Coordinator, 1865 Broadway, New York, NY 10023, USA

Contributors

Tristam Carrington-Windo

Tristam Carrington-Windo BSc, MA, PG Dip TST, Dip Trans, MITI, MIL, MTA worked as an editor of biographical reference works in Germany for two years. He is now a scientific and technical translator who has worked with the German market since 1980 managing the English version of the publicity material for a small group of direct clients. He has published German language courses and is a visiting lecturer at the University of Westminster.

Eyvor Fogarty

Eyvor studied in Aberdeen, Moscow and London. After some years as a staff translator, she worked for various presentation and media-related companies, then rounded off her education by training on the shop-floor as an electronics repairman. She is now a full-time freelance and is actively involved in helping newcomers of whatever age and career background to get launched in the language professions. She has been a Council member of the Institute of Translation and Interpreting and the Fédération Internationale des Traducteurs, and chaired the Organising Committee for the XIIIth FIT World Congress.

Geoffrey Kingscott

Geoffrey Kingscott is a translator with some 30 years' experience, who today runs a translation and language consultancy company, Praetorius Limited. This company specialises in monitoring developments in language engineering worldwide, and examining how they can be applied to the translation process. Geoffrey Kingscott has written and spoken widely on translation matters, particularly as General Editor of Language Monthly (1983-88) and its successor journal Language International (1989-96).

Sean Marlow

Having graduated from St Edmund Hall, Oxford, Sean began his translation career with Randall Woolcott Services Ltd in Gerrards Cross as a semi-technical translator and translation verifier. After three years there and a year at Tek Translations he worked in the software industry for a time. He currently works as a Project Manager for ITR, International Translation Resources, specialising in software localisation.

Siân Marlow

Having graduated in German and Swedish from St David's University College, Lampeter in 1990, Siân worked as a translation verifier at the Translation Division of Randall Woolcott Services Ltd in Gerrards Cross. She subsequently moved to Aardvark Translation Services Ltd in Ascot to take up a post as a Staff Translator. Siân currently holds the position of Scandinavian Section Leader at Aardvark.

Peter Newmark

Peter Newmark BA (Cambridge), FIL, Laurea (honoris causa, Trieste), was formerly a student of F.R. Leavis and Anthony Blunt. Since 1981 he has been a part-time lecturer in the Department of Linguistic and International Studies at the University of Surrey, and since 1984 he has run the translation option of the EFL Summer School at the University of Westminster. He was President of the Institute of Linguists from 1989 to 1993 and is now a Vice-President. He was previously Head of Department and Dean of the School of Languages (now Professor Emeritus) at the Polytechnic of Central London, now the University of Westminster. He is the author of Approaches to Translation (1981), A Textbook of Translation (1988), which won the BAAL Annual Book Prize in 1988, About Translation (1981) and Paragraphs on Translation (1993). He contributes Paragraphs on Translation once in two months to The Linguist and has written numerous papers and articles on principles and practice of translation and on foreign language teaching. He has lectured and taught in about 30 countries and has acted as consultant to several departments of translation. He is a member of the British Association of Applied Linguistics and an active and long-standing member of Amnesty International.

Rachel Owens

A graduate in Swedish and German from St. David's University College Lampeter, Rachel worked briefly as a trainee accountant before going on to the University of Surrey where she was awarded an MA in Translation (Swedish to English). She subsequently worked in-house as a staff translator at Aardvark Translation Services Ltd and gradually became involved in teaching translation at the University of Surrey. After three years she went freelance and stepped up her teaching commitments. She currently works full time at the University of Surrey teaching translation from Swedish and Norwegian to English, primarily at postgraduate level.

Catriona Picken

Graduated from London University in 1957 with a degree in French, Spanish and Dutch. After 30-odd years as a staff translator for a major international industrial corporation, became a freelance translator and consultant in early 1984, specialising in general technical translation, from Dutch, Italian and French into English. For many years, has been a member of Aslib Technical Translation Group. Founder member of the Institute of Translation and Interpreting. Served on its Council and chaired or served on numerous commitees. Edited the *Proceedings* of several 'Translating and the Computer' Conferences and ITI annual conferences. Edited the Proceedings of the 13th Congress of the Fédération Internationale des Traducteurs, Brighton, 1993. Edited and contributed to the first two editions of The *Translator's Handbook*. External examiner and occaisional lecturer at the Universities of Bradford, Kent, Salford and Westminster.

Clare Rutzler

Clare Rutzler gained a degree in Modern Languages from Salford University specialising in Information Technology. She is currently employed by Syntegra, the systems integration department of British Telecom, as an Information Technology support representative for sales persons working throughout Europe.

Geoffrey Samuelsson-Brown

A translator, lecturer and writer, Geoff originally worked as a design engineer and became involved in translation while working as a technical editor at Volvo's Technological Development Centre in Gothenburg. He returned to the UK in late 1977 to work as a Senior Project Engineer with responsibility for technical documentation at the Building Services Research and Information Association in Bracknell. Some of this work involved monitoring and abstracting Scandinavian publications on building services. This ultimately led to his becoming a full time freelance translator in 1982. This work has now developed into Aardvark Translation Services Ltd with a staff of 12 full-time translators, administrators and project managers. When he is not running Aardvark, he acts as a series editor for the publisher Multilingual Matters Ltd who published his bestseller A Practical Guide for Translators.

1983 to 1990 saw Geoff teaching Norwegian and Swedish undergraduate and postgraduate students of technical translation at the University of Surrey. He is also a regular speaker at events arranged by the Institute of Translators and Interpreting, the Institute of Linguists, and the Fédération Internationale de Traducteurs. He has acted as international guest lecturer in Copenhagen, Oslo and Stockholm at annual meetings of translator organisations.

Klaus-Dirk Schmitz

With a diploma in computer science and mathematics from the University of Saarbrücken, Klaus-Dirk went on to complete his doctorate in applied linguistics, information science and computer science in 1985. He has since worked as Executing Head of the PCs in Electronic Language Research project, a university lecturer and Project Manager for Electronic Linguistic Data Processing in the Training of Translators and Interpreters at the University of Saarbrücken. Since 1992 he has been Professor of Translation-orientated Terminology Science in the Department of Languages at the Fachhochschule Köln. He is also President of the Gesellschaft für Terminologie and Wissenstransfer e.V., and the Rat für deutschsprachige Terminolgie. Furthermore he sits on the Infoterm Advisory Board (Vienna), the TermNet Board and the TermNet Executive Committee (Vienna). He is also a member of the Advisory Board of the Terminology Committee of the German

Standards Association (DIN) and several German and international standards committees for computational aids in terminology.

Chris Schröder

Chris is the founder and managing director of The AngloNordic Translation Company Ltd, which specialises exclusively in translation from Danish, Finnish, Norwegian and Swedish to English, primarily for clients in the Nordic countries. With a degree from the University of Cambridge and Postgraduate Diploma in Translation from the University of Surrey under his belt, he worked first as a staff translator in Denmark and the UK before turning freelance to concentrate more on his specialist fields, pharmacology and environmental science. Besides translating and managing AngloNordic, he is a part-time associate lecturer at the University of Surrey, teaching technical translation from the Scandinavian languages at both undergraduate and postgraduate level.

Harold Somers

Harold Somers is Senior Lecturer in Computational Linguistics in the Department of Language Engineering, UMIST, Manchester. He has been teaching and researching in the field of Machine Translation for 20 years, has been involved in several research projects, including the European Commission's Eurotra programme. He is the co-author of An Introduction to Machine Translation (Academic Press, 1992) and is the editor of the journal Machine Translation.

Lucas Weschke

After completing his first degree in Modern Languages in 1981 (Bristol Polytechnic), Lucas Weschke worked for ten years in the computing industry, specialising in computer networking and office systems. During this time he lectured extensively throughout Europe and Scandinavia, and frequently worked on special projects within multinational teams in continental Europe, making good use of his foreign languages (German and French). he then followed an MA course in translation (University of Surrey) before embarking on a career as a freelance translator in 1991. He specialises in technical translation and undertakes teaching and consultancy assignments.

Index

INDEX